# Shared *Sorrows*

*Our ashes were mingled in the ovens*

# Shared *Sorrows*

## A Gypsy family remembers the Holocaust

Toby Sonneman

UNIVERSITY OF HERTFORDSHIRE PRESS

First published in Great Britain in 2002 by
University of Hertfordshire Press
Learning and Information Services
University of Hertfordshire
College Lane
Hatfield
Hertfordshire ALIO 9AB

British Library Cataloguing-in-Publication-Data.
A catalogue record for this book is available from the British Library.

ISBN 1 902806 10 7

The symbol on the frontispiece is that of the Romany-Jewish Aliance
(copyright Ian Hancock)

*Front cover:* Sophie Höllenreiner with her children in happier times
with a picture of one of the women's barracks at Auschwitz
*Back cover left:* Rosa Mettbach in foreground with figures from the past, her sisiter
who died at Chelmo and sister-in-law who died at Auschwitz
*Back cover right:* Toby Sonneman in foreground with her father as a young man and
great aunt Else Sonneman, shot by the Einsatzkommando in Lithuania

Design by Geoff Green, Cambridge CB4 5RA.
Cover design by John Robertshaw, Harpenden AL5 2JB
Printed in Great Britain by J. W. Arrowsmith Ltd. Bristol BS3 2NT

# Contents

❧

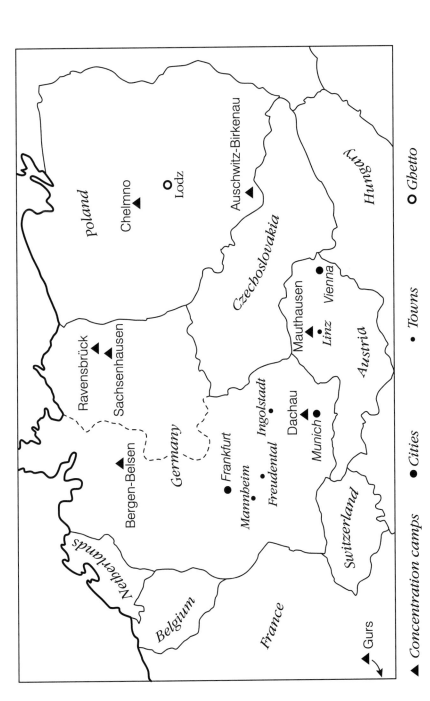

▲ Concentration camps   ● Cities   ● Towns   ○ Ghetto

Map showing the location of places and camps mentioned in the book.

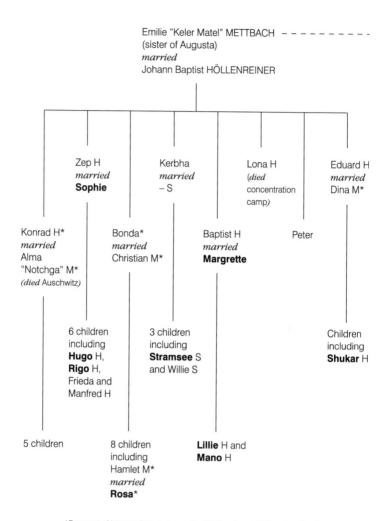

Emilie "Keler Matel" METTBACH – – – – – – – – – –
(sister of Augusta)
*married*
Johann Baptist HÖLLENREINER

| Zep H | Kerbha | Lona H | Eduard H |
|---|---|---|---|
| *married* | *married* | (*died* | *married* |
| **Sophie** | – S | concentration | Dina M* |
| | | camp) | |

Konrad H*
*married*
Alma
"Notchga" M*
(*died* Auschwitz)

Bonda*
*married*
Christian M*

Baptist H
*married*
**Margrette**

Peter

6 children
including
**Hugo** H,
**Rigo** H,
Frieda and
Manfred H

3 children
including
**Stramsee** S
and Willie S

Children
including
**Shukar** H

5 children

8 children
including
Hamlet M*
*married*
**Rosa***

**Lillie** H and
**Mano** H

*Because of intermariage between the Mettbach and Höllenreiner families, these names appear in both family trees.

H = HÖLLENREINER  M = METTBACH  S = SCHÖNBERGER

The family trees of Emilie and Augusta Mettbach

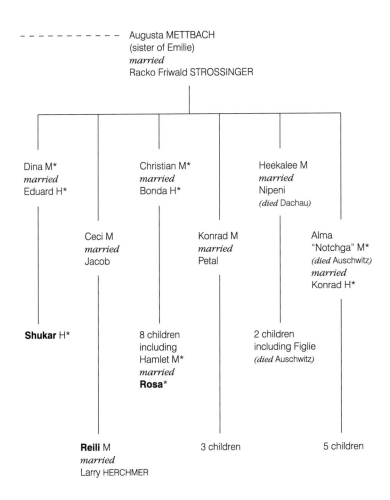

Augusta METTBACH
(sister of Emilie)
*married*
Racko Friwald STROSSINGER

Dina M*
*married*
Eduard H*

Christian M*
*married*
Bonda H*

Heekalee M
*married*
Nipeni
*(died* Dachau)

Ceci M
*married*
Jacob

Konrad M
*married*
Petal

Alma
"Notchga" M*
*(died* Auschwitz)
*married*
Konrad H*

**Shukar** H*

8 children
including
Hamlet M*
*married*
**Rosa**\*

2 children
including Figlie
*(died* Auschwitz)

**Reili** M
*married*
Larry HERCHMER

3 children

5 children

This family tree is based on notes left by Reili Mettbach before her death and it is not known why she and her sibling took their mother's family name of Mettbach.

**Bold type** indicates people interviewed for this book.

# *In human terms*

ᐁ

It has been called 'the forgotten Holocaust' – the Nazi persecution of the Gypsies. Though tens of thousands of books have been written about the Holocaust, perhaps only a couple dozen have fully considered that Gypsies, along with Jews, were victims of Nazi crimes against humanity. And of those couple dozen books, most take a scholarly approach, an approach which is essential and valuable but is not intended for the lay reader.

Today, seventy years after Hitler came to power, few readers know much about what happened to Gypsies under the Nazis, though interest in the topic is strong. So many years after these events occurred, this story still has not been told fully, still has not been adequately recognized. And this lack of recognition impacts not only how we understand the past, but also how we see the present. Without full acknowledgment that Gypsies were victims of the Holocaust, too little attention is paid to the current situation in Europe where Gypsies are frequently victims of prejudice and racially-motivated mob attacks.

I have always believed that real recognition is dependent upon caring, and that, in turn, is dependent upon making a personal connection. Works of scholarship, which detail Nazi policies toward Gypsies or debate whether policies toward Gypsies and Jews differed in philosophy, approach their subject in a necessarily cool and objective light – and readers rarely forge a personal connection. These works have given me a vital historical context for understanding what happened to the Gypsies under the Nazis, but scholarly debates, while undeniably important, were not of great importance to me as I wrote this book. Instead, my premise was caring about the people, and my intent was to tell a very human story, the story of a family of Gypsies in Germany and how they were affected by the Nazi tyranny.

∾

The idea for this book was born of my lifelong interest in Gypsies − a feeling of connection to this people so innate to me that I can't even remember its origin − and my own identity as the Jewish child of a Holocaust survivor. I was raised on my father's stories of his life in Germany, before and during the Nazi rise to power, and of his escape from Germany to America.

I am steeped in my father's stories, my personal history lesson. Long before I knew what Kristallnacht was, my father told me how he and his family hid in the attic on that night of destruction that marked the violent beginning of the Holocaust and how he walked the next morning through shards of broken glass and smoldering rubble for his long-awaited appointment at the American Consulate. Long before I understood why Jews were persecuted in Nazi Germany, I learned how my father had lost his job because of Nazi laws; how his aunts and uncles and cousin had been murdered in concentration camps; why he had decided to flee his homeland. And long before I understood the complexities of friendship and betrayal, I heard the story of how my father's best friend had joined the Nazi Party and warned him, time and time again, to get out, telling him, "We're going to bury the Jews."

Though I wasn't always eager to hear these stories when I was a child, as an adult I have grown to value them more and more. I find they have taught me truths about a time and a place that I would never have understood from history books. For example, from my father's stories, I knew about the paradoxes of the Nazi government which, in 1933, forbade all youth organizations save for the Hitler Youth, yet issued my father a permit to be a qualified leader of the Jewish youth movement. I learned about the contradictions of a government that, in 1936, caused my father to lose his job because he was Jewish, yet immediately granted him unemployment compensation. I heard about my grandmother's sister, who was protected from Nazi anti-Semitic measures because she was married to a non-Jew from an important family; she was allowed to live freely in Germany while her siblings fled to America or were murdered by the Nazis.

As my father told me these real personal stories, including the paradoxes and contradictions of the time, I gained a view that predisposed me to understand something essential about the stories of Gypsy survivors too – for the Nazi policies toward Gypsies were sometimes inconsistent or contradictory as well. In human terms, these contradictions didn't lessen the suffering, or the crime. The Nazis committed murder when they sent my great-aunt Frieda to the gas chamber in Auschwitz, and it was no less a crime because they had spared her sister, Rahel. Similarly, the Nazi crime against the Gypsy people could not be mitigated because some Gypsies had been spared.

If my father's stories nurtured a kind of familiarity with Germany and the Holocaust, as well as encouraged a particular way of seeing history, it was my meeting with Reili Mettbach Herchmer that gave this idea its root and brought it to fruition. Reili was born a Sinti Gypsy in Germany in 1931 and had spent her childhood in hiding, on the run and in a concentration camp – due to Hitler's racial policies toward Gypsies. The Nazis deprived her of education: at liberation, she was fourteen years old and had only two years of schooling. Her literacy skills were minimal but she knew she had an important story to tell and she felt strongly about telling it.

People should know what the Nazis did to the Gypsies, just like the Jews, she said.

When I went to Colorado Springs to talk to Reili in 1991, I was immersed in discovering how deeply the Holocaust had affected my own family and, at the same time, in discovering the deep connection I had with the Gypsies. All of this feeling was embodied in my meeting with Reili. We were as sisters who had never met before, freshly acquainted, yet recognizing instantly the depth of our bond. She felt deeply connected to Jews, and I felt deeply connected to Gypsies. She had the story to tell; I had the interest and the means to tell it. When we traveled together to Germany to talk to members of her extended family, our personal connection was welded to a greater purpose: the story of families, Gypsy and Jewish, and their profound sufferings under the Nazis.

∾

I am greatly saddened that Reili will never hold this book in her hands, for it is her book as much as mine. Reili died in November 1999 after a series of strokes. She was sixty-eight. Though I take some comfort in knowing that Reili read and liked a shortened version of this book in my master's thesis, *In the rain one sees no tears,* and that she realized my commitment to telling this story, I will forever miss my Sinti sister whose generosity of spirit enabled me to turn ideas and hopes into reality.

The writing of a book is a kind of journey, and though a physical journey is at the heart of this book, the internal odyssey that it spurred lasted much longer. When I traveled to Germany in 1993 I met again with Reili and had the chance to talk with the members of her extended family who had suffered under the Nazi racial policies. Here, looking at their faces, hearing their words, seeing their tears, the past became even more real to me, the significance of the story even more vivid. And when I traveled alone, wandering along a ribbon of sites that held meaning in my family's history, the journey acquired ever more layers of complexity as the threads of past and present twisted and entangled, and the stories of Gypsy and Jewish families entwined.

The oral histories that I recorded from Reili, my father, and members of the Mettbach-Höllenreiner family in Germany, form the basis for this book. In addition, I have also chosen to depart from traditional oral history by exposing the seams of these unconventional interviews: recording my own role and my personal involvement, as well as recording my observations, conversations and activities with the families, to add another layer to the understanding of the present-day life of the Sinti in Germany. My confrontation with my own family's past in Germany weaves yet another thread through this text.

I hope that the stories of a Gypsy family set against the backdrop of a Jewish family will give readers a perspective that is broader than that of just one person, yet far more personal than that which considers a whole population. As this is not an exhaustive study, I have here only considered what happened to Sinti Gypsies in Germany and Austria. The reader should be aware, however, that Gypsies, both Sinti and Roma, throughout Western and Eastern Europe suffered profoundly in the Holocaust.

Throughout this book I have tried to illuminate the events of these families by placing them in accurate historical context, and in this endeavor I have relied upon several invaluable sources. These sources are credited in the end notes and bibliography. A personal/historical chronology, map and kinship diagrams are my own contributions and are designed only to aid the reader in tracing the events and relationships of these families.

One other stylistic choice I would like to note is the use of italics throughout the book. When quoting people's own words about their experiences under the Nazis, I have used italics to increase readability, while other quoted conversations are indicated by quotation marks. All other descriptions of people's thoughts, speech or actions are based on interviews or other factual sources.

Although no work based on people's memories can vouch for 100 percent accuracy, I have checked these memories against historical sources whenever possible. To the best of my judgment and knowledge, these stories are both important and true.

# Chronology of two families

This chronology is not intended to be comprehensive, but is selected to show the historical context that most involved the people with which this book is concerned, as well as the personal family events.

| | |
|---|---|
| 1438 | ∾ Kaiser Albrecht II gives the Höllenreiner family a coat of arms, with a crown and ox design, in recognition of their old and strong family line |
| 1899 | • Bavaria establishes the *Information Agency on Gypsies* to collect genealogical data, fingerprints, and photographs |
| 1926 | • Bavaria adopts *Law for the Fight Against Gypsies, Vagrants and the Workshy* to mandate registration of all Gypsies; this law becomes a model for other German states<br>∾ Shukar's father receives an identity pass for Bavaria |
| 1929 | • The national police commission establishes the *Center for the Fight Against Gypsies in Germany*, with headquarters in Munich |
| 1933 | • January: Hitler is appointed Chancellor of Germany, ushering in the Third Reich.<br>• February: German government takes away rights such as freedom of speech, press, protection from invasion of privacy<br>∾ *Die Frankfurter Zeitung*, the liberal newspaper started by my father's great uncle Leopold Sonnemann, is taken over by the Nazis<br>• March: First concentration camp opens at Dachau, Germany<br>• April: Nazis lead nationwide boycott of Jewish-owned businesses in Germany; Jewish civil servants, including teachers, are fired in Germany |

• July: Jews, Gypsies and disabled are classified as "inferior
peoples"
• Laws are passed to allow the forced sterilization of Gypsies,
disabled, African-Germans and others considered 'unfit'

| 1935 | • Nuremberg Laws, announced at a Nazi party rally in Nuremberg, classify Gypsies, along with Jews and blacks as minorities with 'alien blood,' and forbid mixed marriages between them and those of German blood |

1936
• The *Racial Hygiene Research Center,* a scientific institution
to register and classify Gypsies and Jews, is established as
part of the National Health office, with Dr. Robert Ritter as
director
• The *Central Office to Combat the Gypsy Menace* is established
in Munich, co-ordinating all German police agencies, along
with the *Interpol* in Vienna, to intensify police harassment
and control of Gypsies (it is renamed the *Central Office to
Combat the Gypsy Nuisance*, and moved to Berlin in October,
1938)
• Jewish doctors are barred from practice; other Jewish
professionals lose their jobs
∾ On Nazi orders, my father is dismissed from his job with
a pharmaceutical company; he is, however, allowed to collect
unemployment insurance
• July: First German Gypsies are arrested and deported to
Dachau concentration camp

1937
• Ritter's unit of the *Racial Hygiene Research Center* begins
systematic genealogical and genetic research. Ritter and his
co-workers try to establish a link between heredity and
criminal or asocial behavior
• Gypsies are officially excluded from the army, but the
military's racial policy is not enforced until 1942 or 1943

1938
• March: the Anschluss, incorporation of Austria into the
German Reich
• May: Decree requires the registration of all migrant
Gypsies
• June: Gypsy Clean-up Week, June 13–18 results in arrest of
1,000 Gypsies who are deported to concentration camps.
In late summer and fall about 3,000 Gypsies in Austria are
also deported to concentration camps

• September: Able-bodied Gypsy men are conscripted for work in Burgenland
• November 9–10: During the night of pogroms called Kristallnacht (Night of Broken Glass), Nazis burn synagogues and loot Jewish homes and businesses across Germany. Nearly 30,000 German and Austrian Jewish men are deported to concentration camps.
ↅ November 10: On the morning after Kristallnacht, my father walks through the rubble, hides a Torah, and keeps his appointment at the American Consulate in Stuttgart
• November 15: All Jewish children are expelled from public schools; segregated Jewish schools are created
• December: Himmler calls for "the resolution of the Gypsy question (*Zigeunerfrage*) based on its essentially racial nature." All Gypsies in the Reich are required to register with the police

1939    ↅ My father leaves Germany, takes a ship from Holland, and arrives in the US on March 17
ↅ Reili's family flees Germany with false passports, traveling to Italy and Yugoslavia
• March: German troops invade Czechoslovakia
• September: Germany invades Poland. World War II begins
September: Gypsy adults in Vienna are forced to work on public projects, Rosa's older brother and sisters are ordered to forced labor in Vienna
• October: Hitler extends power of doctors to kill institutionalized disabled persons in the 'euthanasia' program
• October: Registration and census of Gypsies is enforced in Austria
ↅ In Vienna, Rosa's family is measured and fingerprinted for 'anthropological research'

1940    • Spring: Germany invades and defeats Denmark, Norway, Belgium, Luxembourg, the Netherlands, and France
• May: Planned deportation of German Gypsies to Poland begins but is halted in October 1940. Some 3,000 Gypsies are deported to Poland
• October: Jews in Mannheim and other cities in Baden-Wurttemburg are deported to concentration camps in France
ↅ Frieda Berger, my grandmother's sister, is deported to Gurs concentration camp

• November: Creation of Lackenbach, a special internment camp for Gypsies in Austria
• Trainloads of Gypsies are added to Jewish deportation transports from Vienna
∾ Rosa's family is arrested in Vienna and deported to Lackenbach

1941
• March: Gypsy children are expelled from public schools in the Reich
• April: Germany invades Yugoslavia and Greece
∾ Reili's family flees from Yugoslavia to Romania
• November: Gypsies from Lackenbach concentration camp in Austria are deported to Lodz Ghetto in Poland
∾ November: Rosa's family is deported to Lodz Ghetto; Rosa escapes from the transport
• December: Gassing of Jews using mobile vans begins at Chelmno extermination camp in Poland.

1942
• January: Nazi and government leaders meet at a villa in Wannsee, a lakeside town on the outskirts of Berlin, to discuss the "final solution to the Jewish question"
• January: Deportation of 5,000 Austrian Gypsies from the Lodz concentration camp to Chelmno to be killed in mobile gas vans
∾ Rosa's parents, siblings and extended family members are among the 5,000 Austrian Gypsies deported from Lodz and killed at Chelmno
∾ Rosa is captured, sent back to Lackenbach and escapes again in spring
• Gypsies are discharged from Germany's army, navy, and air force
• April: Germany invades Yugoslavia and Greece
∾ Rosa travels from Vienna to Munich, lives with the Mettbach family, marries Hamlet Mettbach
• Nazi extermination camps in occupied Poland begin mass murder of Jews, Gypsies, and others in gas chambers
• June: Germany invades Soviet Union. The Einsatzgruppen, mobile killing squads, begin mass murders of Jews, Gypsies, and Communist leaders
• August: Vichy officials hand over the prisoners of Gurs to the Germans, who deport them to Auschwitz, where they are gassed

∾ My grandmother's sister, Frieda Berger, is deported from Gurs to Auschwitz, where she is murdered
• September: Gypsies are transferred from Buchenwald to Auschwitz to build the Gypsy enclosure in Birkenau
• October-November: First group of Austrian and German Jews are deported to ghettos in Eastern Europe
∾ Reili's family continues to try to escape Nazi forces, traveling in Bulgaria and back to Yugoslavia
• December: Japan attacks Pearl Harbor; Germany declares war on United States
• December: Himmler orders the Auschwitz decree, dictating that Gypsies must be deported to Auschwitz-Birkenau

1943
• March: Most Gypsies in Germany, including those in Munich, are arrested and sent to Auschwitz
∾ Sophie, her husband, Josef, and children (including Hugo, Manfred, and Rigo) are deported to Aushwitz; Margrette, Johann, Mano and Lilly Höllenreiner are also deported to Auschwitz
∾ Hugo's friend is shot to death on the 'playground' in Auschwitz
∾ Shukar's parents' home in Munich becomes a refuge for Gypsies in hiding
∾ Rosa goes to a doctor for post-partum complications and is arrested, jailed and then deported to Auschwitz
∾ Reili and her parents are arrested in Yugoslavia and sent to a forced labor camp

1944
• March: Germany occupies Hungary
• May-July: Hungarian Jews are deported to Auschwitz-Birkenau; most of them are gassed
• April-July: Transports take some of the younger, able-bodied Gypsies out of Auschwitz to other camps, mainly Ravensbrück (for females), Buchenwald and Flossenburg
∾ July: Rosa is sent out of Auschwitz on a transport to Ravensbrück, then to a labor camp in eastern Germany; she escapes, is captured and is sent to jail
∾ Sophie and Josef Höllenreiner and their children are sent to Ravensbrück, Mauthausen, and Bergen-Belsen. Josef and Manfred are separated from Sophie and the younger children.

ᖫ Sophie's husband, Josef, and her older children, Manfred
(12) and Frieda (14) Höllenreiner, are subjected to forced
sterilization in Ravensbrück

ᖫ Margrette and Lillie are sent to Ravensbrück, Mauthausen and Bergen-Belsen

ᖫ Stramsee and his mother are involuntarily sterilized in the
hospital of a small town outside of Munich

• August 2: The Gypsy camp at Auschwitz-Birkenau is
liquidated; approximately 3,000 Gypsies are gassed in a
single night

• Hungarian Jewish witness, Noemi Ban, hears screams of
the Gypsies in the gas chambers

ᖫ November: Rosa is returned to the labor camp and tortured; put in a dark and narrow cement bunker for four
weeks

ᖫ December: Rosa is allowed to join the other prisoners on
Christmas Eve

| | |
|---|---|
| 1945 | • January: Nazis evacuate Auschwitz; prisoners begin 'death marches' toward Germany; Soviet troops enter Auschwitz |

• January: Nazis evacuate Auschwitz; prisoners begin 'death
marches' toward Germany; Soviet troops enter Auschwitz

• Prisoners are consolidated in concentration camps in
Germany; Bergen-Belsen becomes hideously overcrowded
with severe problems of malnutrition and typhus

• Hugo's cousin dies of typhus in Bergen-Belsen; her corpse
is eaten by rats

• April-May: concentration camps are liberated

• May 7: Germany surrenders; the war ends

ᖫ Sophie and her children leave Bergen-Belsen, without
release papers

ᖫ Margrette stays with Lillie in Bergen-Belsen until her son
arrives to take her back to Munich; she claims an apartment
from a wife of a former SS officer

ᖫ Mano tries to escape from Sachsenhausen but collapses.
He is found on a road near Hamburg and taken to France

• November: War crimes trials held in Nuremberg, Germany

1946    ᖫ Johann, Margrette's husband, returns to Munich

ᖫ March: Mano is adopted by a French couple

ᖫ December: the French assistance organization locates
Mano's parents

# Shared *Sorrows*

chapter *one*

# *A bit of sweetness*

ↄ

Rosa examines the piece of cake carefully, testing its weight and texture with the tines of her fork. The golden yeast dough, its edges rose-hued with fruit syrup; the lush red-purple flesh of the juicy plums; the crumbly sand-colored streusel topping. Satisfied with what she sees, she lifts a forkful of cake to her mouth and chews it thoughtfully.

"I like this *Kuchen*," she says to me. "This is a good one."

Rosa is over seventy but the deep lines and bumps of her face make her look ten years older. She has walnut-brown skin lined with wrinkles and gleaming mahogany eyes under thick black eyebrows. You can see that her dark grey hair was once black. She pulls it back tightly in a bun but curly pewter wisps of it escape, softening her expression. I notice her hands because she brings a cigarette to her mouth almost continually – her fingers are slender and agile, her fingernails manicured.

Rosa is a Gypsy, though she prefers to identify herself more specifically. "My people are the Sinti," she says, the Sinti being a subclass of the ethnic Gypsy population who settled in northern Europe in the early 1400s. Rosa was born in Austria but now lives in Germany, in a two-bedroom high-rise apartment on the outskirts of Munich with her six-year old grandson. A tiny woman, she seems both frail and tough at the same time. Frail when she is in the grasp of one of her periodic spasms of coughing and her small thin frame seems too delicate to withstand the onslaught. Tough when she is angry

Rosa Mettbach, 1993

and she scowls, her arched eyebrows lowering, dark eyes flashing as she barks harsh commands to her daughter and grandson. Then her voice and expressions seem too large, too intimidating for such a slight person. But now, pleased by the *Kuchen,* she smiles sweetly and her two gold teeth glimmer beside the white ones, echoing the gold and pearls of her necklaces and the small gold rings on her ears.

I am gratified that she likes the cake, a *Zwetschgenkuchen* that I chose from a neighborhood pastry shop, a *Konditorei.* I'd considered the extravagant glazed and whipped cream confections in the display case but had finally settled on this plainer cake because I knew how special it was. Baked only in the autumn when the tiny purple-blue plums are ripe, *Zwetschgenkuchen* evokes the golden October of the countryside, the lingering of the year's last harvest. I know this cake because my grandmother brought the memory of it with her from the old country. From *this* country, Germany. From Before.

My Jewish grandmothers were able to bring few treasures with them from their homelands. One fled poverty, discrimination and the threat of pogroms in Russia; the other barely escaped ghettoization and the then-inconceivable horrors of the Holocaust in Germany. So the family heirlooms did not consist of antique furniture, silverware or crystal but instead took the form of recipes for special pastries, remembered by my grandmothers and brought to America.

My mother's mother, my Baba, the one who had come from Russia and spoke Yiddish more often than English, was famous for her *Schneckenudeln* – cinnamon rolls. The yeast-risen, raisin-filled buns were small and hearty; they were plain – lacking icing, nuts or glazes – but very good and I always associated them with my Baba who wore her grey hair wound into a bun the same snail shape as the sweet rolls.

For special occasions – Sabbath or holidays – Baba made strudel, rolling the fine dough into a huge rectangle on the dining room table. I loved to watch her slight form as she moved around the table, plying her rolling pin energetically, then stretching the dough with her hands until it was thin and even, then filling it with a succulent mixture of apples, sugar and raisins or jam.

My father's mother, the grandmother we called Oma, was also a wonderful pastry chef. She brought her renowned *Mür-beteig* pie crust with her from Germany – a dense but elegant pastry made with butter, flour, sugar, a beaten egg and a touch of brandy – and filled it with sweetened cherries, gooseberries, currants or apples in season. And she successfully transplanted 'S' cookies, a tender, rich butter cookie in the shape of the first letter of our last name. It was considered such an essential delicacy at all celebrations that we'd come to think of it as the family cookie.

And then there was *Zwetschgenkuchen*, a German yeast

cake topped with slices of sweetened plums. My Oma used to make this cake, then my mother learned to make it for my father and finally I taught myself how to make this beautiful, aromatic pastry for my friends and family. Every autumn, I'd pick the ripened dusky blue Italian plums, layer the slices of blue-skinned yellow fruit in overlapping concentric layers on a circle of sweet yeast dough and bake until the fruit turned a rich, rosy, purple-gold.

As Rosa and I sit on the sofa savoring forkfuls of the *Zwetschgenkuchen* and drinking sweet creamy coffee from thin china cups, we reminisce about shared pastries. Stumbling between her broken English and my fragmentary German, we talk about the recipes that crossed the ocean, bringing sweet remembrances of the old country. Rosa takes my hand. "I will make an *Apfelstrudel* for you," she promises. "*Morgen.*" Tomorrow.

She is true to her word. By the time I awake the next morning, she's already mixing the flour, oil, egg and water into a bowl.

"Have some coffee," she urges, gesturing to the pot on the stove. I sit at the kitchen table drinking coffee from a frail china cup, watching her as she gathers the dough into a ball and kneads it to baby-skin smooth elasticity. She rolls it out into a long rectangle across her kitchen table and then places her hands underneath, stretching the dough thinner and thinner, just as my grandmother did long ago.

Looking at Rosa's strong slender hands moving beneath the translucent sheet of dough, I find myself wishing that only this, this shared fragmentary memory of sweetness, had brought us together. But as I watch her roll the strudel dough expertly around the sliced apples and sprinkle the top with sugar, I can't help but look at the faded blue Auschwitz tattoo on her right forearm. Pale numbers, preceded by a 'Z' for *Zigeuner*, the German word for 'Gypsy' which derives from the Greek root meaning 'untouchable' and the German root for 'vagrant' or even 'criminal'. Rosa hates the word *Zigeuner*,

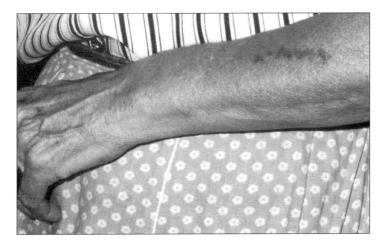

Rosa's Auschwitz tattoo

the word that the Nazis seared into her skin to show that they considered her, and all her people, to be subhuman. That faded tattoo reminds her, every time, of the Nazi genocide that destroyed her entire original family.

And it is this that has brought me here, this kindred history of bitterness and pain that Rosa's people share with mine. That faded tattoo is a too-familiar shadow of the abyss; it stirs the ghosts. As a child, I stole secret glances at similar tattoos on the arms of my parents' friends, German and Austrian Jews who came to our home to visit, to *schmooze* over coffee and pastries. When did I first learn to connect images of unspeakable horror and humiliation with these brands forged on human skin? When did someone – my mother? – first explain the name? Behind a closed door, in a whisper choked by regret: "Auschwitz."

There. There in Auschwitz and in Chelmno, there in Belzec and in Treblinka, there in Sobibor and in Majdanek, there were other sorts of ovens, ovens that produced not sweet pastries but only bitter ashes. In the Gypsy language, *Romanes*, there is a saying: "Our ashes were mingled in the ovens." There had our peoples been inextricably bound.

chapter *two*

---

*A bitter root*

༄

I can't remember when I first became interested in Gypsies – it seems as if I was always drawn to them – but at first it was simply a romanticized fantasy that I did not connect to my own Jewish identity. Who were the Gypsies? What were they like? I read about them, discovered that many of them lived in the United States and, when I was eighteen, I approached some Gypsy fortune-tellers on Maxwell Street, the vibrant, tawdry street market of my hometown, Chicago. I kept returning to talk to the fortune-tellers and eventually they invited me in to their apartment over the storefront. Somehow they let me hang around – that time and the next and the next – and over the next couple of years, I became acquainted with the large extended family, visiting them from time to time, relishing the chance to be in such an exotic environment. The sprawling second-story apartment was decorated with brightly patterned curtains, drapes and bedspreads in the same fabrics as some of the women's long skirts. I'd sit with the women and children observing people coming and going, listening to animated discussions (about food, cars, clients, relatives) that alternated between English and *Romanes,* the Gypsy language. To justify my presence, I took photographs of the family and brought them prints; once, they invited me to Easter dinner in their home.

This 'contact' didn't really give me much insight or knowledge of the Gypsy language or culture but I was not easily discouraged. I studied anthropology in college, wrote letters to Jan Yoors, the Belgian author who had lived with the Gypsies as a child, and determined that I, too, would get to know some Gypsies. Propelled by my naiveté and a strong sense of adventure, I traveled alone through Europe for four months the summer I was twenty – and by late autumn I finally came to realize the foolish nature of my quest. I had eaten meals in the caravans of the Gypsy Travellers in England, had been ridiculed by a group of young Gypsy men in France and had gazed longingly at horse-drawn caravans of Gypsies on cobbled streets in Romania, but I hadn't gotten to know much about the Gypsies at all. I was too young, too ignorant – and on top of that, I was a single female, highly unlikely to be welcomed in their closed communities. Without a purpose or a contribution to make, I could no longer justify my interest in the Gypsies. Still, I hoped to return to that interest, someday – when I had something to give, some reason to be among them.

∞

It was twenty years before I returned to the Gypsies and though this time I had a personal connection that justified my presence, I was also aware of its limitations. I needed to know I could not 'become a Gypsy' or even come to know them very well before I could return to them. I needed to understand my own identity before I could begin to examine theirs.

I was almost forty before I began to re-examine my own heritage and started to realize more fully the weight of my family's connections to the Holocaust. Not that I had been unaware; my father, after hiding with his family during *Kristallnacht* in November 1938, had escaped Nazi Germany in early 1939. I was born in America ten years later and grew up on my father's stories of his homeland's treachery, stories of the relatives who had been murdered by Nazis, stories of his own efforts to flee and to secure visas for his family. My mother was less talkative but I knew that her parents had left

Russia to escape anti-Semitic pogroms and policies in the early 1900s; the families that they left behind fell victim to the Nazis. My parents sought out the few relatives we had and cherished them all because our extended family in Europe was nearly all destroyed.

Still, I thought of the Holocaust as a horror that did not touch my own life with the force and impact that it had on the lives of my parents and their generation. Looking back, I can't pinpoint when or how that changed for me, but I do remember that one spring, when I was reading a familiar passage from the Passover Haggadah – 'In every generation one must see oneself as having personally come forth from Egypt' – I was suddenly struck by its meaning.

Similarly, and in some mysterious way, I was coming to see my personal involvement in the Holocaust. I would look at my face in the mirror and imagine my relatives who had been killed, simply because they were Jewish. Did they look something like me? In the Jewish tradition, one names a child to remember dead relatives; my parents had named me for their mothers' two favorite sisters, both of whom died at the hands of the Nazis. To bear their names was an honor, I now realized, and also a responsibility – to remember not only their lives (of which I knew so little) but also their deaths. And so I began to ask my parents probing questions, trying to learn some details of my ancestors' experiences.

I began with my namesake, Toba. She was my maternal grandmother's favorite sister and she was murdered by the Nazis in Russia. Her sons had immigrated to France but were arrested there and taken to Auschwitz where they were killed. My mother met Toba's daughter, Genia, the only survivor of that family, in Kibbutz Negba in Israel many years ago and gave her the one remaining photograph of her mother. Genia has now died too, and when I pressed my mother for further details about her aunt's death, she said she didn't know any more. "My mother never dwelt on how the family died and probably didn't know exact details," she said to me, reprimanding me gently for 'dwelling' on tragedy. Except for those few relatives who emigrated before World War II, my grandmother's entire family in Russia was destroyed, as was the Russian family of my grandfather. Many more of my father's family from Germany survived, simply because they had more warnings and more opportunity to leave. But nearly all of those who remained in Europe died. There was

Else Sonnemann

Else Sonnemann, my father's aunt, a doctor in Munich who used to take my father with her sometimes when she went on her hospital rounds, buying him an ice cream afterwards. According to the family stories, Else refused to work as a doctor for the Nazis. I thought of her when I read an account by Lucie Adelsberger, a Jewish doctor forced to work for the Nazis in Auschwitz. Perhaps if Else had agreed to serve, she too would have worked in the Gypsy camp in Auschwitz, bearing witness to disease and medical experiments that prisoner-doctors like Adelsberger were powerless to prevent. Else was deported to Lithuania in 1941, where she was shot and killed by the Einsatzkommando.

My paternal grandmother's brother, Moritz Hermann, was a farmer in the village of Freudental, Germany, living with his wife, Sidonie, and their son, Adolf; they were deported to Auschwitz where they were murdered. My paternal grandmother's favorite sister, Frieda, whose name I bear as my middle name, Friedl, was a divorcée who lived with my father's family in Mannheim and sold sewing machines. She was deported with other Mannheim Jews to the concentration camp in Gurs, France, in 1940. My father tried to save her, pleading with the State Department to help get her out but his request was refused. In 1942, she too was murdered in the gas chambers of Auschwitz.

∽

Why dwell on the negative? my mother asked me. I couldn't quite explain; I just felt a burning need to know more. I began to read books about the Holocaust, especially Holocaust memoirs, almost obsessively immersing myself in the horrors of survivors' lives so I could know about those who did not survive.

At the same time, I began to read again about Gypsy history, and now I realized something I had known but had not fully absorbed before: for hundreds of years in Europe, the Gypsy people and my people were deeply connected by the tragic history of ethnic persecution. Both had been targets of Hitler's plan for racial purity; both had been victims of mass murder in the concentration camp and the gas chamber.

Yet there seemed so little public awareness of the *Porajmos*, the Gypsy Holocaust. And now, so many years later, there was another compelling reason to pay attention to history. An epidemic of racially motivated mob attacks against Gypsies had broken out across Europe, from Germany to Romania. Gypsies in Europe were scapegoats, targeted by skinheads and ordinary citizens alike. Shocked by the horribly familiar connotations of these attacks, I wrote to Dr. Ian Hancock, a Romani (Gypsy) rights activist and professor of linguistics at the University of Texas in Austin. Was there anything I could do to help the Romani cause? I asked. He encouraged me to phone and write to Gypsies and Jews around the country, to see whether we could find enough support for a coalition organization.

In early 1991, Ian Hancock and I co-founded the Romani-Jewish Alliance, a human rights organization to recognize the shared history of Jews and Roma and to draw attention to their current struggles. For the next five years I served without pay as co-Chair and newsletter editor of the small organization. I wrote articles about what was happening to Gypsies in Europe; about mob attacks throughout Europe; about the Gypsy babies in Romanian orphanages; about the ignored story of the Gypsy victims of the Holocaust. I wrote letters to public officials and ambassadors and newspaper editors to win recognition of the plight facing Gypsies. And I continued to read.

Though I was naturally drawn to the subject of Gypsies and the Holocaust, I had discovered only one full-length book in English, *The Destiny of Europe's Gypsies* (by Donald Kenrick and Gratton Puxon), along with a number of articles scattered in various obscure publications. And I searched in vain for personal accounts, for memoirs from Gypsy survivors. The memoirs I'd read by Jewish survivors had touched me powerfully, had given me the connection to imagine their lives as my own. I wanted to understand the Gypsy experience as well on such a personal level. To know a person as the world knows Anne Frank is to give that person and others like them a voice; to acknowledge their pain is to acknowledge their lives. Without that voice, that personal voice, Gypsies were reduced to a faceless number in a history book, relegated to an impersonal footnote.

Why was there such a dearth of personal memoirs from Gypsy survivors? The long silence about what has been called 'the forgotten Holocaust' of the Gypsy people has only recently been broken. But for a long time after the war, the Nazi genocide of the Gypsies was not fully acknowledged, and thus few people sought to record their testimonies. A primary reason for this lack of recognition was the theory that, unlike Jewish victims, Gypsies did not experience racial persecution. Since Nazis often classified Gypsies as 'asocials' or criminals, some historians maintain that the Gypsies were not targeted for *racial* persecution and genocide. This argument was also used by the German courts to refuse reparations for Gypsy victims of the Nazis. Yet the Nazis bestowed the 'asocial' classification on Gypsies even if they had committed no crime. Despite clear evidence that an entire ethnic population – including infants and children – had been branded as socially inferior, Germany's post-war courts decided that the Nazis had not persecuted Gypsies on *racial* grounds.

This denial of racial persecution may also stem from old prejudices and myths: prejudices that label Gypsies as thieves and child-stealers; myths that encourage the public to think of them as romantic figures that exist only in the past or in fairy tales, thus denying their legitimate ethnicity. In the United States, where Gypsies routinely mask their own identity, the public is often unaware that real Gypsies exist and that they are a valid ethnic group with a distinct language and culture. While Gypsies *are* recognized as a real people in Germany, too frequently stereotypes and prejudices rule out any sympathy. In the recent past, Gypsies were often not only denied reparations but also vilified for seeking them. Although these attitudes are beginning to change, they are deeply entrenched.

This lack of attention to the Gypsy experience of the Holocaust is often attributed to the smaller number of victims. It's true that in pre-war Europe, the Gypsies made up a far, far smaller segment of the population than the Jews. In pre-war Germany, for example, while 500,000 Jews lived in a total population of 67 million, there were only 30,000 Gypsies. Yet of this small population, a mere fraction – 5,000 – survived, a proportion of losses similar to that of the Jewish population.

Is it only the group with the highest number of victims that deserves acknowledgment for their suffering? I think that few would agree with such a crass approach to history or to humanity. Still, until recently few non-Gypsies have deemed the memoirs of Gypsy survivors worth retrieving. While tens of thousands of testimonies from Jewish survivors have been recorded and archived, the number of testimonies from Gypsies is woefully small. Serious efforts to record oral testimonies in Germany and other European countries have been undertaken only in the last decade.

Public understanding *is* changing, if slowly, and recently there has been more interest and scholarship about the Gypsies' experiences. Yet other reasons contribute to an ongoing gap in the historical record. Superstition and fear often inhibit Gypsies from talking about the ill fate that befell them, while experience has shown them no practical purpose or emotional value. Some survivors have told their wrenching stories many times in applications for reparations but to no avail. Now Gypsy survivors are aging, dying off and their stories are dying with them.

"The most urgent research now needed is *oral history* with Gypsy survivors," wrote Gabrielle Tyrnauer in a paper for the U.S. Holocaust Memorial Council in 1985. With every year that passes, that need becomes more urgent. I read Tyrnauer's paper in 1991 and agreed, with a passion. Inspired by Dr. Tyrnauer's efforts to record oral testimonies from Gypsies in Germany, I decided then and there that I was going to help in the effort. Yet despite my resolve, I wondered how I would locate these survivors. Few of them lived in the United States, and fewer still were willing to reveal their identity, much less talk to an outsider (a *gaje*, or non-Gypsy) about their painful experiences. I kept asking Dr. Hancock if he knew any Gypsy survivors I could talk to and he kept saying no, he didn't. But I heard the hesitation in his voice and I persisted. Finally, he told me there was someone in Colorado who just might be willing to talk to me.

The woman Hancock mentioned was originally from Germany and had been in a concentration camp as a child. I wrote her a letter proposing an interview and she wrote back. Yes, she would talk to me as long as I didn't use her last name. Audio recordings were fine, but not video. She didn't

Reili Mettbach Herchmer, 1993

want her neighbors to know she was a Gypsy. Later she told me, "I didn't want my children to have to live with that. I didn't want them to go to school and if a pencil was missing, have the other kids say, 'the Gypsy took it.'" She was proud of her identity – but privately. I accepted her terms willingly, glad that she had agreed to talk to me.

I called and we chatted for a while. Her German name was Bregunda but she told me to call her Reili, her nickname in *Romanes*. Would I like to come visit her this summer? she asked. She said I'd be welcome to stay at her home with her and her husband, Larry. They had an extra bedroom. Why not make it a week so they could show me around?

In July of 1991 I flew into the Denver airport and looked around for Reili. She had told me she'd be wearing a red carnation so I'd know who she was. She needn't have worried. Tall and statuesque, with high cheekbones, caramel-colored skin, and long, wavy, silver-streaked black hair gathered into a clasp at her neck, sixty-two-year-old Reili was more beautiful than anyone else in the airport crowd that day. She had accentuated her dramatic appearance with a glittery appliquéd cream-colored blouse and matching long skirt and silver Native American jewelry. Combined with her physical attributes, this attire completed the illusion that she was an American Indian. (She later told me that even Native Americans asked her which tribe she belonged to.)

During the week that I spent with Reili and Larry, talking, eating together, recording her memoirs, driving around the countryside and telling each other about our lives, we became fast friends. I'd been prepared for suspicion and distrust but with Reili this didn't seem to be an issue. Perhaps it was because of my German-Jewish heritage and strong sense of connection with Gypsies, or perhaps it was because we liked to talk to each other, laughed and cried at the same things, and simply got along.

I listened, rapt, as Reili told me long, fascinating stories about her relatives in Germany, and their varied experiences of persecution under the Nazis. Would they be willing to let me record their memories? I asked. Yes, sure, Reili said – if we could just go to Germany together. In Germany, everyone knew they were Gypsies, she explained, so there was no point in trying to hide their identity. And they trusted her – their relative who lived in America. If I came with her, they would by extension trust me. And be willing to talk.

What a remarkable offer. I felt I had been grasped by fate, or at least by lucky circumstance. The opportunity I'd longed for was actually possible now. Except for one problem. Money. It was all very well for me to find the funds to pay for a plane trip from Washington State to Colorado, but to pay for two people to go to Germany for several weeks was out of the question. I didn't even have a job, much less the resources for a project of this nature. I tried to calm myself and I applied for a grant. When it was rejected, I whittled away at my proposed budget until it was just enough to pay for the bare bones and applied again. This time – by now it was May 1993 – I got it.

Elated, I called Reili with the happy news that I could pay for both of our plane tickets to Germany. We started planning. "October is the best time of year to go to Germany," Reili said.

At last, in October of 1993, my unlikely project had become reality. Reili had agreed to serve as both my translator and my 'contact,' introducing me and explaining my role to her relatives. We were here at last, staying with Reili's cousin, Rosa, in Munich for two weeks and traveling to smaller towns in Bavaria to talk to other relatives. And for me, it was especially meaningful to be in Germany – in Munich and Stuttgart, in Mannheim, Heidelberg and Freudental, the towns that my father had known as a boy and as a young man. When I traveled to Europe more than twenty years before, I had assiduously avoided Germany; all my associations with the country were negative. But it was only through being in my father's homeland that I could realize the depth of the losses that my father and his relatives sustained, only through being in Germany that I could begin to understand the depth of the pain that Gypsy survivors still experienced.

∞

The people I spoke with in Germany are victims still living in the country that caused and condoned the mass murder of their people, and they are understandably bitter. Many of them believe that contemporary Germans place no more value on the lives of Gypsies than the Nazis did. But they agreed to talk to me, and in doing so they were both generous and courageous. They talked to me because I was Jewish, because I was American, because I was Reili's friend – but mainly they talked because they wanted the world to know what happened to them. They talked because they believed that people should hear their stories, stories that are both unique and common, the stories of their experiences in the *Porajmos*, the Great Devouring.

∾

The Gypsy culture has little in common with the Jewish culture; Gypsies and Jews have been bound more by difference from the majority and its effects – marginalization, persecution and suffering – than by anything else. Jews and Gypsies are Europe's oldest non-Christian minorities. Both were peoples without territory, foreigners everywhere, ostracized and often despised because of the difference of their language, food restrictions, dress and other customs, the color of their hair or their skin.

Gypsies, or *Roma*, arrived in Europe from India in the middle of the thirteenth century and were mistaken for the Islamic conquerors that the Christian establishment so feared and hated. The error is recorded in the name 'Gypsies' which is derived from 'Egyptians' and was applied loosely to any exotic Eastern peoples.

Prejudice and superstition followed on the heels of the Gypsies' arrival in Europe, and was soon legitimized by legislation. Medieval Christians, who associated dark with evil, responded viciously to the migration of this dark-skinned people. Just as Jews were accused of killing Jesus, folktales propagated the legend that Gypsies had forged the nails with which Jesus was crucified. Likewise, while Christians accused Jews of drinking the blood of Christian babies in secret rites, they accused Gypsies of stealing babies and children, even eating them. These attitudes were evident as late as the eighteenth century, when hundreds of Gypsies were brought to trial for cannibalism in Hungary. After more than 200 were executed, the alleged victims were found alive and well.

The pervasive prejudice against Gypsies in Europe became legalized in two different forms: forcing them to stay and work, or forcing them to leave. In the Balkans (Moldavia and

Wallachia – the area that is now Romania) Gypsies filled the employment vacuum left by men fighting the Crusades and became so important to the economy that slavery legislation was adopted to prevent them from leaving. Approximately half the Gypsy population was enslaved for over five hundred years, from the mid 1300s until abolition in 1864. Meanwhile, the other half of the population managed to flee, dispersing through the continent until they inhabited every county in northern and Western Europe by about 1500.

The separate histories of these two population groups have fractured a strong sense of cultural unity but various Gypsy groups do share a cultural and linguistic core. The basis of their culture derives from India's caste system and is centered on a complex set of pollution taboos encoded into every aspect of life. Basically, Gypsies divide the world in two: Roma (Gypsies) and *gajé* (non-Gypsies), ritually clean and ritually polluted. Gypsies have survived as an intact population with a cohesive culture because of stringent rules that prohibit prolonged contact with *gajé*, who are regarded as both defiled and defiling. Hygienic, dietary, moral and social codes are all founded on this idea of ritual pollution.

Soon after Gypsies migrated to northern and western Europe in the 1500s, oppressive laws were enacted to forbid them to settle and to restrict them from practicing their traditional trades. By the 1600s, laws in Germany, Finland and England had decreed that it was a hanging offense even to be *born* a Gypsy and in some places 'Gypsy hunts' treated Gypsies as wild game (*Freiwild*) and declared 'open seasons' when they could be tracked down and hunted for sport. Public warning signs showing a Gypsy being flogged and branded were posted at the borders of a territory to deter Gypsies from entering. In some German states, all adult Gypsies faced torture, flogging and branding; if they returned, they were liable to hanging without trial. Other countries attempted enforced assimilation, forbidding Gypsy language and culture. Although the nineteenth century, with its Romantic interest

in the Gypsy as 'noble savage', brought a diminution of out-
right persecution, Gypsies were never accorded equal status as
citizens.

It is the *treatment* of Gypsies in Europe that is so similar
to that of the Jews. Like Jews, Gypsies were also the victims of
cultural attack: in books, sermons, drama and popular art,
both peoples were demonized. Both groups were subject
everywhere to persecution, fines and heavy taxation if they
tried to settle, barred from trades and prevented from settling
in the center of towns and villages. While both groups became
known as wanderers, they migrated mainly to escape persecution and to earn a living. Since both Gypsies and Jews were
pushed to the outskirts of town, they lived close to one
another and had ongoing contact. This made for a cross-cultural
exchange that is most evident in music. Gypsy musicians
played at Jewish weddings; Jewish violinists borrowed Gypsy
strains. Many Hassidic tunes of Eastern Europe are rooted in
Gypsy culture. Klezmer and Gypsy music influenced each
other profoundly – one of the only sweet effects of prejudice.

Never were the fates of the Jews and the Gypsies more
tragically intertwined than during the Holocaust, when both
groups were deemed 'parasitic alien races' and targeted for
racial extermination. There were differences, yes – Nazi policy
toward Gypsies was inconsistent in the early years and one
can hardly overlook such anomalies as the Gypsy 'family
camp' in Auschwitz, where Gypsies were allowed to stay in
family units and retain their own clothing for some time
before the entire camp was 'liquidated.' But those who wish to
maintain that Gypsies were *not* victims of a Nazi plan for
genocide will point only to those differences.

To me, though it's important to acknowledge the differences, it's even more important to recognize the similarities:
the methodical persecution through a pattern of exclusionary
legislation, arrests, deportations, concentration camps and
eventually mass murder – which historian Dr. Sybil Milton
documented so well. Comparing the Nazi treatment of Jews

and the Gypsies, eminent historian Raul Hilberg says, "The fates of the two communities were inextricably linked. It's not a question of whether one wants to talk about both – one has to… During the years 1933 to 1945, the parallels between what happened to the two communities, in my view, predominate over the differences."

But were Gypsies included in the Nazi's plan for a 'final solution'? As Benno Müller-Hill writes, this question is "inappropriately phrased." Like Müller-Hill, I believe that "the desire to exterminate Jews, Gypsies and mental patients was more important than any 'total plan.'" I believe that it is more important to recognize that anti-Semitism and anti-Gypsyism stem from the same bitter root than to emphasize the uniqueness of each group's experience.

Gypsies acknowledge this connection with Jews. Along with her other jewelry, Reili wears a gold Star of David around her neck. "To remember my Jewish brothers and sisters who died in the camps," she explains. Like many Gypsies, Reili regards Jews as a kindred people, but the reverse is not often true. Except for an eccentric handful of people who claim Gypsy ethnicity as a means of establishing both individuality and identification with a group, no people has ever proclaimed brotherhood (or sisterhood) with the Gypsies.

Yet I believe that my Jewish ancestors in Germany were not so far from that feeling of kinship that I want to reclaim. My grandfather, a music critic and writer in Mannheim, once wrote a poem called "The Gypsy" about a Gypsy violinist. I like to think that I take after the German side of my family in their affinity for writing, for my great-grandmother was also a published writer and my great-great uncle, Leopold Sonnemann, was the founder of the distinguished liberal German newspaper, the *Frankfurter Zeitung*.

When I began to pursue my interest in Gypsies, my father sent me a copy of his father's poem, roughly translated, and I was struck by the content. It described the coarse crowd that gathered round to listen to a musician: *Thin people, fat people,*

Leopold Sonnemann, 1909

*sit around me, stupidly shaking their heads, with commonplace smooth faces, clapping with tankards, smacking with thick tongues...* the poem begins.

This insensitive crowd is entertained by the Gypsy violinist who seems almost unaware of their presence as he plays his violin.

*Plays and sobs... sobbing out of his deep, deepest soul. Out of his fiddle's soft strings, sobs and shouts to the stars...*

Then the crowd begins to applaud: *Clapping, clapping, all of them, with their fat red hands ...* A profound emotional moment is desecrated and the narrator runs from the crowd, searching for the solitude to recall the powerful music.

*And I go, plunge, race, like lashed with a whip, fleeing away – until I am alone, totally alone again to hear those sobs – those sobs of a soul.*

# Der Zigeuner.

Dürre Menschen,
Feiste Menschen,
Sitzen um mich,
Wackeln blöde
Mit des Alltags Glattgesichtern,
Klappern mit den Deckelgläsern,
Schmatzen mit den dicken Zungen,
Schmatzen — und da oben spielt und
Schluchzt jetzt einer auf der Geige,
Schluchzt aus tiefer, tiefster Seele . . .

Aus der Geige weichen Saiten
Schluchzt und jauchzt es zu den Sternen,
jauchzt, wie nur Zigeuner jauchzen —
Daß im Innersten erschauernd,
bebend fühle ich: ein Großer,
Größer wird dies einstens werden,
Der mit solcher Kunst gestaltet.

Bebend fühl' ichs, blicke um mich —
Dürre Menschen,
Feiste Menschen,
Sitzen um mich,
Wackeln blöde
Mit des Alltags Glattgesichtern,
Klappern mit den Deckelgläsern,
Schmatzen mit den dicken Zungen
Und dann — klatschen, klatschen alle
Mit den roten, fetten Händen —
Und ich gehe, stürze, rase
Wie vor Peitschenhieben flüchtend
Fort, — bis einsam ich, ganz einsam
Wieder höre dieses Jauchzen —,
Dieses Schluchzen einer Seele . . .

*Der Zigeuner*, poem by Kurt Sonnemann, published in 1925

∾

So often the Gypsies of literature, because of their real-life associations with music, dance, travel and colorful dress, are merely metaphors for freedom, passion and expressiveness. We use what we like – the exotic, the romantic – and disregard the rest. But it is only when we also acknowledge sadness and pain that we recognize the whole person – the whole people – and that we can even begin to approximate the truth. My grandfather heard the pain of the Gypsy in this plaintive song. I imagine that he hoped that his readers would hear it as well, would taste the bitter with the sweet.

Bitter and sweet. Every year at Passover, I celebrate like Jews the world over by remembering that we were once slaves, by eating horseradish to remember the bitterness of our persecution. But we also eat a little *charoset* – a sweet mixture of fruit, nuts and wine – with the horseradish to make it a bit more palatable. I've always marveled at the sensation of the two substances in my mouth: the sharp, hot horseradish with the softly spicy sweetness of the charoset. The tastes do not blend but remain distinct, a rich complexity in my mouth, the bitterness of the horseradish always dominant.

For the most part there is little sweetness to be found in recalling slavery and even less in recalling the tragedy of the Holocaust, the *Porajmos*. But those moments of sweetness do come: when a survivor thanks you for listening, even as she says she will not sleep for days. When Rosa and I talked of shared recipes, when she made the strudel for me, when she showed me photographs of her dead relatives and I listened to her story of imprisonment and torture and escape, and acknowledged her pain, we ate the sweet together with the bitter. Though the bitter still prevailed, the bit of sweetness gave us the strength to swallow that bitter root.

# chapter *three*

# *The family album*

&

"She's stubborn; don't rush her," Reili advises me when I wonder when Rosa will be ready to tell me her story. It's my fourth day here and I'm eager to begin interviewing. Already the days are slipping by.

It's eight a.m. and Rosa is still asleep. I've slept well too, on a firm bed, softly embraced by the feather pillows and comforter. But Reili's been up for a while and has made a pot of coffee and boiled water for tea. She's dressed for the day in a crisp white embroidered blouse, tucked into a long, full denim skirt with matching embroidery. Though she'll probably stay in the apartment all day, she looks ready for anything.

Reili's long skirts remind me of the stories she's told me about the grandmother who raised her, a healer and fortune-teller who wore colorful sweeping skirts. *They knew she was Sinti by the way she dressed.* She must have looked like the stereotypical picture of the Gypsy woman, I think, even though she didn't travel in caravans or horse-drawn wagons but instead tended a farm outside Berlin. *People came from all over for her remedies; that's how she made her money. She was known, people came to the property. She had the customers, steady.*

Reili's family doesn't fit the stereotype of the traveling Gypsy; instead, like many Sinti, they have been settled for generations. *Our Familie had been in Germany for over four hundred years*, Reili tells me.

Ironically, it was the Nazis who documented evidence of the family's long presence in Germany. *The papers are in*

*Berlin. And that's what they were interested in: the pure Sinti with no intermarriage, fifty years back, a hundred years back. The Nazis told us that when they made that survey on our* Familie. *They measured the heads, they checked the whole background, they went through old papers and they proved it. Pure, pure, no intermarriage.*

The systematic genealogical and genetic research on Germany's 30,000 Gypsies, to which Reili refers, was designed to prove their racial inferiority – and it led directly to their murders at Auschwitz and other concentration camps. But the racial research resulted in policy decisions that were inconsistent. Before 1942, most of the Nazi measures against Gypsies were directed at *Mischlinge*, or those of mixed ancestry, while 'pure' Gypsies were temporarily protected from such measures. In 1942, however, the distinctions between the two groups were dropped and all Gypsies became subject to Nazi policy of racial persecution.

∾

*They picked the better* Familie, Reili says of the genealogical and genetic research conducted by a special unit of the Reich Department of Health. *I don't know why they picked us. I'm not bragging about it.* Reili laughs when she says this. *But it was the fact!*

I wonder why Reili thinks that only the 'pure' families were picked for this research, as evidence shows that the Nazis registered and collected data on all Gypsies and part-Gypsies in Germany. But even more, I wonder how Reili can talk so calmly about the Nazis' racial persecution of Gypsies that affected her so profoundly.

"Fifteen, twenty years ago, I couldn't have talked about it," Reili tells me. "I would have got too angry and upset. I was hateful. Bitter."

Now, perhaps because she was able to start a new life in the United States, perhaps because of her strong religious beliefs, she is able to talk about her experiences fleeing from the Nazis with her parents and enduring the wretched conditions of a concentration camp.

Reili's neighbors in America know that she is from Germany and was interned in a concentration camp, but they don't know that she is Gypsy. Why are you so dark? they ask her. "I tell them not all Germans have blond hair and blue eyes."

I know Reili is proud of her ethnicity, even though she wants to disguise it for one very specific reason: "I didn't want my children to suffer from the prejudice, she says. The Sinti are always going to be looked down on, regardless what, Toby. Regardless what. And that's what I want to prevent for my children."

Still, Reili believes it's important for people to know what happened to the Sinti; that's why she's here with me in Germany, helping me with this project. "In Germany, it doesn't matter," she told me, when we were still in the United States. Germans recognize the identity of the Gypsies, she said, so there's no point in being secretive.

"All the Sinti will talk to you about everything because they're branded as Sinti anyway," she assured me before we left.

Yet now that we're here, people don't seem quite as eager to talk as Reili led me to believe. I worry that Rosa is postponing the interview, that we have no plan yet to go to see the other relatives. Sitting around the kitchen table with Reili in the morning before Rosa is up, I confess my anxieties.

"I don't want to keep asking her," Reili says. "She'll let us know when she's ready."

I bite my lower lip and keep silent, counseling myself to be patient and to respectfully follow Reili's lead. After all, she is the real authority here. I am just a guest, an outsider. And if not for her I would not be here at all.

૭

Rosa shuffles out the bedroom in her house slippers, her hair flying in untidy wisps about her wrinkled face. Dressed in the same blouse, cardigan sweater and checkered wool skirt that she wore yesterday, she seems startled by the fact of another morning. *"Guten Morgan,"* she says to us, on her way toward the bathroom. After she emerges, with her hair brushed and pulled back into a tidy bun, she settles into her chair at the table.

*"Schlaft gut?* I no can sleep." She shakes her head. "Whole night I cough. No good."

There is a silence while she lights her first cigarette of the day and begins to cough again – a deep guttural hacking that lasts for some minutes. As the violent cough overwhelms her, Reili and I are awkwardly quiet, unable to help, as we wait for the cough to run its course.

Afterwards, I offer her a glass of water or a cup of coffee but she refuses. Instead she gets two raw eggs and a bottle of non-alcoholic malt, and brings them to the table to mix her daily morning concoction. She separates the two eggs carefully, puts the yolks in the bottom of a glass, fills the glass with the dark brown malt liquid, stirs vigorously and drinks it down. My own stomach is weak from the insults of international travel and I can hardly bear to watch her drink this potion. But she claims that the drink is what keeps her going. *"Ja* – it opens up my lungs."

After she gulps down the breakfast drink, she spends about ten minutes sorting through a variety of pill containers in a large plastic box to find her four morning pills. She washes these down with a cup of coffee and smokes a couple more cigarettes.

From the next room, the television blares, as inane and abrasive in German as it is in English. Jethro, Rosa's six-year-old grandson who lives with her, clicks on the set as soon as he gets up each morning, then stumbles sleepily to the living room couch. Rosa brings him a container of banana milk for his breakfast and he washes it down as he watches TV, still dressed in his pajamas. Although Jethro eventually wanders back to his room, to dress in jeans and a flannel shirt, and to play with his favorite plastic super-hero figures, the TV set stays on for most of the day, permeating the apartment with the irritating chatter of American sit-coms and game shows, dubbed in German.

Reili and I wash the breakfast dishes, help Rosa sweep and vacuum the apartment and then, our work finished, settle in the living room around the coffee table, to talk some more.

The decorative touches of Rosa's living room remind me of Gypsy homes I've seen in America. Lace curtains on the windows, dark red velvet curtains in between the living room and the bedrooms, lace crocheted doilies on the coffee table, intricate, richly colored Persian rugs. On one of the walls, in an elaborate gold frame, there is a photograph of Rosa as a young woman with her husband, Hamlet, in military uniform.

"How lovely Rosa looks," I remark.

"Rosa was very beautiful when she was young," Reili agrees. "She had the eyes that wouldn't quit."

Reili points to a nearly empty wooden armoire. "Rosa used to have so many beautiful things. That cupboard was full. All the carpets on the floor are the real thing. When Hamlet died, she had to sell most of her good things to pay for his burial."

Rosa just shrugs her shoulders and takes another puff of her cigarette, as if she cares nothing about the material goods she lost. But noticing my interest in the old photograph, she goes to a bureau drawer and pulls out an album.

"Look – I show you something." She opens the old photo album and I look over her shoulder as she turns the pages: page after page of black and white photographs of people, taken from before the war. Elegantly dressed young men and women, an older couple, a grouping of men with violins, a mother with her children.

"*Tot, tot, tot.* . ." Dead, dead, dead. . . Rosa points to each picture. "Litzmannstadt, Litzmannstadt."

These are photographs of her family, all of whom died in

Rosa with her photo album

Litzmannstadt, the German name for Lódz Ghetto in Poland, the first locality in Poland to be used for the mass murder of Gypsies in a camp setting. Rosa herself was spared because she escaped from a transport taking her family from a transit camp in Austria to Lódz.

Rosa pauses by a photograph of her sister, a handsome woman with long blond braids, holding two smiling young children. Her sister could have been a symbol for the concept of 'Aryan' with her classic Germanic looks. She reminds me of Marko, the son of Reili's cousin, who met me at the airport. Large-framed, blond-haired, blue-eyed, the young man looked like an archetypal German youth. I'd never have guessed that he was a Sinto, a Gypsy. Indeed, many of the Gypsies I meet here challenge my preconceptions. Although Reili and Rosa and many of the other Sinti who I meet in Germany have 'Gypsy looks' – thick, dark hair, dark eyes, high

Photographs from Rosa's album

cheekbones, and golden-brown skin – others look as far from the stereotype as Marko or Rosa's sister.

I linger at the picture. The mother and children look so happy... and so Germanic. The two children are even wearing lederhosen.

Rosa's sister and her children, all of whom died at Lodz (Chelmno)

Rosa brings me back to reality. "Dead. All of them. In Litzmannstadt."

Litzmannstadt. Łódz. By the autumn of 1941, a section of the Jewish ghetto at Łódz had been designated the *Zigeuner-lager*, or Gypsy camp. During five days in early November, 1941, five transports, each carrying a thousand Gypsies from Austria, arrived in Łódz Ghetto. Adolf Eichmann had personally given the orders to send the transports.

At first the Gypsies were allowed to play their violins and guitars, and Jews who lived on the other side of the barbed wire fence heard the melodic strains of Gypsy music. But soon the Germans forbade any more music. Silence ensued, interrupted only by screams from the tortured prisoners.

Drunken German soldiers attacked the Gypsy section at night, beating and raping the prisoners. They smashed all the windows of the houses, exposing the weakened, starving Gypsy prisoners to the bitter winter cold. There were no sanitary facilities, no medical help. Within two weeks, an epidemic of spotted typhus fever raged through the camp and hundreds fell victim. Workers piled the disfigured corpses into carts, more and more of them each day.

While the Jewish ghetto in Lódz existed for four years, the Gypsy section existed for only about two months, and in those two months over 600 Gypsies died, mostly of typhus. In December 1941 and January 1942, those who hadn't died of typhus were loaded onto three-ton trucks, 200–300 people at a time, until the camp was empty. The trucks, with their human cargo covered by tarpaulins, drove toward the extermination camp of Chelmno on the River Ner. The camp authority made promises to the Gypsy prisoners: They would be fed and transferred to a work camp in the East. But first, they had to bathe and have their clothes disinfected.

Guards accompanied the Gypsies, two by two, into the camp building, up a flight of stairs and into a heated room. They told the inmates to undress and then walk downstairs, wearing only their underwear. Then they were to walk through a doorway marked with a sign: 'To the bath.'

They would travel to the bathhouse in a covered truck, they were told.

Then the guards dropped the pretense, beating the prisoners and forcing them into the truck – which was actually a mobile gas chamber. The truck doors were slammed shut. The motor roared and engine exhaust poured into the sealed van. Screaming and moaning penetrated the walls of the van. Five long minutes of these terrible sounds. Then the screaming subsided. Guards drove the van to the nearby forest and dumped the corpses. Then they returned to the camp building to load the next group of Gypsies going to the 'bathhouse.'

Gypsy survivor accounts from Lódz Ghetto are almost

A page of Rosa's album

absent – there is only one known survivor who was transferred to a labor camp with a small group shortly before the liquidation. Everyone else was murdered. This blunt fact is driven home to me by Rosa's tragic photo album. Her finger, pointing to each person. Her voice, telling me each name. Each one, followed by the litany. "*Tot*. Dead. Litzmannstadt."

༅

Just as I think again that this would be an ideal time to record her memoirs, the door opens and Rosa's daughter, Velda, comes in, pushing a baby stroller and accompanied by her friend, Lilly.

Rosa slams the album shut, leaps up and sprints to a dresser on the other side of the room. She pulls lace tablecloths and sheets out of a drawer. "This is very good – the Battenburg lace," she says, giving me a few delicate lace doilies.

Rosa supplements her pension by selling lace that she buys in Czechoslovakia, Reili explains to me, and Lilly, the only woman she knows who has a car, has offered to drive her to her customers' homes. Before I know it, Rosa yanks off her apron, gathers an armful of lace and leaves with Lilly. Within ten minutes, my hopeful plans for the day are crushed. Rosa won't return for hours. No interview today, I think.

But in the early evening, after Rosa returns and the supper dishes have been washed and dried, Rosa surprises me. "We can do the interview now," she says. I quickly check my tape recorder, already set up on a small table in Jethro's bedroom. Rosa takes off her apron, gathers her cigarettes, a lighter and an ashtray and we begin.

## chapter *four*

# *Before and after*

໑

*Everything was fine before the Germans came.*
Rosa was part of a large family: seven sisters and two brothers. The family followed the Sinti traditions, speaking Romanes in the home and strictly forbidding intermarriage with non-Gypsies. When she describes their life in Vienna, it sounds quite attractive. Her father and brothers were employed as musicians and one brother played his violin in Vienna's finest restaurants. The family was on friendly terms with their non-Gypsy neighbors, and frequently invited them to their home for an afternoon of conversation accompanied by coffee and cake. She doesn't recall any prejudice against the Sinti when she was a young child. *The people in Vienna are not like the Germans*, she says.

*Everything was fine before the Germans came.*
Before: this is almost a sacred time zone to many survivors. All life, joy, good, occurred in the Before time.

Yet long before the Nazis came to power, the Gypsies had become Europe's scapegoat, discriminated against and persecuted by both church and state. The Nazis didn't have to create legislation against the so-called 'Gypsy menace'; it already existed. In Germany, Gypsies had been photographed and fingerprinted like criminals from 1922. When the Nazis took over, however, a new rationalization was given for persecution: the allegedly inferior racial character of Gypsies.

Eugenics, the idea that hereditary improvement of a race could be achieved by genetic control, had gained favor as a tool for social change in the United States in the 1920s, when tens of thousands of Americans were declared 'moral imbeciles' and subjected to involuntary sterilization. In the 1930s, the eugenics movement became popular in Germany as well, forming the basis for the Nazis' extreme race theories and measures that eventually caused millions of deaths. When Hitler came to power, the Nazis determined to discriminate against, or persecute, all who were *Gemeinshchaftsfremd*, alien to the community. And this designation was defined in terms that were ideological, social, and – most importantly – biological.

Needing proof that the Gypsies were inferior to the 'Aryan' Germans, Nazis confined many Gypsies to internment camps, *Zigeunerlager,* where scientists registered them and collected racial and genealogical information which often resulted in loss of citizenship and the involuntary sterilization of Gypsy prisoners. In Vienna, where Rosa lived, the International Center for the Fight Against the Gypsy Menace was established in 1936, and the German police were instructed to give the center full support.

ও

Rosa says she first became aware of Nazi policies against Gypsies when she was just ten or eleven years old – in 1934 or 1935 – soon after Hitler came to power in Germany. The Nazis had just passed laws classifying non-Europeans, including Gypsies, as second-class citizens in Germany. "In Europe, only Jews and Gypsies are of foreign blood," the legal commentaries stated.

Rosa's family, and other Austrian Gypsies, had heard that German Sinti were being arrested and sent to internment camps. But there were speculations that they themselves might be spared if they changed their occupations from musicians to factory workers. They'd also heard that the 'pure' Sinti – those who hadn't intermarried – would not be sent to the

Rosa Mettbach, Vienna, 1940 (*Print courtesy of Ludwig Eiber*)

*Zigeunerlager.* These rumors came about through the uncertain and shifting policy of the Nazis, as they searched for a solution to the 'Gypsy question.'

Rosa was fourteen in 1938, a critical year for the Gypsies, as it was for the Jews. The *Anschluss*, or incorporation of Austria into the German Reich, on 13 March marked the end of sovereign Austria, and the country was named *Ostmark*, a province of the Reich. Gypsies were prohibited from voting in the plebiscite for the 'reunion' of Austria with the Reich. The Nuremberg laws were implemented in the *Ostmark* and a decree issued in May required the registration of all migrant Roma and Sinti by June 1938. In June, national raids against 'anti-socials' took place throughout the Reich; 'clean-up week' or Operation Work Shy resulted in the arrest of about 1,000 Gypsies who were deported to concentration camps. August saw the first attempted mass expulsion of Gypsies in Germany as several hundred Gypsies were forcibly removed from the left bank of the Rhine and relocated to Berlin and Frankfurt. And on 8 December 1938, riding the tails of *Kristallnacht* a month before, SS Chief Heinrich Himmler signed the first law directed specifically against Gypsies. The Decree for Combating the Gypsy Plague required the more systematic registration of all Gypsies, based on the research of the racial scientists, and recommended "the resolution of the Gypsy question based on its essentially racial nature."

Austria's 11,000 Gypsies were now to be treated the same as those in Germany. Discriminatory measures which had evolved in Germany over a period of years were adopted in Austria in just a few months. Himmler ordered that all Austrian Gypsies above the age of fourteen were to be fingerprinted and a copy of the prints sent to the Reich Criminal Police Office in Berlin. Austrian Gypsies were forbidden to leave the country. They were forbidden to marry persons of German blood. They were subject to compulsory labor at public works. Sporadic arrests began, and within a few months, 2,000 male Gypsies had been sent to Dachau (and later to Buchenwald and Mauthausen) and 1,000 female Gypsies had been sent to Ravensbrück.

Anti-Gypsy measures were most aggressive in the

Burgenland, the easternmost province of Austria where most of the country's Roma and Sinti lived. The governor of the Burgenland, Tobias Portshy, referred to Gypsies as "parasites" and called for their sterilization. In the spring of 1938, a debate erupted over whether Gypsy children, like Jewish children, were to be barred from public schools. Austrian officials wanted to expel the Gypsy children but didn't want to provide separate schools for them as the children still had a legal right to public education. The solution was to banish only those Gypsies who were considered a threat. Now, since the school officials considered *all* Gypsy children 'pests,' it was easy to get rid of them. In Vienna, schools barred Gypsy children on the grounds that they constituted "a threat to the moral character of the German children." Due to these regulations, Rosa was removed from school.

By the end of 1938, it was impossible for Gypsies to ignore the restrictions and persecution by the Nazi regime. Gypsies presented a special problem for the Nazis: since they had come from India, they were true Aryans and so they would have to be reclassified, as 'asocials.' More and more often, Roma and Sinti were stereotyped as criminals, vagabonds or asocials, simply because of their race. More and more frequently, they were subject to arbitrary arrest and detention. Rosa's family, like the other Sinti families, was forbidden to leave their district. Despite the law, Rosa and her sister did once leave their district: *To look for something to eat,* she explains. They were caught. As punishment, the police shaved all the hair off their heads and kept them in jail for three days before sending them home.

In Austria's Burgenland province, a decree issued in September 1938 prohibited Gypsy musicians from performing publicly, and called for the conscription of able-bodied Gypsy men to work in public works projects such as construction, roads and stone quarries. By fall of 1939, this decree was implemented in Vienna and Rosa's brother, the musician who played in Vienna's finest restaurants, was told that he could no longer perform. Along with three older sisters, he was sent to forced labor on the streets of the city.

For Gypsies in the Burgenland, the situation was even worse. In June 1939, 3,000 Romanies were deported from the Burgenland to Dachau and Ravensbrück. The next phase, the deportation of all Gypsies from Austria, had been planned, but had to be delayed because transport capacity was insufficient. Reinhard Heydrich, head of the SS Secret Police, issued a decree prohibiting Gypsies from changing their registered residences and mandating the systematic registration of all Gypsies in Austria. The census and registration took place from 25–27 October 1939. Along with the others, Rosa's family members were measured and fingerprinted.

She tells a story – the first of many involving cigarettes – of how she and two of her sisters were summoned to the registration. Defiantly, the girls decided to use the opportunity for a little mischief. They rubbed cigarette tobacco in their eyes, so the whites of their eyes turned yellow. When the examining doctor saw them, he feared that they had a contagious disease and so he released them.

She laughs at the memory: a small victory in the face of unrelenting Nazi persecution.

∾

Rosa is a native speaker of both German and Romanes. Yet she chooses to tell me much of her story in English, even though Reili is there to translate from the German. Rosa's English, which she learned after the war when she sold goods to American soldiers, is fragmented and often rough – she frequently uses verbs in the wrong tense and sometimes she is unable to find the words she needs at all and reverts to German. It is a great effort for her to speak in English, and I know that her account lacks the fluidity and detail it would have had recounted in her native tongue. Yet there's something striking and significant in her choice to tell this painful tale in English. She wants to tell it to me – and, through me, to other English speakers. She looks at me intently as she talks. She is trying to translate memory, to translate language, across generations, across cultures. It is this attempt to translate memory that I cherish in Rosa's story.

❧

*Rossauerlände – all of them knows it.*
The Rossauerlände police station and jail in Vienna was a holding area for the Roma and Sinti facing deportation to Lackenbach, a *Zigeunerlager*, or internment camp for Gypsies, established in November 1940. In late 1940, Gypsies were taken to this collection center and jailed.

*The police and the SS put us in there – a big area with barbed wire around it. Rossauerlände – everybody: Jews and Gypsies, Sinti or not Sinti – they take all of them. Or go to work or not go to work – egal. Equal. All of them. We were in there for six, seven months.*

I ask her if she can describe the day that the police came to her home to take her family away. She shakes her head and her eyes cloud with pain.

*Oh.* Her voice cracks. *I no can think of that.*

*Then, Lackenbach,* she continues, bluntly. *We all cried.*

"What did you think was happening?"

*We cried. Kill 'em, kill 'em, all of them.*

Lackenbach was in Austria, near the Hungarian border. It was located on the site of a former pig farm and, in 1940, the camp was utterly unsuited for human habitation. While the officials took over the walled storage buildings, the Gypsy prisoners had to sleep in damp stables, often sodden after a rain. As many as 200 people were pushed into one room. Water and sanitary facilities were lacking, and prisoners had to clean the latrines with their bare hands. As one prisoner recounted, "We were taken there from …our clean houses and caravans into poverty and dirt." Only in late 1941, after a

Gypsy women marching to work in the Lachenbach internment camp. (*Mauthausen Museum Archives, courtesy of United States Holocaust Museum Photo Archives*)

typhus epidemic made guards vulnerable to the disease, did living conditions improve to the standard of other internment camps, with dormitory barracks, a sanatorium and toilet and washing facilities.

Lackenbach was run by the Vienna Kripo, Criminal Police, rather than the SS and thus it was never officially classified as a concentration camp. But, as Kenrick and Puxon write, "Conditions hardly differed. No high voltage electric fence was built but the usual roll-calls, corporal punishment and forced labour went on. The prisoners were permitted, however, to stay in family groups."

Prisoners lived in barracks, without heat during the winter, and the terrible unhygienic conditions caused epidemic outbreaks of disease. Camp officials responded to outbreaks of typhus by sealing off the prisoners, leaving them to suffer the ravages of the disease on their own. In between epidemics, inmates – even children – had to work building the camp, or in the farms or on the streets of the area, having been 'lent' to private firms or farmers for forced labor. Strict discipline was enforced at work and even talking was forbidden. Though workers were to receive 10 percent of their wages, ex-prisoners remembered that they received only enough to cover the three cigarettes they were allowed each day. The rest went to the camp authorities.

Any infractions of camp rules were punishable by solitary confinement, corporal punishment and starvation. Anyone caught trying to escape Lackenbach was brutally beaten, deprived of food, sentenced to hard labor or sent to a concentration camp.

One of the more difficult realities of everyday life at Lackenbach was the poor food, served in meager portions. Soups and stews made from turnips or rotten cabbage. Inedible cheese. Peas and beans full of maggots.

*We ate food intended for pigs. My sister and her children cried for a piece of bread. But what you going to do? Nothing.*

And there was the Camp Commandant, Franz Langmüller. Rosa remembers him striding through the camp with the whip that he always carried. Arbitrarily, he would stop to beat the prisoners. He showed no mercy. At his trial after the war, Langmüller was accused of responsibility for 287 deaths, including an incident in which 35 to 40 children were poisoned, probably as a result of a medical experiment.

After nearly a year in Lackenbach, an announcement came. The prisoners were to be transferred to another camp. Another work camp, the prisoners thought. Probably not too far away. How could they guess then that they were being deported to their final destination in Poland?

In order to carry out the plan to rid Germany and Austria of all Gypsies, the Nazis had decided to use part of the Jewish Ghetto in Lódz, Poland, and five thousand Gypsies were to be sent from various locations. The first transports arrived in Lódz in October 1941, and by November the whole consignment had arrived.

Again they were loaded into a cattle car. It was a November

day – cold and bleak. Inside the cattle car it was almost totally dark, warm and airless from the density of bodies crammed together. This transport was headed for Poland – to a place that the Germans called Litzmannstadt.

*My people goes with the Jewish people to Litzmannstadt – Lódz, you say today. Lódz.*

The guards packed the train car tightly for maximum efficiency. After all, they had orders. And so what if some of these people died? They were expendable anyway, "life unworthy of life," the Nazis said, like the handicapped and the Jews.

*So many that we thought we would suffocate. Everyone – children, old people.*

Rosa must have suspected that the place they were going would be even worse than the place they were leaving. Otherwise, she could not have left her family. But just before the train started moving, Rosa and a few other girls escaped by crawling through an air hole on the opposite side from the loading doors.

*I ran away. I crawl up – and go.*

She would never see any of her family again.

## chapter five

# *I can do nothing for you*

༽

"Did anyone help you escape?" I ask Rosa.

*No, no. I had an aunt – my Tante. I go to her. And my Tante, she's an old, rich lady. Had two houses, big ones. Very nice houses. Lots of money, lots of gold, diamonds, everything. I go – I have nothing.*

Rosa explains all this rapidly, as if to race past the moment of her escape and what it signifies. The finality implicit in the escape. The way she wrenched her own life out of the clench of death that would devour her family whole.

"How did you find your aunt's house?"

*I know the area. It's not far from Vienna – maybe 50 kilometers.*

Accompanied by one of the other girls who had escaped, she found her way to her aunt's home, in the countryside not far from Lackenbach, and they stayed with her aunt for eight days. Her elderly aunt wanted her to stay longer but Rosa feared that the Nazis would discover her hiding place and arrest both the girls and her aunt.

"How come your aunt hadn't already been arrested?"

*A little later. They got her, too.*

With some money that her aunt had given her, Rosa and her friend left the luxury of the country home, to hide in the surrounding forest. For months the two girls lived in the woods, begging for food from farmers during the day, sleeping in barn haylofts at night. But one day, Rosa's friend went out to look for food and never came back.

Alone now, Rosa decided to go back to Vienna where she was taken in by a non-Gypsy neighbor, a woman whose husband was away, serving in the military. *She give me something to eat, to sleep.* The other neighbors, who knew what had happened to her family, said nothing to the authorities, and the women, who had been friends with her mother, brought her supplies.

*One brings me shoes, one brings me a dress, a blouse...*

She lived there for five or six months. *But the woman's husband was a military man. I no trust him, and she no trust him either. I go. She said, "When my husband leaves, come back."* Rosa went to other acquaintances to ask for protection and they also allowed her to hide. But soon she was discovered and arrested again.

"How did you get caught?" I ask.

*Hunger. I was hungry, I needed something to eat. I went out on the street, and they caught me.*

Some Hungarian Sinti had turned her in, to try to save themselves, she believes. Rosa tried to give the police a phony name, but they knew who she was.

*They say, "No, no. You're Rosa. You were in Lackenbach."*

*They caught me and returned me. They took me to the Elizabethpromenade and put me on a train to Lackenbach. There, they gave me 25 lashes.*

Rosa had been returned to this dismal camp. *Lackenbach.* In agonizing pain from the whipping, her skin torn open and raw, she couldn't sleep. What had happened to her family after they left here? she wondered. They were gone, and now she was here, again. The people in the Gypsy camp of Lackenbach had all been brought here since her escape; she didn't recognize anyone.

*Nobody from my people. All of them to Litzmannstadt. All of them died,* she says – though she didn't know this at the time. *These were new people, who had been in hiding.*

Rosa was seventeen. She was sent out to work hauling rocks.

*Then the typhus broke out.*

Lice carrying the disease lived in the straw mattresses and in people's hair. People died in the night and, when they were pulled out of their straw-lined barracks in the morning, their necks were covered with a solid mass of lice. Rosa raked her hands through her thick, wavy hair and pulled out handfuls of lice. She doused her hair in kerosene to kill the lice. These measures weren't enough. Soon all the prisoners' hair was cut off to control the lice-spread epidemic.

*I was over there four months. Then I go again. Sshvvvveet!* Her hand darts in front of her, cat-like, to show the nimbleness of her escape.

A cousin had warned her to leave. *"Otherwise, you'll end up in Auschwitz,"* he said. Already, rumors about Auschwitz were raging. *Everyone had heard about Auschwitz, and kill all the people there.*

During a work break, in the spring of 1942, Rosa saw her chance. She took off, running into the woods.

*That time, by myself – I go alone.*

*I go to Vienna. No money, nothing. I think it was March. I can't say exactly – March, April, May.*

Again Rosa went to see some people she knew in Vienna, and they gave her a little money. She decided to use it for a train ticket to Germany. But why would she go to Germany then, into the very center of the Nazi terror? Her rationale was based on personal factors. All the Sinti Gypsy families she knew in Vienna were gone, deported. She knew from experience that she wouldn't be able to hide successfully there any longer. She also knew that many Sinti lived in Munich and that they'd welcome her.

*When you run and you know Sintis – you can go,* she explains.

She had nice clothes that she'd received in Vienna but she had no papers, no identification. Rosa took her seat in the train and surveyed her surroundings. The only other passenger with her in the train compartment was an elderly military man from Hungary, wearing a uniform decorated with medals. He could be a threat, she thought, but his face was kindly.

After every stop, the train inspector walked through the cars, checking the papers for each passenger. Rosa anticipated this check every time and went to hide in the lavatory before he could reach her compartment. Soon, her seatmate caught on.

On the Austrian-German border near Salzburg, there was another inspection, but this time Rosa didn't have enough time to get out of her seat. *That's the end of it,* she thought. She leaned her head into the corner and pretended to be asleep. The inspector moved toward her, intending to wake her up but before he reached her, the military officer intervened.

*"Leave that girl alone,"* he said. *"She's been checked ten times since Vienna. Let her sleep. I know she has identification."*

The inspector thanked the officer for the information and moved on through the train, closing the compartment door.

*"Now you can open your eyes,"* said her seatmate. Rosa could hardly believe her fortune. Before she knew what to say, the man had opened up a suitcase full of food and offered it to her. *"I guess you haven't had anything good to eat for a long time,"* he said.

As the train pulled into the Munich station, Rosa got up and gathered her bags. At the door of the compartment, she turned to the man who saved her life and whispered her thanks.

The Hungarian officer smiled at her kindly. *"I wish you much luck, little Gypsy girl,"* he said.

*He is a good man — never forgot that man.*

In Munich, Rosa found the Sinti neighborhood and a generous family, the Mettbachs, offered her shelter. She didn't know the Mettbachs personally but she had heard of them.

How did she know where to find them in Munich, a city she had never seen? *I never see it before in my life. Never. Over there, Sinti, over here Sinti. All Sinti were running, hiding. They all knew about each other.*

Johann ("Hamlet") Mettbach, around 1941. He was discharged from
the army in 1942, and assigned forced labor in a BMW plant.
(*Print courtesy of Ludwig Eiber*)

The family that had taken her in included a handsome
young man, Hamlet, who lived with his parents and siblings
in the house. He was on leave from military service on the
Russian front and he and Rosa fell in love.

Perhaps because of a specific connection in the military,
Hamlet's family had been spared deportation but this protec-
tion could not include his new love. Nazi policy towards the
Gypsies was sometimes inconsistent because local police,
rather than the Gestapo, were in charge of deportations of
Gypsies and so sometimes local connections could spare a

family. Thus, Hamlet, a full Sinto, still served in the German army, although he was discharged later in 1942, and ordered to compulsory labor in a BMW plant. Still, in 1942, he lived quite openly in Germany – but Rosa could not. She had no local connections and she was both a foreigner and an escapee.

By Sinti law, Rosa and Hamlet were married, but they couldn't marry under German law. That kind of attention would have resulted in Rosa's arrest. She had already twice been arrested and taken to a *Zigeunerlager*. Rosa had no illusions about what would happen if she were caught.

She lived in Munich for about two years until her son was born. She gave birth to her child in the hospital but left the day after the birth so she wouldn't be discovered.

*Everybody (could) see that I am not German.*

Rosa left the hospital with her husband and son and went to the country for six weeks to recuperate, staying in a farmhouse belonging to a friendly non-Gypsy woman, but then she fell ill from postpartum complications and needed to go to a doctor in Munich.

The visit was her undoing. The doctor treated her but as soon as she left, he reported her. She was arrested on the street outside the doctor's office, taken to the prison in Munich, and interrogated.

*"Where is your baby?"* asked the police officer.

*I have no baby,* Rosa answered.

The officer struck her. *"Who has your baby?"*

*Nobody,* she insisted. *I have no babies.*

*"Oh, I know who has your baby,"* he said.

*They found out the child came from Hamlet,* Rosa explains. *One day he* (the policeman) *said to me, "No - you're not going to go to your baby. Your baby will come to you."*

Sure enough, after a day or so, her sister-in-law came to visit Rosa and brought her baby.

*And the baby – oh, the baby was sick! He was only seven weeks old then.*

The police officer told the sister-in-law that Rosa would

be sent to Vienna, but Rosa, with no illusions, contradicted him.

*Nein,* she said, shaking her head. *I'm going to Auschwitz.*

Then Hamlet came to talk to the police. A different officer was on duty and Hamlet persuaded him to release the baby. The officer assured Hamlet that his wife would only be sent to Vienna.

*Don't lie like that,* Rosa reprimanded him. *I'm going to go tomorrow, on the transport to Auschwitz.*

*Hamlet, he no can do nothing. They told him, be glad that you're on the Russian front. Otherwise you'll be in a concentration camp.*

*And Hamlet, he didn't have any cigarettes. He was nervous. He forgot; he didn't bring cigarettes. So Sizer* (the policeman) *gave me a pack of cigarettes. And Hamlet took the baby.*

I imagine this exchange: the baby's life for Rosa's, with a pack of cigarettes thrown in to sweeten the bitter bargain.

*How I felt when Hamlet took the baby and I know I have to go…* Her voice trails off.

*The next day, I go. In the morning, five o'clock, on the transport – to Auschwitz.*

Meanwhile, Hamlet had taken the sick baby and placed him in the children's ward in the hospital. He'd explained to the head doctor that he had a girlfriend in show business and that when he'd come back from the Russian front she'd left the baby behind with nobody to care for him.

*The doctor said, "Well, there's not much I can do for that baby. He's awful weak, awful sick. I'll do the best I can. But he's sure a dark child."* He took the basket and put it next to him on the desk.

The transport Rosa was on stopped in Vienna to load more prisoners, and one of the Viennese policemen, after looking through the papers, recognized her. It was a man who had known her mother, who had been good to the family.

The policeman looked at her sadly. *"I can do nothing for you any more,"* he said. Slowly he shook his head. *"I can do <u>nothing</u>*

*for you, more. I can do nothing for you — you're going to Auschwitz."*

He paused. Then, speaking softly, he told her the worst news: *"And your mother died – in Litzmannstadt."*

## chapter six

# *The sky was grey*

∾

*They bring me to Auschwitz in the night. I see nothing,* Rosa says, pausing to puff on her cigarette.

*And the train went right into the concentration camp. I see nothing, you know – it's dark. Coming over there, open the doors. Bang, bang, bang, hitting us. Open the doors. Lots of them (on the transport). Only two men and one woman Hungarian Sinti; the rest Jews. And no children. Men, women. Over there I see nothing.*

*"Schnell, schnell, schnell, schnell, schnell!!!"*

Guards beat the prisoners as they emerged from the cattle car at night. *Hitting them when they came out. Take us off.* As soon as they arrived the prisoners were branded with tattoos. Rosa and the other Sinti were tattooed with the letter 'Z' for *Zigeuner*, followed by numbers.

*Put the number there.* Rosa points to her arm.

The guards herded the prisoners into the shower room and forced them to strip. For both Gypsies and Jews, this was the ultimate offense, a brutal humiliation.

*The young women and the men, all of them, in one, naked, naked. You have to take it all off, your dresses and that. Oh, you don't think of nothing more.* Her voice is heavy with disgust, humiliation, shame.

*Then you had the shower. And the old ones, I never see them no more. Maybe kill them.*

Rosa was separated from the Jewish prisoners and sent to the Gypsy camp at Birkenau, the so-called 'family camp.' Following Himmler's decree of December 1942, a special camp had been set aside for Gypsies in Birkenau, the large camp near Auschwitz.

The gassing of Jews was already underway when Gypsies were sent here, to Camp BIIe (*Zigeunerlager*), in 1943 and the first half of 1944. When Jews arrived in Auschwitz, they were separated into two groups. Those considered fit for work were taken to the camp, while those considered unfit for work were taken directly to the gas chambers. In contrast, Gypsy families did not undergo the selection on the platform, and men and women were not separated but were interned together as families. They often kept their own clothing, though a black triangle was attached to signify 'asocial' status.

The family camp at Auschwitz-Birkenau was the only concentration camp where Gypsies were treated differently from other prisoners, and why families were not separated is still a matter of speculation. Perhaps it was because they were being kept for medical experiments, for a show to the Red Cross, or because guards feared violent rebellion from the Gypsies if extended families were separated. Whatever the reason, this difference in treatment only postponed their inevitable murder. Altogether, some 23,000 Sinti and Romani Gypsies were sent to Auchwitz-Birkenau, and 20,000 of them were killed there.

The Gypsy family camp was only 400 feet from the crematoria and the air was saturated with the smoke of burning human flesh. Still in family units, the Gypsies were crammed together in thirty-two damp and filthy windowless wooden barracks – converted horse stalls that rested on waterlogged soil. About 500 people were housed in each barrack which held three tiers of bunk beds, with a whole family assigned to each bed. Sometimes as many as a thousand people were crammed into a barrack which was ventilated only by slits in the roof. During the winter, cold seeped in through the wooden walls. With an unreliable water supply, frequently contaminated water and only the most primitive latrines, the conditions of the camp were described as "extraordinarily filthy and unhygienic even for Auschwitz, a place of starving babies, children and adults."

As in Lackenbach, malnutrition and abysmal sanitary conditions frequently led to typhus and other disease. Prisoners were regularly deloused to try to control the typhus outbreaks but even this was not effective. Overcrowded hospital barracks offered only the most primitive facilities and little in the way of food or medicine. Over half the Gypsies deported to Auschwitz-Birkenau died as a result of the poor conditions.

Rosa knew many of the Sinti there and all of them asked her questions, hoping she would bring them some new information about their families.

*Everybody wants to know something. Maybe from a father, maybe from a son, maybe from a mother.*

Though many of the Gypsies in Auschwitz-Birkenau were not sent to work, some were chosen to work on the digging and building of the campsite. Rosa was put to work with a crew of Gypsy women, who leveled the ground and carried rocks in their hands and skirts.

*And you have to sing – a military song. And a Gypsy band had to play.*

*And then one day a doctor came – took all the children and put them in one block. Dr. Mengele.*

The infamous Josef Mengele, who had a doctorate in anthropology and a second doctorate in medicine, had been camp doctor of Auschwitz since May 1943. Two months before his arrival, Gypsies transferred from Bialystok had brought in an epidemic of typhoid and Mengele's first assignment was to control the spread of the disease. His response was characteristic: he selected several hundred of the sickest prisoners and sent them to the gas chambers.

The German Gypsies were sent to Auschwitz at about the time Dr. Mengele arrived. They had already been subjected to a thorough anthropological investigation by Dr. Robert Ritter (a psychologist who specialized in 'criminal biology') and his colleagues at the Racial Hygiene Research Center. Dr. Ritter's research team also helped Dr. Wagner of the Kaiser Wilhelm Institute of Anthropology, who was engaged in a study of Gypsy twins and had reported on hereditary eye anomalies. To aid this research, Mengele set up an experimental barracks in the Gypsy camp and killed Gypsies by intracardiac injections so that he could send their eyes to his former teacher, Professor von Verschuer, and other scientists at the prestigious institute. In one case, Mengele ordered that an entire family of eight be killed so that their eyes could be dissected and sent to Berlin. In other medical experiments, Gypsy women were impregnated through artificial insemination and their fetuses aborted at different stages of development. Also, women in advanced stages of pregnancy were infected with typhus fever.

Children were Mengele's favored subjects for medical experiments that caused illness, deformities and death, and he was particularly interested in dwarfs and twins. He acted perversely, giving the starving children candy, then selecting them for barbaric experiments with typhus, desalinization of sea water or tolerance of freezing water. After they died – from typhoid, starvation or lethal injections – they were dissected, their organs examined and often sent to the Kaiser Wilhelm Institute. Thus did scientific research consummate its treacherous union with Nazi ideology.

Those child-victims who lived for a short time after such horrendous experiments could frequently be seen in the Gypsy camp, with grotesquely swollen heads and other deformities.

Rosa's eyes narrow as she remembers Mengele's impetuous, sadistic personality.

*I see him many times. He is very good to the children. Give the kids enough to eat, make everything for the children, all so he could make experiments.*

Away from the operating table, Mengele was known to treat the Gypsy children with special kindness, giving them food, sweets and sometimes toys, even taking them for brief outings. In turn, the children regarded him with affection and called him 'Uncle' or 'Daddy.' Yet he had no compunction about killing those same children – in the name of science.

*All of them knows it! Over there, nobody says anything. When the kids died, you know. And you see kids with large swollen heads.*

Of course, it wasn't only Gypsies who were subjects of Mengele's experiments. Mengele often selected Jewish subjects from the train platform for his 'research.' One of the Jewish boys who fell victim to Mengele's savagery was my father's cousin, Adolf Hermann, sixteen years old at the time of his death. His parents had arranged for him to live with his aunt in Belgium, hoping he would be spared the Nazi terror in Germany, but both Adolf and his parents were deported to Auschwitz and murdered there – Adolf as a result of one of Mengele's experiments.

Rosa tells a story that I've also read in other accounts, about a young Gypsy boy, about four years old, who was Mengele's personal favorite. The doctor, it's said, liked to take the boy with him on his rounds of the camp and frequently displayed the boy's talents in singing and dancing. According to various accounts, the boy, dressed all in white, often stood beside him on the selection ramp for the Jewish transports, while Mengele decided who was to be sent to the gas chamber. At last, this Gypsy boy, too, was murdered. It was said that Mengele personally brought him to the gas chamber.

❧

Mass murders of Gypsies in Auschwitz began in March 1943, with a group of about 1,700 Gypsies, and continued with two more mass killings in May 1943. By the spring of 1944, in response to a severe labor shortage in Germany, Gypsies considered fit to work were selected for transfer to various concentration camps in Germany. Healthy, younger Gypsies and those who had served in the military and agreed to sterilization were selected for transfer.

*Then, one day, we all had to stand for a selection. Military men, go this way. The old ones, go that way and the mothers with children, go that way too.*

Rosa understood how the selections worked. The ones who were sent to the right were considered fit for work, while the ones sent to the left were destined for the gas chamber.

She was ordered to the left.

Panicked, she boldly addressed the official. *I know that whoever goes that way, goes to the crematorium,* she said. *Why did you send me over there? I can work!*

*He says: "You have a little baby."*

*No,* she insisted. *I have no baby.*

*"Okay, then you have no baby. You go over there."* The officer allowed her to join the group on the right.

Rosa breathed again. Her life had been spared, once more. *The last minute.*

She joined the other Gypsies who were to be sent on transports – those who had, for the moment, escaped the jaws of death. The condemned prisoners left at Auschwitz-Birkenau cried out to the few people who had a slight chance at life.

*Then everybody called, "When you see my husband, tell him." "When you see my son or daughter tell them."*

Rosa pauses, her eyes watery. *Reili, I cannot explain how that was.*

It is quiet in the room while Rosa reaches for another cigarette.

*The sky when they burned them wasn't blue – it was grey. And the smell – oh!*

She stops, holds the cigarette to her mouth and slowly draws in the smoke. I am reluctant to break the silence, loath to move on past the tragic image, the line of people condemned to die. I'm not ready to shift the focus back to her own survival. What an enormous weight on this small woman, I think.

Strangely, at this moment, the door opens and a visitor

announces his arrival. Abruptly, we are jolted out of the country of memory.

"It's a good time to stop," Reili says maternally. "We can continue tomorrow."

I nod my head and shut off the tape recorder. But like a wakened dreamer struggling in vain to finish an interrupted dream, I carry the last image with me: the heavens, dark with the smoke of burning flesh. The cry of people going to their deaths rings in my ears.

∾

Later, when I describe Rosa's testimony of the selection to Dr. Sybil Milton, then resident historian for the United States Holocaust Memorial Museum, she says that Rosa couldn't have been at Auschwitz-Birkenau when the camp was liquidated and she suggests that Rosa's memory has jumbled some of the events she experienced into a sort of impressionistic collage.

But I wonder if her memories aren't fairly accurate, after all. Of course, she didn't witness the liquidation of the Gypsy camp but surely she remembers the smoke of burning bodies from the crematoria. The Gypsies were well aware that people were being murdered and their bodies burned – they constantly smelled the odor of burning flesh. And from the summer of 1944, rumors that the Gypsies would be killed had spread through the Gypsy camp. In *The Destiny of Europe's Gypsies*, authors Kenrick and Puxon note that SS men sometimes came to the Gypsy camp in the evenings and took girls off to dance in their barracks; through this contact, the Gypsies knew about their approaching annihilation.

Once, just to quell the unrest caused by these rumors, Nazis took Gypsies from the main Auschwitz camp and loaded them onto trains that ran on a siding alongside the Gypsy camp at Birkenau. The Gypsies at Birkenau, seeing their own people alive and apparently being transported for work, calmed down. The train, however, returned to the Auschwitz camp in a roundabout way and the Gypsies were unloaded.

Selections of healthy, younger Gypsies and decorated veterans that took place after April 1944, resulted in males being sent to Buchenwald and Flossenburg, while females were sent to Ravensbrück. These selections apparently continued until 2 August, the very day of the liquidation, and may have been made by Mengele himself.

Rosa, on one of these last transports, was sent to Ravensbrück. Wouldn't the prisoners who remained at Auschwitz-Birkenau, who were not selected for transport, have been cognizant of their own impending death? Wouldn't they have cried, have begged the others to tell their relatives of their fate?

Even Auschwitz camp commander, Rudolf Höss, who ironically called the Gypsies his "favorite prisoners" described this kind of reaction: "In camp, when a selection of people for work took place and families had to be separated, there were moving scenes full of suffering and tears," he wrote in his postwar confessional autobiography. "The Gypsies would calm down only when told that they would be together later on."

On 2–3 August 1944 (the date of this liquidation varies slightly from one account to the next), on the order of Heinrich Himmler, Nazis began the annihilation of the Gypsy camp. A final selection of adults took place even on this last day. A large group was loaded into a train and said their goodbyes through the barbed wire. Rosa may have been among the prisoners on this last transport of Gypsies from Auschwitz-Birkenau.

In the late afternoon, Dr. Mengele checked the children's block and sent some twins to the main camp. Although Mengele is said to have initially opposed the mass murder of the Gypsies, once it was ordered he worked tirelessly to carry it out. Some say he even ferreted Gypsy children out of hiding and personally drove them in a car to the gas chamber, "drawing upon their trust for him and speaking tenderly and reassuringly to them until the end."

At about eight o' clock in the evening the trucks arrived. "The Gypsies knew what was in store for them, but the Germans tried to allay suspicions," write Kenrick and Puxon. "Everyone was given a ration of bread and salami as they came out of their quarters and some believed at first they must be going to another camp." In an attempt to mislead them further, the trucks took off in a different direction from the crematoria. The light of the August evening lingered and only under cover of darkness did the trucks drive their Gypsy prisoners directly to the gas chambers and crematoria.

"I did not see it," wrote Rudolf Höss in his memoir (written in a Polish prison while awaiting execution) – "but Schwarzhuber told me that no liquidating action of the Jews was ever as difficult as the liquidation of the Gypsies."

At first perhaps the Gypsies were not aware of what was about to happen. But when they saw the first of the six trucks, fully loaded with Gypsies, turn in the direction of the crematoria, they began screaming and crying. They tried desperately to defend themselves but their struggles were futile. According to one source, the broken pots and torn clothing strewn about the vacant camp attested to the resistance of the Gypsies. Even more telling are the witness accounts from Jewish survivors at nearby camps who remember the horrifying screams of the victims. "Betrayal!" "Murder!" they screamed.

Some time after I spoke with Rosa, I talked to a Hungarian Jewish survivor who was interned in a nearby barracks in Birkenau that night in August that has been called *Zigeunernacht*, or Gypsy night. Noemi Ban was twenty when she heard the screams and wails of the 3,000 Gypsies being sent to their death. More than fifty years later her memory of that night was still vivid.

"And here it happened what I will never, ever forget," she

said. "We were, one hundred of us, in a room. Without cover, without anything, just on the bare floor. The cold is still running on me as I'm talking about it, because all of a sudden what we heard was that heavy trucks were coming. We felt by the noise that it was not our camp – somewhere, somewhere a little bit over.

"Then when the trucks arrived, the motors stopped. We heard yelling, German orders, the ever, ever-present German Shepherd dogs were barking. And then, *screaming...*"

Noemi's voice dropped to a whisper: "I never, *ever* forget that scream."

"And they must have been put on those trucks, and I heard the trucks going and then nothing – quiet in the night. This about ten times. Coming the trucks. Orders yelled. Dogs barking. Screams – terrible screams. I never heard such a screaming before. They must have known."

Hearing these chilling cries, Noemi and the other prisoners shivered with fear. All night, flames roared from the chimneys of the two crematoria, lighting the camp with an eerie glow. Only the next day did they find out what had happened when a guard halted their questions, saying, "Oh, we took care of the Gypsies."

Later they learned that the whole camp had been liquidated, everyone murdered. Hearing this, Noemi said, all her childhood images of Gypsies passed before her eyes. "The Gypsies on the side of the road. Their tents. Their colorful outfits. Their disappearance, their beautiful music. And that shook me, to my very deep self, because I know that I am in the same situation, and we are all. We were under one umbrella, all of us.

"In one night, all of them, all of them killed. And I heard that, I heard that. That is my very vivid memory."

Noemi paused for a long time, as if she were finished, but then she spoke again.

"As I talk about it I can hear it, their screaming. And smelling that – I never forget it. Always that cloud about us, the ash, and that terrible smell, the burning. That was a terrible screaming."

∞

Though Rosa may not have been physically present to hear the despairing cries of those ripped from their homes and families, plunged into a chasm of pain and loss, eternally condemned to unfinished lives, I believe the agonizing screams haunt her as much as they do Noemi. Those who survived after powerlessly witnessing these crimes are also condemned, crushed by the impossible burden of their memories. These survivors (a title that carries no honor or glory for those who bear it), left alone with only the private nightmares of the horrors they have witnessed, must reduce their experiences to words, using a painfully inadequate, clumsy language for this necessary – yet unsatisfactory – task of the telling.

*I cannot explain how that was*, Rosa had said.

And yet, I think she *has* begun to explain how it was. Listening to Rosa today, I heard the cries of her people, mingling like wisps of smoke with the cries of my people. And I was chilled – I *am* chilled – by the echo of their agony.

# $\mathcal{S}$*tains on the table*

$\infty$

I hoped to hear the rest of Rosa's story today but Lilly arrived early in the morning and offered to drive Rosa to Austria so she can try to sell lace to her customers there. Maybe we can talk to some of the other relatives, I suggest to Reili. Not yet, she says. They live more than a hundred kilometers away from Munich and we'll have to wait until her cousin Shukar can borrow a car from his son so that he can drive us there. I press on: When will this happen? Reili tells me, in effect, to back down. She says she doesn't want to ask Shukar too often or too directly.

"Don't worry," she tells me. I'll try not to, I say. But I'm utterly dependent on others, unable to make plans or ask direct questions. It's making me nervous.

"Go look around Munich," Reili urges. She knows it will do me good to get out of this smoky apartment, where my anxiety about the work is heightened by the background noise of the television and shrill arguments between Rosa and her daughter and the children. "Too much *Schtress*," says Reili, pronouncing the word in German. I ask her to come with me but she declines. She's not interested in being a tourist in Germany where she grew up. She left here after the war, some forty years ago, when she married an American soldier, and she has returned only a few times, to see her relatives. Munich holds no charm for her.

I have my prejudices about Germany too. As a Jew from Germany, my father raised us – my brother, two sisters and me

– to despise all things German. He never bought anything "made in Germany" and if anyone even mentioned buying a Volkswagen – the very car inspired by the Nazis – he delivered a scathing denunciation. From my father I absorbed a strong distaste for the German language which I am still trying to undo. As I listen to the German of Reili and Rosa and the other friends I meet here in Munich, little by little I try to overcome my bias against the language. But it's easy to understand my father's revulsion. I think of how the German government systematically denied him all the rights of citizenship – even taking away his job – simply because of his Jewishness. How my father's friend and former classmate who joined the Nazi party told him, "You'd better get out of Germany. We're going to bury the Jews."

My father had been lucky indeed to get out – by the time he made up his mind that he no longer wanted to live in Germany, the means for departure were already severely restricted and only a set of fortuitous circumstances enabled him to leave. He waited nearly a year for his appointment with the U.S. Consulate, and then it was scheduled for the day after Kristallnacht. Almost stiff with fear, he walked through the streets of broken glass and smoldering rubble, past the SS guards at the train station and at the consulate, to keep his appointment for a visa. Six weeks later, with ten dollars and some clothes packed in a brown steamer trunk, he took a train to Holland and boarded a small ship bound for America. He arrived in New York on 17 March 1939 – St. Patrick's Day. In honor of his allegiance to his new country and to the haphazard luck to which we owed our lives, the green shamrock had come to take its place in our personal family crest, alongside the Star of David.

After my father became an American citizen, he adamantly rejected any sense of German nationality or even German heritage. When my childhood friends talked of being part Irish, Italian or French, and I came home and asked if I was part Russian and part German, my father responded sternly. "No. You are all, 100 percent, American. You are Jewish and you are American. You are not German."

This rejection of German nationality was typical of German Jews after Hitler. "Fine specimens of humanity, those Germans, and to think I'm actually one of them!" wrote Anne Frank (who was born in Germany to German-Jewish parents) in her diary in 1942. "No, that's not true, Hitler took away our nationality long ago. And besides, there are no greater enemies on earth than the Germans and the Jews."

All the Gypsies I've met here would say the same thing. Most of them stayed in Germany – "Where can I go?" asked Rosa – but they despised it. They called non-Gypsies "Germans" and called themselves "Sinti" as if they weren't really living in Germany, as German citizens.

Yet Munich, where my great-grandparents lived and my father often visited, *is* a charming city to walk around. The ancient gate of Sendlinger Tor and the cobbled streets. The magnificent churches: Gothic, neo-Gothic, rococo, baroque. The food market, the *Viktualienmarkt*, with its fresh fruits and vegetables, flowers, cheeses, sausages, olives.

At the entrance to the bustling food market, a colorfully dressed couple cranks a hurdy-gurdy and works invisible strings so their brightly painted marionettes will dance. There are juice stands with all kinds of fresh juices. I order the red currant. *Johannisbeersaft.* Deliciously tart, it awakens the slumbering taste buds of my childhood and I remember: Currants. *Johannisbeeren.* Gooseberries. *Stachelbeeren.* I've hardly ever seen these berries commercially grown or sold in America but my parents planted the related shrubs in our little backyard on the south side of Chicago long ago, and every summer my mother makes gooseberry pie and currant jelly.

The one affection for Germany that my father retained was his love for food, German food. When I was a child, my father would join me in the kitchen in the late afternoon for a *nosh.* I'd sit on the lower steps of the creaky wooden stairway that led from the kitchen to the attic dormitory-style bedroom

I shared with my sisters. My father, with his hooked nose and dark mustache, sat on the opposite side of the tiny tongue-shaped pink and white Formica table. His severity softened and gave way to delight as the two of us devoured dark crusty rye bread spread with sweet butter and sprinkled with sugar. Sometimes he took us to a German-style beer garden where we ordered big steins of root beer and ate liverwurst sandwiches on rye bread. On special Sunday evenings I'd watch, mouth watering, as my father cooked *Kaiserschmarn* for supper – a sweet, egg-rich chopped pancake, served with lemon juice and cinnamon sugar – and listened as he told us once again the story of Kaiser Franz Josef of Austria (who may have eaten the more regal version of the dish with raisins and nuts) who was said to have loved it so much, he offered to give all of Austria in exchange for a dish of it.

My father would travel across town, a thirty-mile round trip to the north side of Chicago, simply to buy a decent loaf or two of bread, and perhaps some pastries, from a European-style bakery. I have inherited the same almost-obsessive love of bread and have also been known to travel long distances to buy a loaf of bread, *real* bread – that is, bread with a good crust.

Munich is full of such breads: dark and hearty and wholesome, laced with seeds and grains. Rye, pumpernickel, farmers' breads, white – all with crackling crisp crusts and the hard rolls, sprinkled with seeds or salt. When I try to cut myself a slice from a dense, round loaf of dark bread, Rosa yells, "No, no! You don't do it that way!" and taking the knife from me, she shows me how to hold the loaf on its side, slicing it so the knife never touches the surface below. She has meat and cheese for sandwiches but I prefer to eat the bread unaccompanied, except, perhaps, for a thin layer of sweet butter. Like the famous Munich beer, it is so full-bodied and filling that it seems to satisfy the most basic needs for nourishment.

Pastries are another story. The *Kuchens* and *Torten*: plain, sweetened yeast doughs topped with streusel or with fruit, and the glorious whipped cream confections that my father bought on special occasions, deriving immense pleasure from giving us these fanciful sweets. Designed to delight the senses, they are to food as lace is to fabric: impractical and unnecessary, yet beautiful and treasured above all. One cannot help but admire these gorgeous creations. The pastry shops, *Konditorei*, sell bread and pastries at the counters and serve customers tea and coffee, pastries and light lunches at the tables. It is here that I see gooseberry and currant pies, the likes of which I have never seen in America—intensely colored, glossy green or red berries topped with a towering cloud of golden-crusted meringue.

My father tells a story of my uncle who used to bribe the express train conductor to make an unscheduled stop in his hometown – just so he could get off and have a piece of his mother's currant pie. I am more familiar with the cherry pies that my grandmother made. But when I was a child, washing down my Oma's rich delicate German *Mürbeteig* pie crust with swallows of brash American Coca-Cola, I never realized how fortunate I was even to know my grandparents, never contemplated their wrenching departure from their home-land. With the help of my father and the distant American relations who had helped him obtain a visa, they had escaped Germany in 1939, not long before all the Jews in Mannheim, including my grandmother's sister, Frieda, were deported to concentration camps in France. Because there were no more ships from Europe to the United States then, my grandparents had to endure a tortuous train trip through Siberia and around the world to come to America, to a brown brick apartment building on the south side of Chicago, just blocks from our house.

But they were lucky to get out at all. So many – like my grandmother's sister and brother – did not. None of the Gypsies I've met had even a remote chance of getting a visa to the United States. Reili's family fled but were later captured in Yugoslavia. Many of her relatives stayed and were rounded up in the mass deportation of Gypsies to Auschwitz in March 1943. Five of every six Gypsies who lived in Germany before 1933 did not survive the Nazis. My hosts in Germany are survivors living in the nation that betrayed them.

∾

In the late afternoon, I walk onto the Marienplatz, the town square. A crowd gathers in the October sunlight, their eyes uniformly turned upward to watch the Glockenspiel, a mechanized display of jousting knights and dancing barrel-makers that takes place twice daily in the clock tower of the neo-Gothic *Rathaus*, the city hall. A Munich tourist requirement. "Be sure to see it, Toby," my father had told me.

I imagine my father as a young boy, coming here to Munich in the summers to visit his grandparents. I imagine Reili and her cousins as children in Munich. The strong element of fantasy in this city would delight any child who saw the Glockenspiel, the fanciful marionettes and puppets, or the wonderful playthings in the toy museum just opposite the *Rathaus*. For a moment I let myself relax into the simple childlike pleasure of wonderment. But I feel too disconnected to blithely enjoy without memory, to be a simple tourist here. My own family's past and the bitter experiences of my Sinti friends weigh heavily upon me. For the tourists, the present moment here in Munich is an opaque cloth, laid over the table of the past. But for me the cloth is translucent, almost sheer, with a dark stain spreading beneath its surface – sometimes, sometimes bleeding through.

## chapter *eight*

# *I no like the German people*

℘

"I sell nothing," Rosa says. She's returned from Austria looking weak and worn, discouraged. She gives us an account of her elderly customers in Austria. One of them was sick, another in the hospital and a third had died.

Sitting on the sofa, Rosa eats from a platter on the coffee table, gnawing on a fat-laden roast pork leg and a little bread, smoking her cigarette, sipping a cup of creamy, sweetened coffee. I haven't seen anyone eat any fruits or vegetables here yet. When I eat some grapes and carrots I've brought from the market, Rosa and Velda both ridicule me. "You eat like a rabbit. Why don't you have some meat?"

Food is often a sensitive issue. Though it's easy to bridge a cultural gap with a shared memory of strudel or *Zweschgenkuchen*, other foods can present more of a challenge. Like kidneys. Shortly after I arrived here, Rosa returned from the market with a bundle wrapped in white butcher paper.

"Now I make the Sinti cooking for you," she declared proudly, unwrapping the package to reveal a gleaming mound of slippery reddish-brown ovals. She sat next to me at the kitchen table, cutting slices of the raw organs into a bowl of water while I watched squeamishly. The water turned blood red. How am I going to get out of eating this? I wondered.

Then I remembered a story that my father often told about eating food in the home of his hosts. After he had arrived in America, and tried in vain to find a job in New York, the relatives who had guaranteed his immigration and in effect saved his life, the Lovemans, insisted that he come to stay with them in Nashville. All expenses paid. My father was given a generous welcome at their mansion and, after he was shown his room, he was invited to sit at the massive dining table for a traditional Southern meal. Fried chicken, biscuits with honey and a platter of a bright orange, glazed mushy substance my father did not recognize: candied sweet potatoes. He thought it looked repulsive, unlike anything he'd ever eaten but, not wishing to offend his hosts, he accepted a generous portion. The soft, sticky-sweet vegetable sickened him, but he knew it would be rude not to eat it. So instead, he ate it hurriedly – as he'd learned to do as a child when he'd had to take cod liver oil – holding his breath, swallowing rapidly and following each bite with a piece of bread. By this method, he soon consumed the entire portion.

"Oh, you must really like the sweet potatoes!" Mrs. Loveman said with delight, as she ladled more of the dreaded dish onto his plate.

"My mother raised me that you should be able to eat anything," my father explained, as he retold this story to me recently. "And if I had refused the first meal in the home of the people who had saved my life, I wasn't so sure they would have helped me the way they did afterwards, to help bring my parents out of Germany."

The moral of my father's story hit me as I watched Rosa cook the kidneys in a sauce with oil and sugar. The smell turned my stomach, and when Rosa asked me if I was hungry, my first instinct was to say no. But then I realized that all this effort had been for my benefit. Maybe nobody's life depended on me eating kidneys but my expression of gratitude certainly did.

"I'd like to try it; it looks good," I told her.

Rosa gave me twice the portion I asked for. "You try it. Maybe you no like. Then I throw it away."

My stomach balked at the raw visceral taste – but fortified by the memory of my father's sweet potato tale, I was determined to be polite. Not all bonds were formed with sweetness. Sometimes one had to swallow bitterness for the sake of respect.

"How you like the Sinti cooking?"

"*Schmeckt gut.*" Tastes good, I assured her, with all the enthusiasm I could muster. "*Sehr gut.*"

Somehow, I managed to finish everything on my plate – and Rosa smiled broadly.

∾

This evening, Rosa hasn't prepared a special meal and I'm no longer the focus of attention, so I feel free to eat grapes. There are other sorts of tensions manifesting here tonight in the constant petty arguments between Rosa and her daughter, Velda. A tall, thin woman with long, straight black hair, Rosa's daughter would be lovely if she didn't seem so nervous, so unhealthy. Sitting across from Rosa, with her long, full skirt covering her crossed legs, Velda chain smokes cigarettes, chats with Lilly, coos at the baby and yells at Jethro or Rosa.

Rosa asks Velda to get something for her from the kitchen but Velda doesn't do it immediately. Instead she smokes her cigarette and tends to the baby.

"You don't respect your mother!" Rosa yells angrily at Velda.

Velda yells back. Then Rosa holds out her arms to Jethro, takes him on her lap and hugs him sweetly. For a minute or so, this looks like a loving tableau but then Jethro starts wiggling and Rosa abruptly yells at him too. "Get off my lap!" Her voice is shrill, harsh.

Privately, Reili has told me she can see both Rosa's and Velda's perspectives. "It's no life for Velda," Reili says. To meet her filial duty, Velda has to haul the baby carriage into the subway and travel across town and up the elevator every day to come to her mother's apartment, only to have Rosa order her about and yell at her. The children are an additional source of conflict between them. Rosa has taken care of her grandson, Jethro, since he was a baby – ever since Velda's Sinto husband left her. (According to Reili, Rosa spoils the boy with too much candy, television and a lack of discipline.) In contrast, Rosa has never accepted Velda's baby's daughter – because the baby's father is a *gajo*, a non-Gypsy. When the baby's father lived with Velda, Rosa refused to even meet him. She wouldn't have him in her house. Velda has since left her *gajo* boyfriend but Rosa is still cold toward their baby, her granddaughter, and still seems resentful of Velda too. The tensions between mother and daughter abound, layered with the conflicts between the old ways and the new ways, Gypsy and non-Gypsy, young and old.

"You shouldn't be so hard on Velda," Reili says to Rosa, after Velda and Lilly and the baby leave. "Her life is not easy."

Rosa, curled up on the sofa, pats the cushion beside her and tells me to sit next to her. She listens to Reili quietly for a while, then wrinkles her face and launches into a litany of complaints against Velda's ex-boyfriend. She defends her decision not to let him come into her home, a traditional Sinti home.

It's not right, she says, the way young people act nowadays. "They don't respect their elders anymore," Rosa complains. "The young people won't even give me a ride somewhere or give me a cup of coffee when I visit. The old ways are gone." But worst of all, Rosa says, young Sinti are marrying Germans. By 'marrying' she seems to imply all love relationships; by 'Germans' she clearly means non-Gypsies.

"I no like the Germans," Rosa says, frowning severely. She tells a story about an eighty-year-old German man who lives in their apartment. One rainy day, Velda left the stroller in the entryway instead of hauling it upstairs. The man was so furious about this infraction of the building rules that when he saw Velda, he yelled at her and slapped her. Velda slapped him back.

"Good for her!" Reili interjects.

Rosa continues. One day, after this incident, Rosa ran into the old man by the mailboxes in the entryway. He eyed the envelope with her pension check. "Why can't I get a pension check when you *Zigeuner* (Gypsies) get a pension?" he asked provocatively.

"Why can't you get a pension? I'll tell you why," Rosa snapped back. "It's because you are a Nazi swine. You ever call me a *Zigeuner* again and I will call you a Nazi swine again."

"I no like the German people!" she says again, raising her voice emphatically. "Why they kill the Sinti? If a person steals, does something wrong, you put him in jail. But you no take the grandparents, the little babies, kill them all..."

Fuelled by the strong emotions, she rouses from her fragile, exhausted state. Her eyes flash, fiery and defiant. "If someone is good to me, I am good to them. I give them everything I have, my last piece of food. But if they are mean to me ..." She pauses and her eyes narrow viciously, "I am *mean.*"

Her weak, sickly body tenses like an insect shell, as if to hold in the force of her anger. This old woman has fire in her still, I think. I would not want to cross her.

"I'd like you to say these things on the tape recorder tomorrow," I suggest hopefully. Her opinions and interactions with Germans are an important part of her experience that I'd like to get on the tape. I'm also itching with curiosity about the rest of her story. What happened to her after she was spared death in Auschwitz? What happened to her baby? Hamlet?

I refrain from asking any of these questions now because I want the telling to be fresh for the tape-recorded testimony. Rosa says she'll tell me the rest of the story soon, but first she wants to get her chores done. She gets upset when she talks about the Nazis, she says.

"I know it's very hard to talk about," I say. "You can stop the recording whenever you need to. Just tell me and I will stop."

"No. I tell you, Toby. I don't tell nobody else no more – but you I tell."

I shouldn't let myself be flattered, I think. It's not uncommon for a Holocaust survivor and an interviewer to form a special bond of trust. But I am touched all the same.

Just then, Rosa gets up from the sofa and walks out of the room, into her bedroom. When she comes back, she hands me a silver necklace. "This is for you, so you remember me."

The lovely old necklace, a delicate silver filigree flower and leaf design with tiny glittering stone, reminds me of something that my Baba, my mother's mother, would have worn. Holding it in my hands, for a moment I think that Rosa, too, reminds me of my Russian Baba, with her small bones and hair wound into a bun and her wrinkled old face still lively with the fire of youth and strength.

I am about to slide into a morass of sentimentality when I remember how difficult Rosa can be, how opinionated, intolerant, and critical she is sometimes. She's not a child's romanticized image of a loving grandmother, I remind myself, but a complex human being with a mixture of characteristics, some endearing, others alienating. Flawed like everyone who is real, everyone who lives outside of fiction. Yet despite Rosa's flaws, I feel a genuine warmth for her, for this old woman who is not my grandmother but who reminds me of my connection to the past. A past before Nazis, when my people and Rosa's were linked by more subtle and delicate threads, before blunt words like 'crematorium,' 'ash' and 'extermination' described our commonalties. Now only old people like Rosa can make the past live on in their stories, remembering the traditional Sinti communities which, like those of the European Jews, were eradicated by the Nazis.

I thank her and hug her and clasp the slender chain around my neck.

chapter *nine*

# *I never was a child*

Ⰽ

In German the word for 'survivor' is *Überlebende*, literally "over or above living." Rosa fits the description well. "She's a real, true survivor," Reili says, after one of Rosa's fierce coughing attacks. She tells me that Rosa has recovered from several hospitalizations when others thought she would die, and we both marvel at her sheer physical persistence. Emotionally, of course, she has also bridged the ruins of ordinary living and the memories of what can hardly be called living, to resume her life once again with Hamlet and her children. All her explosive feistiness, her squabbles with the family, attest to her energy for this life.

I have always been grateful that I am not the daughter of a concentration camp survivor. Though my father could be called a survivor, I consider him more of a refugee, and though I don't discount the pain of his experiences, I believe there is a vast difference. My father was never in a concentration camp, like many of my parents' German and Austrian friends, never watched his parents or siblings being beaten or killed. He did not hide from the Nazis for years in attics or barns, or undertake a series of harrowing escapes. He did not cry out in the night from his nightmares, as did the survivor parents of one of my friends, waking the children with their screaming.

The children of concentration camp survivors who are themselves also survivors carry an especially heavy burden. Who can imagine it? Reili carries it, along with many of her cousins. They are the child survivors – in their sixties now.

Reili Mettbach, first row on far right, with her extended family, about 1938. The young man in the middle of the picture, wearing a plaid jacket, is her uncle Eduard, who was killed in Dachau (see chapter 21). (*print courtesy of Ludwig Eiber*)

I talk to Reili and her cousins: Hugo, Shukar, Mano, Stramsee. There are other of her cousins, too, like Lilly and Rigo whom I will interview briefly along with their mothers, and others like Bluma and Manfred and Frieda, whom I won't be able to talk to. They all experienced the Nazi regime, and all of them but Reili live in Germany still. Some of them will give me detailed interviews while others will speak only sketchily of the events of their childhood. Yet each of their stories illustrates a piece of what happened to Gypsies in Germany during the Nazi regime. And perhaps each can shed some light on the burden of the child survivor of a survivor.

*I never was a child*, says Reili. *My life was so old and serious and scary that I didn't act as a child.*

When Reili was eight years old, in 1939, her mother and stepfather began to plan their flight from Germany. They had plenty of reason. Anti-Gypsy sentiment, always present in

Images from a German publication showing the daily existence of Gypsies. The caption at the right reads "Such rest stops only plague the next community." (*Library of Congress, courtesy of United States Holocaust Memorial Museum Photo Archives*)

Germany, had been steadily increasing since 1936. Newspapers accused Gypsies of every crime imaginable. Hate-filled expressions, such as 'asocials,' 'parasites,' 'alien blood,' or 'the Gypsy plague' came from every segment of society. . Not only officials, but also academics and even ordinary citizens called for a "solution to the Gypsy question." Some demanded sterilization; others recommended imprisonment.

By 1938, the Nazi regime was ready to respond to the growing hostility toward Gypsies and the demands that "something" be done. A research unit in the Ministry of Health, established in 1936, had already been locating and classifying Germany's 30,000 Sinti and Roma. Dr. Robert Ritter, a psychologist who directed the unit, hypothesized that although Gypsies had come from India and had once been 'Aryan,' they had inbred with 'lesser races' so that now, he claimed, 90 percent of them were not 'pure' Gypsies. Ritter,

Dr. Robert Ritter, Director of the Department of Racial
Hygiene and Population Biology, and his assistant, Eva Justin,
take blood from a Gypsy man during a racial examination
in the Gypsy internment camp in Landau.
(*courtesy of Bundesarchiv, Koblenz*)

whose previous work in 'criminal biology' forecast his conclusion, contended that 'part-Gypsies' or *Mischlinge* were *racially*
predisposed to 'asocial' and criminal tendencies, and he
advocated resettlement of *Mischlinge* in closed colonies and
sterilization.

Ritter's research unit was relocated from the Ministry of
Health to the Central Police Headquarters, under the control
of SS Chief Heinrich Himmler, and in 1937 Himmler
instructed the Central Office to evaluate the findings of the
research on Sinti and Roma. Shortly after the evaluation, the
research findings became policy. On 8 December 1938, Himmler issued the Combating the Gypsy Plague decree, which
declared that "...the proper method of attacking the Gypsy

problem seems to be to treat it as a matter of race." The decree ordered the registration of all Sinti and Roma living in Germany with the Reich Criminal Police Office to determine their "racial affinity." Gypsies would have to submit to a thorough racial-biological examination. Applications for weapons were to be denied. Traveling and camping in "hordes" was prohibited. Marriage was severely restricted.

In March 1939, the Criminal Police issued instructions on how to implement the decree. All Sinti and Roma had to carry passes: brown for 'pure' Gypsies, light blue for part-Gypsies, and grey for non-Gypsy travelers. Every police headquarters was to establish a unit for Gypsy problems and designate one or two persons to be responsible for the Sinti and Roma. The instructions were unequivocally racist, as evidenced by this statement: "The aim of the measures taken by the state must be the racial separation once and for all of the Gypsy race from the German nation, the prevention of miscegenation, and finally the regulation of the way of life of pure and part-Gypsies."

With the decree and the instructions, the anti-Gypsyism of the late 1930s now had a legal basis.

*The time came when they said we should leave because it was bad.*

Not everyone agreed. Reili's aunt Dina and her family decided to stay, as Dina's husband was a decorated soldier serving in the military.

*The rest of the* Familie *in Munich said, "They're not going to do anything to us, we're citizens here, nothing's going to happen."*

By then −1939 − Himmler's Combating the Gypsy Plague decree and the instructions for carrying it out had ensured that any Gypsy with a fixed address in Germany was registered with the Nazis and would be all too easy to find. And freedom of movement was also restricted by law. Police regularly checked identity papers, harassed and arrested those without proper identification.

*So my step-grandfather was a good forger. He could forge*

*passports. But he couldn't really read and write! So he made us all false passports, with other people's help. And they took all the gold. The Sinti use gold for their bank account. They wear it too and enjoy it but it's a banking for them.*

Along with a couple of families from her stepfather's side, Reili and her parents took the train to Italy. They were not used to a traveling life; they had no horse-drawn wagons or caravans or trailers. Instead, they came from families that had been settled for generations, and lived in houses and apartments just like their neighbors. Now this small band of refugees was on the move, and constantly feared discovery. The parents cautioned the children to hide their identity.

*The only thing that was drilled into us: Don't talk to strangers, don't tell where you come from, don't tell you're Germans. We blended in with the Italian people because we're dark too. We had enough money to support ourselves at first. It was okay for a while in Italy. We were dressed decently and we'd rent a house. We all lived together and it wasn't so bad.*

While the first wave of arrests, deportations and confinement was taking place in Germany and Austria, many Gypsies were able to elude capture for a time by traveling to other countries, as Reili's family had. But from 1941, the second wave of arrests began in the invaded lands of Belgium, Holland, France, Italy, Poland and the Soviet Union. In France, Gypsies had been restricted and confined even before the German occupation in 1940. In Mussolini's Italy, large-scale roundups of Gypsies had likewise occurred even before the war began and became more efficient after German occupation.

*The Hitler and the Duce made the truce, so the German troops came in. We moved farther out, farther out. To Sicily. Then it got too complicated. We had to leave Italy.*

Reili's childhood is a tangle of hasty departures, of increasing poverty, of fear.

*Then we went by train to Yugoslavia. It was okay the first time. We had enough money left and we lived about the same way.*

*We weren't suffering the first couple months. We had money to get by with – we had to budget; we had to sell gold. We stayed in Yugoslavia until the Germans came into Yugoslavia. Then we went to Romania.*

Fleeing from the second wave of persecution, Reili's family had been caught in the third wave that affected the Balkans, Hungary and Romania. In the Balkans, as in Russia, Nazi policies towards Gypsies were wildly inconsistent. Some Gypsies remained relatively free, while others were held in concentration camps or deported, and still others were killed in mass executions at the hands of German troops, civilians, and Fascist militia, like the Croatian Ustashi. In Romania, tens of thousands of Gypsies were deported to Transnistria, Hitler's newly conquered area of the Ukraine.

*And we were there for a couple of months. Then the same thing happened: the Germans came in, in Romania.*

*So we went to Bulgaria. Same thing happened.*

*Then we slowly ran out of money. It had gotten tight. So we went back to Yugoslavia again because it happened the same thing in Romania, in Bulgaria. So we went to Yugoslavia and there it really got bad. We ran out of money. I had no more shoes to wear; I was barefooted. We couldn't stay in cities so we stayed on farms. We slept in barns and we had to live on what we found. People gave us food, we found corn that was in the field, and berries. That's how we survived.*

Did she understand why they'd had to flee, why they lived like this, in such fear?

*In those days, parents didn't explain much. They just said, "Be quiet, don't do that, don't do that." You didn't ask any questions: How come? or Why? You just did it.*

In every country, Reili's family was helped by the local Gypsies who were often the Roma, the other major group of Gypsies in Europe.

*We found Romanian Gypsies, we found Yugoslavian Gypsies. Culture-wise, we didn't have much in common but it was a bad time so they recognized us, we recognized them.*

The Roma and Sinti shared a cultural and linguistic core, but a historical separation caused distinct differences. Both groups, indeed all Gypsies, came to Europe from India in the middle of the thirteenth century, but while about half the Gypsy population was enslaved for over 500 years in the Balkans (from the fourteenth to the nineteenth century), the other half of the Gypsy population dispersed through northern and western Europe. This created two separate Gypsy cultures. Once slavery was abolished, between 1856 and 1864, however, the Roma spread throughout Europe, so now the two groups often live in proximity.

The Roma and the Sinti recognize each other as Gypsy brethren but do not share similar cultures. In addition, Reili's family's long history of sedentary behavior clashed with the traveling life of many of the Roma they met. Although Roma and Sinti were often unfriendly to each other before the war, during Nazi persecution attitudes were different. It was a different time. Now Reili's family had also been forced to travel, as refugees. Now Roma and Sinti had a common enemy, so it was more important to help one another.

*We didn't agree with a lot of things they did, they probably didn't agree with a lot of things we did, but we stuck together. They helped out.*

"By force of circumstance, their particular predisposition, and their mode of life, the Rom had sooner or later, and practically without exception, come in contact with elements of the Resistance or become involved in some aspect of anti-German activities," writes Jan Yoors in *Crossing*, an account of his involvement in the resistance movement with the Rom. Yoors details how the Rom hid fugitives in their wagons and smuggled rationed goods, explosives and small arms for the resistance, shuttling in and out of forests and deserted places as they were accustomed to doing without arousing much suspicion.

Perhaps through the influence of Romani friends, Reili's family also became involved with the resistance. They'd been helped by a band of partisans and, in turn, Reili's family aided them when they could. One day, the partisans asked Reili to take a message to a group of partisans in another village.

*They picked me to bring the message there because I could speak Yugoslavian. And I blended in with the Yugoslavian kids: I was dark, skinny, barefooted, raggedy. Who paid attention to a kid?*

*And they said to walk on the railroad tracks so I don't get lost. Go to the next village and somebody will wait for me there. They said when you get there and you see a light, then you stop there and somebody will come and pick them up and you tell them... And they told me what to tell them.*

*And they brought me to the railroad tracks. I had a piece of bread. It was stale. My main thing was to get there and eat the piece of bread and tell them what I was supposed to tell them. And I walked down the railroad tracks. It was late evening. There was woods on one side.*

*And on the poles where the telephone wires went, they had three or four Yugoslavians. Partisans. Hung them. And when I walked, I saw the legs and looked up. They already hung there three or four days.*

Had Reili herself been caught helping the partisans, she too would have been shown no mercy. In Transnistria, when two Gypsy children were caught carrying messages to the partisans, they were executed in front of their parents. But Reili couldn't allow herself these thoughts.

*Then you were so hard, you weren't even scared. It looked ugly and I looked down.*

*So I walked on and ate my piece of bread. So I made it to over there and I told them what I had to tell them. It was not many words and they knew what it was supposed to be. And they took me in and then they passed the word and they gave me a bowl of beans. They patted me and hugged me, the partisan women. And my feet hurt, they burned.*

*And then early in the morning, before dawn, they said, 'Now don't walk on the railroad tracks. Walk on the side, in the woods, like you're picking berries or something.' So then I walked back.*

*They were all happy, I didn't have to say nothing. She said, "Did they feed you over there?" I said, "Yes"*

I imagine that children in such a situation would live in constant fear. *We were scared and we had to hide from the SS, they were bad,* says Reili when I ask her what she thought as a child. *Those days the only things you heard: concentration camps, killings, Nazis – and you were scared. They always told you not to be out in the open. You had to do what the parents told you: "be quiet," or "Don't move," or not to do that or not to do that.*

Yet even these harsh warnings didn't have a constant effect. *You know how children are. They tell you that, an hour later you forgot. So it happened again till you saw the Nazis coming through the village. Then you hide again.*

Reili and her cousins even used to go door to door in Yugoslavia asking for food. *Especially on Fridays when they baked cakes and cookies,* says Reili. *That was the custom over there, you can go from house to house and ask for cookies.*

And then – it happened. The three families were living in hiding, in a farmhouse in Yugoslavia when the police broke into their home at four o'clock in the morning.

*I think the ones who turned us in were the Volksdeutsche,* Reili says, referring to the Yugoslavian citizens of German heritage. *They were worse than the Germans.*

Armed with guns, the police yelled, "Gypsies! Gypsies!" as they shoved the group together and rammed them into a truck.

*And everyone was crying and upset. We knew that this was the end, that we had to go.*

At the train station, they were made to fill out identification papers, then loaded into a cattle car.

*And my mother was very sick. Then we didn't know it was a kidney infection. Everybody was crying and screaming and the kids were crying too because the mother cried. And we knew it was bad, bad, that we had to go in the bad camp.*

They were sent to Ravensbrück, then transferred to an *Arbeitslager,* a forced labor camp on the Yugoslavian border, near Marburg-an-der-Drau. Reili's mother was sent to work in the kitchen and her father sent to the men's camp, while she and her cousins joined the other child prisoners, sent to work every day in the rock quarry.

*They cut your hair off, shaved your hair. Take your identity away. So the kapo woke us up at six in the morning. Get up, get up! He banged with his stick. They had a roll call. You had to stand in line, they called numbers you had on the uniform. Number twelve. Number thirteen. Here, here, here, here, here.*

*Then they put you into work details. And there was a rock quarry and you selected the stones and put them in carts. You pushed them down and the next detail had to pick them up and stack them. The SS had guns. They guarded because it was out in the open. The kapo made sure you keep working. They push you: Come on! Keep working! Every day, from morning to night, rain or shine, thirsty, hungry, barefooted...*

*And you weren't fussy. You didn't say, Hey, I have no shoes, I have no socks. No. You just went and went. The only thing is, from hour to hour, you look forward to the piece of bread and the cup of water and get in and collapse and you started the next day. That was it.*

Reili says that she was interned for a year and a half, that she had been in hiding, traveling with her family for more than three years. That would mean the family was captured sometime in 1943 or early in 1944 – but I'm not sure if Reili's dates are accurate.

*I couldn't really tell you exact,* she says. *See, in those days, nobody wrote anything down. My mother probably knew all the dates.*

But Reili's mother is dead and she doesn't keep in touch with the other relatives who were part of the refugee band. Most of her relatives on her mother's side stayed in Munich and were deported to Auschwitz in March 1943, an event well documented in history books.

One thing that strikes me when I interview Reili is that she remembers so few details from the year and a half she was imprisoned. She's not reluctant to talk but it seems that each day blurred into the next, all of them fogged in flat, relentless misery. And this is not unusual for survivors. Giving testimony at the Nuremberg Trials, Marie Claude Vaillant-Couturier explained that "it is so difficult to give a precise date in the concentration camp since one day of torture is followed by another day of similar torment, and the prevailing monotony makes it very hard to keep track of time."

*There was no Sunday, there was no winter day. In the winter-time, they give you thin clothing, just for the meanness of it. They give you wooden clogs, if they fit or if they didn't fit.*

*You just followed orders. You didn't say were too weak. You got beaten, you got hurt, you got taken away. You just don't say, "I don't feel good, I'm tired, I don't want to, I'm homesick, I'm still a child." You just followed orders. You made no waves.*

chapter *ten*

# *Inconsistencies*

∾

Reili's mother had cast her fate with her husband's family when she decided to flee Germany and the Nazis. But her sister, Dina, made a different choice. She would stay in Munich with her children, she said, since her husband, Eduard, was now serving in the German military.

*"I can't leave with the kids,"* Dina insisted. *"And my husband is in the military – I think nothing will happen to us."*

Dina and Eduard were proud of their German citizenship. Eduard had been a decorated soldier during the First World War and for some years after the war he had been in charge of training Bavarian police. Now he was serving again, in an élite battalion. They'd moved to Munich with their five children in the mid-1930s and they got along well with their neighbors. Perhaps part of the reason they fit in so easily was that they looked no different from their neighbors. Though plenty of their relatives were dark-haired and dark-skinned, Eduard, Dina and their children had light hair and light complexions.

Shukar, Eduard and Dina's son, is 59 when I talk to him in Rosa's apartment in Munich. He's large-framed, with broad handsome features: blue eyes, slicked-back silvery hair and a warm, closed-mouth smile that conceals his missing teeth. With his light hair and skin color, he could easily pass for a non-Gypsy and, like all the Gypsies I've met, he has two names: his Sinti name, Shukar, which means 'beautiful' in Romanés, and his German name, Ludwig.

Shukar, who wears a  cashmere blazer in a muted rose

Shukar (Ludwig) Höllenreiner, with Rosa's granddaughter, 1993.

shade and pressed trousers, pulls documents out of a briefcase for me to look at: his mother's school report card from 1915, his father's identity passes from 1928 and 1939, and a 1940 proof of citizenship paper from the Deutches Reich.

"This is the paper you had to have after the war," he tells me. "Many Sinti lost these papers when they were deported to concentration camps. Then they were declared stateless and couldn't stay in Germany."

But Shukar's family never had to leave Germany and was never deported. Even though everyone knew that they were Sinti – Gypsies – the family didn't seem to be touched by the increasing restrictions and prejudice. So even when their relatives began to worry in the late 1930s, even when Dina's sister, Ceci, and her family fled Munich in alarm, Dina stayed on. Her children went to school with the other German children. Everything seemed normal.

But soon all this changed. Their food rations were reduced – because they were Gypsies. At school, the seven-year-old Shukar refused to say "Sieg Heil!" and was beaten sharply, a

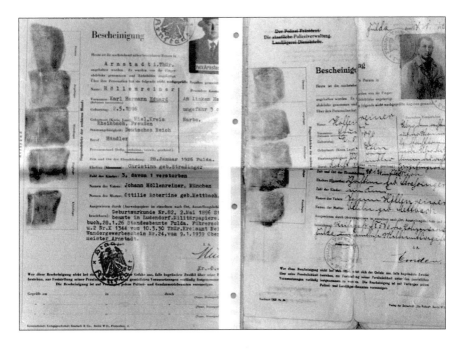

Certification papers for Eduard Höllenreiner, Shukar's father

ruler against his knuckles. *"Don't attract attention to yourself,"* his mother admonished him. *"You must never, never say that you are Sinti."*

A summons arrived. Dina and her children were to report at the local police station right away for registration. They posed in front of a studio camera so photographs could be taken; they sat patiently while the officials wound measuring tapes around their heads and recorded each detail of their facial features. Dina was asked dozens of questions about her family genealogy.

Still, they stayed. One March day in 1943, everything changed. All their relatives – some eighty people – suddenly disappeared. Later they learned what had happened. How the trucks had arrived at the homes at five in the morning, forced the residents onto the street and herded them to the police

The Höllenreiner family, about 1930. Shukar's father is
driving the auto; four of his brothers stand in a line to
the left, and his father, sister-in-law (Sophie), mother,
and sister stand behind and to the front.
(*private family collection, print courtesy of Ludwig Eiber*)

station. Imprisoned them for days. Then packed them into
trains, cattle cars, bound for Poland.

"*They've been sent to a labor camp,*" Shukar's mother told
him. This was nothing new. His grandfather had been forced
to work in a labor camp for six or seven years in the 1930s.

*The Sinti have always been persecuted.* Shukar knew that,
even at seven years old. Everybody knew that. *Before Nazis,
before Hitler.*

ᖇ

Bavaria had a history of especially harsh policies to persecute
Gypsies. As far back as 1899, the Gypsy Information Service
in Munich collected their genealogical data, photographs and
fingerprints. A 1926 Bavarian law mandated the registration of
all Gypsies, and a registration office, the Center for the Fight
Against Gypsies in Germany, was established in Munich in
1929.

Nazis used these legal precedents to continue the persecution of Gypsies. By 1936, there were already 19,000 files on Gypsies in the Munich office and 400 Gypsies from Bavaria had been sent to Hitler's first concentration camp, Dachau, near Munich. In 1938, Himmler moved the Central Office to Combat the Gypsy Menace to Berlin and ordered a more systematic genealogical registration based on the research of 'racial experts.'

Still, up until 1943, the actual harassment of Gypsies may have been less harsh in Munich that in other German cities. Munich had no municipal concentration camp for Gypsies (*Zigeunerlager*) such as those that had been created in Berlin, Dusseldorf, Essen, Frankfurt, Cologne and other German cities between 1933 and 1939. The Gypsy population in Munich was small, relatively settled and assimilated; perhaps they were considered under control. Munich Gypsies had not been included in the earlier deportations of Gypsies which began shortly after the outbreak of war in 1939.

But all this changed in December of 1942. That's when Himmler decreed that the German Gypsies be sent to Auschwitz – including those in Munich.

∾

A letter arrived, from Oswiecim, Poland. It was written in a code, a message that only Dina could understand. *We are hungry, very hungry. Please send food.*

Dina saved the meager ration stamps, skimped on the food for herself and the children and went to the bakery to buy fresh bread. She wrapped the package in brown paper and string and carefully inscribed the names and address: *Arbeit-slager, Oswiecim, Polen.* Then she handed the package to her nine-year old son. *"Shukar,"* she said. *"You must take this package to the post office. Here is some money for the postage."*

The boy walked down the street, the package under his arm. This was an important mission, he thought, to send his relatives food. Where were they anyway? He missed the big get-togethers with all the relatives when they would eat and play music and talk and talk. He missed playing with his cousins. Now his mother said they were forced to work in Poland. Why?

Shukar entered the neighborhood post office and took his place at the end of the long line. There were so many people sending letters and packages this afternoon. Finally it was his turn. He reached the package up to the window. The postmaster inspected it carefully. "*Ah!*" he said loudly, his voice booming throughout the room. "*This package is going to Auschwitz!*"

Everyone in the post office, customers and workers alike, turned to look at Shukar, freezing him with their icy stares. His hand trembled as he handed the postmaster the money, stuffed the receipt in his pocket and ran from the post office.

∽

"*Where is my brother and his family? Why has he been sent away? When will he return?*" Dina stood by the desk of the police officer, demanding information. She was terrified but she kept herself from shaking with fear. She had to know.

The policeman just scowled at her. Insolent woman. "*Be glad you're still alive – because of your husband.*"

Yet how long could this protection last? Not everyone who served in the military was protected, as she well knew. Eduard's own brothers had served in the army ... yet they had not been spared.

∽

It is shocking to see photographs of Gypsy men in military uniforms who were later interned in Auschwitz. Yet many Gypsies served in the military before its racial policy to exclude them was widely enforced.

Of course, both Jews and Gypsies had served in the

Josef ("Zep") Höllenreiner, Shukar's uncle, about 1941 or 1942.
(*private family collection, print courtesy of Ludwig Eiber*)

military during the First World War – one of my father's
uncles fled Germany in 1914 to avoid being drafted, while
another of his uncles was particularly proud of serving as an
officer with the Iron Cross First Class in the First World War
and was such a patriotic German that, despite being a Jew, he
might have even served in Hitler's army if he had been
allowed. Though Jews were excluded from military service
under the Nazi regime, and Gypsies were officially excluded
from the army from 1937, for a while the regulations against
Gypsies were not widely enforced. In 1939, at the beginning of
the Second World War, Gypsy men were, for the most part,
treated the same as other non-Jewish men: they were drafted
into military service. Some, like Eduard, were even awarded
medals for their service.

By early 1941, however, the military's racial policy was

reaffirmed. Army authorities stipulated that no more Gypsies should be called into service. Those already in the army were to be placed in reserve units. Gypsies were to be awarded no further decorations. They were barred from employment in army factories and other top security work, and the police sent the army lists of Gypsies so these policies could be enforced. In early 1942, laws called for the release of Gypsies from the air force, the army and the navy. However, dismissing Gypsies from the army took some time and some Gypsies still served as late as 1943.

Eduard's brothers had been expelled from the army in 1942, along with most other Sinti soldiers. Their military service had failed to protect them or their families from deportation. Since arrests were carried out by local police officials, decorated soldiers were often sent to Auschwitz, even though they were supposed to be exempt.

"The regulations governing their arrest were not drawn up with sufficient precision," notes Rudolf Höss, commandant of Auschwitz, in his memoir. "Various offices of the Criminal Police interpreted them in different ways, and as a result persons were arrested who could not possibly be regarded as belonging to the category that it was intended to intern. Many men were arrested on leave from the front, despite high decorations and several wounds, simply because their father or mother or grandfather had been a Gypsy or a Gypsy half-caste."

But Eduard, Shukar's father, was unusual: he remained in the army even after the 1943 deportations and his family was not deported. Why? Presumably, his dignified military career, along with his connections to the local Bavarian police, was enough to grant him this special consideration. And, as historian Raul Hilberg notes, some Gypsies served in the German army through the war, "for the very simple reason that their commanding officers could not spare them."

Inconsistent – that was the Nazi policy toward the Gypsies. But we often forget that Nazi policy could be inconsistent about Jews as well. My own family bears witness to this. My father was dismissed from his job in 1936 because he was Jewish, yet he was paid unemployment insurance from the same government that had ordered his dismissal. And, though one of my grandmother's sisters was sent to a concentration camp in France and then murdered in Aushwitz, the other sister, blond-haired and blue-eyed, was allowed to live openly in Munich because she was married to the Christian son of one of the richest shipping magnates in Germany.

"His family cut him off from his inheritance when he married a Jewess," my father explains. "But they had such an influence that the Nazis didn't do anything against them or their children." Their daughter found out that she was Jewish only when she told her parents that she wanted to join the *Bund Deutscher Mädel*, the Nazi youth organization for girls.

Similarly, inconsistencies that allowed one Gypsy to live in relative safety while another was deported to a concentration camp were often due to special favors, friendships or connections. Rosa was deported to Auschwitz while her husband was allowed to live with his parents in Munich. Eduard's family also lived openly in Munich while his brothers and their families were arrested, shoved inside a cattle car and transported to Auschwitz. That such exceptions were rare is borne out by the harsh statistics of deaths. Gypsies died at the hands of the Nazis just like the Jews, in proportionate numbers to their population. Yet that there were exceptions and inconsistencies also cannot be denied.

∾

Six months had passed since the relatives had been sent away. No more letters came from Poland. Nothing. Then Eduard returned home. Shukar was overjoyed to see his father at first. But then he realized: his father had been dismissed from the army. Only the intervention of his commanding officer from the First World War had spared him from being sent to a concentration camp. Now that he had been expelled from military service, would the family continue to be protected? He had the best connections in Munich – still, would it be enough?

*Then, everybody shook.*

And the stories his father told! Nazis beating the Jewish prisoners brutally, shoving them into cattle cars like animals. Eduard had always been proud to serve the German nation. Now he no longer knew what to think.

While he had been away, his home had turned into a center for those who had escaped deportation, a refuge for those in hiding. Dina and Eduard took in friends and relatives, any Sinti who needed a place to hide in Munich. *But always with fear.* Frequent checks by the Gestapo made the activity very dangerous.

*You were glad when the person left because you jeopardized your own life.*

But it was impossible to feed the expanding number of people in the house. The family did not have adequate rations even for themselves. To help out, Shukar began to stop at a little grocery store on his way home from school to filch butter and cheese from the counter. How his mother must have worried, grateful to be able to put food on the table but frightened at the risks her son took.

At one time, even Reili hid in her cousin Shukar's house. When was it? They both remember it, but it must have been much earlier, perhaps as early as 1938, before Reili and her parents fled to Italy. Reili would have been seven or eight then, and Shukar only five. Trying to feed so many people on so few rations was a problem even then. Shukar's mother, Dina, took Reili with her to the countryside at night, to help her steal chickens from the farms but they couldn't dispose of the plucked feathers and bones publicly so at first they burnt them in the wood stove.

*"What's that strange smell?"* asked the neighbor the next

morning. After that, they wrapped the feathers and bones in a bundle and took it into the woods to bury it.

∾

1945. *Ah – and then my best life began for me.*
The American soldiers filled the streets of Munich, offering the eleven-year old boy all sorts of new possibilities. They brought food with them. *Oranges, bananas, chocolate, apples.* And Shukar soon discovered they would buy all the black-market cigarettes he had to offer, at astronomical prices. He was rich!

But liberation also meant the return of the survivors. Slowly they straggled back to Munich, converging by the hundreds at Shukar's grandfather's small house – which became an informal information center, a place to look for lost relatives.

The reunions should have been joyous events, but too often they were marred by horror and grief. The survivors told harrowing stories of slave labor, of starvation, disease, and brutality, of clouds of ash and the stench of burning human flesh.

*The worst things, the stories of the survivors. Your father is dead, your mother is dead, your sister, your brother – all the crying when they found out who was dead.*

*Thirty-eight of my relatives died in Auschwitz.*

Among those who did not return were some of Eduard's brothers, the ones who had served in the military. For months and months they did not come, Shukar remembers, and everyone thought they must be counted among the dead. Then at last they did return, bearing a strange tale. They had been taken from the concentration camp, they said, put back into uniform, and forced to serve on the Russian front. Then they had been captured as prisoners of war. Finally, the Russians realized they were concentration camp prisoners and released them.

The survivors were thin, unhealthy and destitute. Their homes and possessions had been confiscated, and they had to rely on other Sinti for help. Reili and her parents stayed with Shukar's family for a while, as did Eduard's brother's family – Josef, Sophie, and their six children, just freed from Bergen-Belsen. Once again, there was seldom enough food to go around.

"Remember when we found a fox and marinated it, and we were so hungry that we ate it?" Reili asks Shukar. "Everybody except you. You wouldn't eat it!"

Remembering the meal of marinated fox, Reili and Shukar laugh so hard that tears cluster at the rims of Reili's eyes. She wipes at the tears with her fingers.

"Oh, I'm glad we can laugh," she says, sighing.

∽

"My father never forgave the Germans for what they did to our people. He despised them to his dying breath. When he talked to Germans, he would say 'You murderers.'"

"How do you feel about Germans?" I ask Shukar.

"After the war, they all said it was Hitler. But everybody was Hitler. I don't trust them. It's not better today. It's still the same.

"Except the young Germans. Many young people are refusing to go into the army. They have a better outlook than the old Nazis."

Shukar pauses a moment. "I'm only telling my story now because the truth might have a chance at being heard in the United States," he says. "In Germany I wouldn't bother.

"I wouldn't tell this to a German. It goes in one ear and out the other. Half of them don't believe you. They think it is a made-up story. In Germany, they say it's all lies."

# $\mathcal{A}$ *matter of surviving*

$\infty$

*Sometimes I saw my mother behind the barbed wire, when we walked by there with the work details,* Reili tells me.

*And one time my mother saw me and she says, "The Americans are coming. Whatever happens, don't move, don't do anything. Just stay in the barracks and wait there till you see me".*

*She was afraid that with all the commotioning, I could get lost.*

*One morning, a week or so later, we didn't have roll call when we were supposed to.* The Nazis had abandoned the concentration camp as the Americans drew closer, so no one was there to inspect the barracks in the morning or to enforce the roll call.

*The camp was under no supervision. And the gates were closed. It happened all unusual. The roll call didn't come, the kapo didn't come. And all was quiet – you saw no movement. So we kids were wondering: it was too quiet, it wasn't the usual thing.*

*And all of a sudden we heard a bunch of noise. And we were afraid to go out and look what happened.*

*Are the Americans here? Are they not here? And all of a sudden we heard a shouting. In every language you could think of: Romanes, German, Polish, Yiddish. Ah, and loud and loud! It was a big uproar!*

*I wanted to run with the rest but Mother had said, Stay there – and I was too much a kid of the escape route; you followed rules. Then all of a sudden she came and she cried and she hugged me. She took me by the hand and we looked for my father and then he came from the other side.*

*The people were laughing and running and crying and doing. And then we saw the gates and the military – the gates were open and the jeeps came in and the trucks came in. Commotioning and crying and shouting and screaming. The military, they tried to make order but the people were crying, passing out, screaming.*

*And I saw military men, the tears just running down their faces. Yes, yes, just running down their faces.*

*Then the Americans, the first thing I remember: they gave me a piece of gum. They didn't want to give you too much food because you were undernourished. Your stomach couldn't take it. They told people, "Don't gobble it up, you'll make yourself sick." They told them to eat slowly. But a lot of them got sick, too sick to move. They had to stay in the camp until they got organized, to get registered.*

*But we took off. We waited for nothing. Did what we wanted to do. They were confused too, they saw so much commotioning. You don't do your paperwork, you don't organize. It was such a turmoil. They gave us ration stuff and then my father came and said, "Let's go."*

"But didn't you think the Americans would help you?"

*We still didn't trust. Why stay there? We wanted to get away. The sick ones, and those who could move, who didn't want to leave the mother, the father, the sick child behind – the Americans got them organized. But we were already gone. We walked and we walked and we walked. Just to get away.*

Of course they didn't think of it then: restitution payments for the crimes of the German government that had imprisoned them. Why would they even consider it? They were so relieved just to be free, to be alive.

*We all of us were malnourished. There wasn't one person who wasn't. But some of them were worse than we were, they were in there longer than we. If you didn't die of sickness, you just wasted away. Till the body gave out. Till the body gave out.*

Against all odds, Reili and her parents had managed to keep alive. Now they were suddenly, miraculously, free – and nobody could have convinced them to spend one more day, even one more hour, in the concentration camp. Yet their sudden departure – before the necessary wheels of bureaucracy had spun into action, producing their documentation – meant that they would later be denied compensation. They had no Auschwitz tattoos, no documentation of release, no proof that they had ever been imprisoned in a concentration camp. *If you had a sick one, you didn't leave them behind. You waited. Then they put out the soup kitchen, nourished those back, found transportation for them, got organized, got the papers and stuff. Those are the ones who had the easiest time with the government. But who thinks about that? You want to get away. You want to get away.*

In any case, the post-war German government routinely denied restitution payments to Gypsy survivors. After the war, Chancellor Konrad Adenauer invited Jewish organizations and the new nation of Israel to form the Claims Conference to negotiate for restitution and administer it to the victims. But the Gypsies, who were viewed with derision and lacked a strong organization, were not invited. And restitution law discriminated against Gypsy survivors. In 1956, the Federal Court ruled that the Gypsies' claims for racial persecution were to be considered only from the 1943 deportation order onwards. This meant that Sinti and Roma who had been classified as 'asocial' and sent to concentration camps before that date had no legitimate claim for restitution. It took years before this was backdated to 1938.

"My cousin was in the concentration camp when she was thirteen years old," said Shukar one day when we were talking about reparations. "Then she survived, she came out, and tried to get money for fifteen years. By the time they changed the law so she could have gotten money, she had already died."

Additionally, the law disqualified many survivors who had not been in officially recognized camps for required periods of time. "Claims filed by Gypsy survivors for homes and businesses impounded at deportation were invariably disallowed, often after investigation by the same policemen who had previously arrested them in the Nazi era," notes historian Sybil

Milton. "Health claims for physical and psychological trauma were similarly disregarded." Many applications for restitution were denied based on the very witnesses, reports and 'research findings' that contributed to their persecution in the first place. In some cases, argues German historian Wolfgang Wipperman, relying on this testimony "was tantamount to asking Adolf Eichmann for expert testimony in compensation cases brought by Jews."

So even if Reili's family had received documentation papers, it is unlikely that they would ever have received restitution payments. This, despite the fact that Reili's schooling had been severed when she was in second grade, and when she was released in 1945 she was fourteen years old and it was too late to return to third grade. This, despite the fact that her health was broken, that malnutrition from the concentration camp had left her weakened and vulnerable, conditions which led her, shortly after liberation, to suffer an attack of rheumatic fever that permanently weakened her heart. Even in later years, when Reili sent testimony by doctors that her heart problems were caused by malnutrition and stress in concentration camps, the claims were denied. "They just said, 'How do we know you weren't born with heart problems?'"

∽

*Then the war was over. We tried to get back to Munich. We walked, we found farmers who gave us a ride on the cart for half an hour, then we'd walk. We slept in the fields. It was springtime. Well, I walked around barefooted with rags wrapped around my feet in January, so it didn't bother you too much anymore. Everybody wants to reach his destination. Ach, we are free! Great! Praise the Lord!*

Back in Munich, they found their old homes destroyed or confiscated. Dina and Eduard's house had been bombed and the family had been evacuated to a small town about forty miles from Munich. Reili's family, along with other returned relatives, stayed with Eduard and Dina's family, sleeping on the floor of the small house. *We weren't fussy,* Reili says with a laugh.

*Then more survivors began to return. My cousin, Hamlet, came back from the war – he was in Russia, his wife, Rosa, was in Auschwitz. They were all scattered, but they were like pigeons, they always come back to the home. So then she showed up, from Auschwitz. Big reunion happened. She told us who died, who survived.*

*So then we slowly gathered the Familie. The other Sinti from the different concentration camps, they all went back to the towns where they started out. Some of them were found, some of them died. And then it got better. We started to pick up our lives. More people came, more survivors. And then it was just a matter of surviving.*

What these survivors faced was utter devastation – for every surviving Gypsy in Germany, five were dead. Reunions became occasions for grieving. As Jan Yoors points out in *Crossing,* those who escaped could do nothing to protect their family members, and for them to survive as isolated individuals was a meaningless existence. "We, the survivors, were condemned to live a fate worse than death – which must be lived to be understood," writes Yoors, who lost his adoptive Romani family to the Nazis. The survivors, as Yoors expresses so well, suffered "the delusional sense of guilt at having been spared, as if we had survived at the price of their deaths, by the betrayal of the murdered, the mutilated, the burned."

*"How come I'm here? How come they didn't take me?"* cried out one of Reili's uncles, who had seen his wife and all five children die.

*Many times when he was in an emotional uproar, he said, "I would have died with them,"* Reili says. *He was the only survivor. So he just could not cope with it. I wish he could have gotten professional help. It's emotions there, you just cannot take an aspirin for it.*

Another of Reili's uncles lost a child to typhus, a daughter who was very close in age to Reili. They had been interned in the concentration camp at Marburg-en-der-Drau together. *We were very close, a couple of days apart. She had typhus. There was no help, there was no medication, it was high fever. I went to eat one morning, and when I came back she was gone from her bunk. And my uncle got word that she was on a pile of corpses in another part of the camp. He went there and found her. She was still alive – but barely, lying with the dead. He tried to pull her out but the guards came and beat him about the head and drove him away.*

*And my uncle can never regroup from that, mentally. He has a problem.*

*He's not a drinking person but he goes out and drinks and he's gone for two or three days and he hates every German and starts a fight and ends up in jail. It's a mental problem. And the people know it so they just bring him home, they excuse him.*

*But always when he saw me, he said, "She would have been exactly the same age as you." I reminded him of her. So really, as a young woman, I didn't want to be around him. I didn't want him to remember when he saw me. And he had good days and he hugged me and kissed me. When he had a bad day, he cried and cried. And I felt bad that he remembered her through me.*

∽

These children who survived are not just survivors themselves but also the children of survivors, the sons and daughters, nieces and nephews of survivors, and they have struggled beyond all reasonable expectations on their passage to adulthood. Though Reili is likely the most well adjusted survivor in her extended family, she is still marked indelibly by her experience and she feels, as many survivors do, the impossibility of conveying it. You have to have survived a concentration camp to know, she says. "They are the only ones who really, really understand it."

Again I'm reminded of Mme. Vaillant-Couturier's

testimony at the Nuremberg Trials. "It is difficult to convey an exact idea of the concentration camps to anybody, unless one has been in the camp oneself, since one can only quote examples of horror; but it is quite impossible to convey any impression of the deadly monotony. If asked what was the worst of all, it is impossible to answer, since everything was atrocious. It is atrocious to die of hunger, to die of thirst, to be ill, to see all one's companions dying around one and being unable to help."

"It's hard for other people to understand," Reili says. "Very hard. If you've never been in there, you can sympathize. But you cannot put yourself... You really don't feel it like those that were in it."

chapter *twelve*

# *Then I realized*

ℳ

It was early in the morning of 8, March 1943 – the sky still dark as lead. Hugo shivered in the cold, despite his wool jacket. He was nine years old and as he stood huddled with his parents and five brothers and sisters outside his house, he wondered why he couldn't go on sleeping in his own bed.

A terrifying pounding on the door had wakened him at five a.m. Sharp voices barked out orders. *Aufstehen! Get up, get up!*

In the dim light, Hugo could make out the uniforms of the police as they swarmed through the house, throwing open every door. One of them spoke brusquely to his parents. "*Pack clothes and food for a few days. You are being sent to work in Poland. Ja, ja, a new job,*" the policeman said impatiently when Hugo's father questioned him. "*Hurry up. Out!*"

Why Poland? Why so early? Why at all? Hugo wondered – but there was no time to explain. His mother told all the children to get dressed – "*Hurry, hurry*" – and be sure to take a warm coat. The policemen – there must have been six or seven of them – pushed them into the street. Now he saw more policemen, shoving other people down the street to join them. They were all Gypsies, Sinti like his family, and Hugo recognized many of them: his cousins, aunts and uncles. All the children looked sleepy-eyed, all the adults bewildered, even scared. "*March!*" yelled the police, when they had assembled all the group. They walked and walked in cold grim silence.

Some of the adults must have known where they were

Deportation of Sinti and Romanies to Auschwitz, 1943
(*Police photo. courtesy of Stadtarchiv Remscheid*)

going. "*The Ettstrasse*", they whispered. "*Ach, lieber Gott*". For on the Ettstrasse was Munich's main prison, with its forbidding thick walls of grey stone. Here, in a communal cell of the prison, they waited for their next order, talking to the friends and relatives imprisoned with them. Hugo's mother gave the children the little food they had brought with them, to supplement the meager rations of the prison.

What next? the adults wondered, as they waited day after day in the prison. They exchanged the terrifying stories they'd heard about labor camps, about people who had been arrested and had never returned. During these four long days of waiting, they speculated wildly, each scenario spiraling along a coil of impending doom.

But for the children life was not yet so dismal. It seemed to Hugo that nearly all his cousins were here with him, as if it were one of the big family feasts, only without food. Certainly this was a bad time but they were in it together and it was bound to get better. As long as there were parents, aunts and uncles, other children, everything must be all right, Hugo thought. The adults would protect the children.

He thought so even after the police came to round them up again, to herd them into trucks that took them to the train station, where again they were pushed together with other families and loaded into a train car. This wasn't a passenger train, Hugo noticed, but the sort of train for transporting animals – a boxcar with no windows, just a slot for a thin trickle of air. All these people – grandparents and babies alike – were shoved inside, the door slammed shut. It was cramped and hot. There was no water and soon they were all parched, their tongues dry and cracked as sun-scorched leather. The adults wailed and moaned, the children sniffled and cried. Only on the second day of this five-day journey did they receive a sip of water – and still no food.

If one could smell shame and humiliation, it would have smelled like the urine steaming from the corner of that dark cattle car, a stench so strong and sharp that Hugo could not smell the rotten meat spread on the stale piece of bread his mother gave him to sustain him. She had saved the bread from the prison, tucking it into her pockets for just such a time as this, when there was no food. Now, as she passed the bread to her husband and children, she imagined it would give them strength for whatever awaited them. It did not. Without refrigeration, the meat had spoiled and the whole family became sick. Their cries disappeared, swallowed in the din of complaints, wails and moans, the relentless clatter of the railroad car shuttling them to the east.

The train stopped, then shook and moved again, its wheels screeching around a sharp curve before it came to a shuddering halt. The door of the freight car unbolted, a thunder of metal. It was night but the harsh bright lights outside blinded Hugo and the passengers as they approached the open door. Where were they?

The arrival of Gypsy prisoners in Auschwitz.
(*Lydia Chagoll, courtesy of United States Holocaust Memorial
Museum Photo Archives*)

"*Raus, raus, schneller!*" Hugo heard the stamp of feet and
strident voices yelling. "*Out, everybody, out! Faster, you filthy
shits!*" Then the whack of metal against bone, as scores of SS
men beat the prisoners with the butts of their rifles, thrusting
them out of the train car. Other guards – sinister looking men
dressed in convict-striped clothing, whom Hugo would later
identify as Kapos – pushed and shoved the prisoners into five
straight rows under the bright lights. *Stand at attention! Eyes to
the right!* Again the guards beat the prisoners with truncheons
and rifle butts when they did not obey. Hugo's uncle resisted
the guard's commands. He was beaten so severely that he
collapsed to the ground.

What was this place that they had come to? Hugo couldn't
see much beyond the lights but what he did see terrified him:
a vast marshy plain, surrounded by a brambly forest of barbed
wire, populated by brutal guards and weak, skeletal prisoners.

And over it all, the smell of death, the smoky odor of burning flesh that drifted and billowed and hung low and thick over the nightmare place, the terrible odor that mingled with the stench of garbage and excrement, the suffocating smell – the smell of death.

*Then I realized*, Hugo says, in his understated way. *It was very bad.*

❧

When I meet Hugo, in October 1993, there is no trace of the frightened boy he had been sixty years earlier. Quite the contrary: I find Hugo's appearance rather intimidating. He's a solidly built man, tall and imposing, with silver hair, black mustache and thick, stern, arched black eyebrows. He wears a dazzling display of gold: a broad gold belt buckle, thick gold rings glittering with diamonds, three long gold necklaces glowing against his chest, his garish silky shirt half unbuttoned to show them off. The strands are solid and heavy, made of narrow, linked rectangles of gold.

"It's all real, real solid gold," he says, as he takes off one of his necklaces and gives it, first to Reili and then to me, so we can feel the weight of it in our hands. The wide diamond-studded gold bands on his wrists were custom-made, he tells us proudly. "They cost 150,000 marks."

"Oh, *schön*, beautiful, *wunderschön*," says Reili, admiringly.

❧

It was called a block, this long dark shed with no windows and only a clay floor, slimy from rain. *"Worse than a sheep's stable,"* Hugo's father said of this building originally designed to hold fifty-two horses. In the morning, Hugo would see that there were dozens of such buildings in the Gypsy camp – and, not far away, two large chimneys spewing the foul-smelling, nauseating smoke. Often, in the days to come, he would see

Hugo Höllenreiner, 1993.

flames shooting upward from the chimneys, the sky painted smoky red from the fire. And always, the air thick with this sick-sweet choking odor.

The night of the arrival, Nazi guards beat Hugo's family and the others until they lined up into military style formations, then marched them into the crowded barracks. Each family was assigned one of the bunks, which were just wooden slabs, stacked in three tiers, covered with thin straw mattresses and threadbare blankets. The other prisoners – hundreds and hundreds of them – sat motionless on their bunks, silently staring at Hugo and the other new prisoners as they came in. Again Hugo wondered: What was this place that they had come to?

How could they have slept that first night in Auschwitz-Birkenau? Though they must have been bone-tired from the miserable journey in the cramped boxcar, and already inured to the constant cries and moans, how could they block out the nightmarish images of their arrival, or the sickening stench of death?

The shock of this terrifying place did not abate. The next morning, they were forced to undress, men and women together, for the Nazis' standard disinfection routine. Their heads were shaved to stubble, their scalps and bodies dusted with a white powder to rid them of lice.

For the women, especially, being forced to display their naked bodies to the SS men was unbearably demeaning. It smashed all their cultural taboos and savagely violated their personal dignity. Even a child of Hugo's age could recognize the suffering of this agonizing degradation and humiliation. *The adults were all around, naked, and they were ashamed.* Hugo's mother cried and cried.

Over the next days, as she watched her children wither away from lack of food, Hugo's mother would have reason to cry again. The food rations were woefully inadequate and they were distributed unfairly in order to provoke conflict among the prisoners. The children in the Gypsy camp, especially vulnerable to malnutrition and disease from contaminated water, died in droves. Those who survived were constantly hungry and during the night, they cried out for bread.

*We hadn't had any food like ham, for example, for two or three weeks. Then they only gave us turnips.*

The older children, those above ten, had to work with the adults, hauling rocks and bricks. *Dirty work in the mud and mire.* Because Hugo was under ten, he was sent to a barracks that had been designated the 'children's nursery.'

*There was a building separate from the camp, with a fence, which was the 'children's nursery' with about two or three hundred children. In the morning we had to go from the camp to the 'nursery' from ten o'clock until three o'clock. There, we could do whatever we wanted. At noon a bell was struck, when the food was given. The first day I was in a crowd when the food was given and I couldn't come near. (After that) I pushed my way to the front, where the tub (of food) came from, and never again received nothing.*

*After fourteen days, I was staggering, weak, miserable, as if I was dead. My mother cried that I was close to death.*

The so-called children's nursery had been instituted in the Gypsy camp for the purpose of propaganda. The barracks' walls were whitewashed and decorated with paintings of fairy tale scenes. In anticipation of a visit from the Red Cross, children's beds were draped with clean white sheets and flowers placed on bedside tables. Outside was a playground with a sandbox, swings and other equipment. Sometimes the children were herded into the playground so the SS officials could take propaganda photographs and films of them playing. But in reality, there was no school and the children had only ragged, filthy clothing and a woefully inadequate diet. Drinking water was lacking and all the prisoners of Birkenau had to drink polluted water from the surrounding swamps.

The children in the Gypsy camp were so close to starving that a Jewish prisoner doctor who worked there reported that they were "all skin and bone," and infections resulted from skin rubbing against bone. Nearly all of the children suffered from malnutrition and disease. Even Rudolf Höss, commandant of Auschwitz, gave evidence that the nursery propaganda was false when he described the many children of the Gypsy camp who suffered from noma, a gangrenous condition affecting the face and mouth, which is rare under normal conditions. It reminded him of victims he'd seen with leprosy, he wrote, and made him "shudder" to see "…their little bodies wasted away with gaping holes in their cheeks big enough for one to see through, a slow putrefaction of the living body."

The children's nursery was also exploited by Mengele, who favored using Gypsy children as subjects in his gruesome medical experiments, and often selected twins or those with heterochromatic eyes (one blue and one brown) from the nursery. Once he experimented with noma victims, giving them medication and special food rations until they improved; then withdrawing the rations until they deteriorated once again. Even though Mengele had hoped to find genetic or racial causes of noma, the research results were overwhelming (and self-evident to the prisoner doctors): noma was caused by the malnutrition and unsanitary conditions of the camp.

With so many children dying of malnutrition and disease, Hugo and his sisters and brothers needed to have some advantage, just to survive. This came about when Hugo's father became the block leader.

*Then it became somewhat better. We received bread and then we didn't have to go to the children's nursery anymore.*

∾

Here is the other reason Hugo and his family survived: they were transferred out of Auschwitz before the Gypsy camp was liquidated in August 1944.

Hugo's parents had already tried to resign themselves to their own death: as early as June 1943, they had witnessed a mass murder in the Gypsy camp. At nine in the evening, the camp had become suddenly quiet and the SS had locked up all the barracks. Hugo's sister, looking through a slit in the wall, could see trucks moving toward one block and the guards beating the prisoners into the trucks. Then the trucks drove away, toward the gas chamber and crematoria, and the people of that block were no more. *Thus we lived eighteen months in constant uncertainty and fear*, recalled Hugo's father of their time in Auschwitz-Birkenau. He counted his father, his brother, and his sister among the victims.

But Hugo's family members, perhaps spared because of his father's military status, were sent to other camps in the Reich. Manfred, Hugo's older brother, was taken with his father to the men's section of Ravensbrück – where both were sterilized

– and then to Sachsenhausen, both camps in the eastern part of Germany. The other five children were sent with their mother to the women's camp of Ravensbrück, and were soon transferred to Mauthausen, in Austria. Hugo remembers walking the ten or fifteen kilometres from the train station to the concentration camp at Mauthausen, atop a high hill. Those who were too weak to walk, who collapsed, were shot as soon as they stumbled or fell.

∾

Hugo has told his story before, when he and other members of his family were interviewed by Dr. Ludwig Eiber for a book and exhibition about the Gypsies in Munich during the Nazi period. At the opening of the exhibition in the spring of 1993, many Sinti were invited to the ceremony with the Burgermeister, the mayor of Munich, at Dachau, and Hugo had read a written account of his personal experiences. Now, as Reili and I are listening to him talk of his experiences, he interrupts his narrative with startling suddenness and leaps up from his chair.

"Wait – I'll get the paper I read to the *Burgermeister*," he says as he walks briskly out of the room.

"What's he doing?" I ask Reili. "I'd rather have him just talk to us, instead of read a paper."

I know that Hugo's written account is valuable but this edited, literary version of events isn't really what I'm after. It's the unexpected nature of a fresh, spontaneous narrative full of personal details that gives oral history its unique value; the emotional nuances in the tone of a voice registering anger, fear, happiness or pain that color each narrative with subtle meaning; the powerful, anguished silences when the voice lapses, failing to find words for the unfathomable, that express the inexpressible.

But Reili quickly suppresses my protests. "Shhh…" she whispers, frantically motioning me to be quiet.

Okay, I think. I don't fully understand the reasons but I'll have to accept a compromise rather than risk having nothing.

It's extraordinary enough just to be here. I lean back in the armchair, taking in the glittery opulence of the room with its eclectic mix of styles. Enormous ornate polished walnut armoires hold collections of antique pewter cups, steins, vases, pitchers and plates. Striped satin brocade chairs and antique carved wooden tables vie for attention with clusters of modern overstuffed chairs, plump white sofas and glass coffee tables topped with lacy tablecloths and extravagant arrangements of fresh flowers. Bright woven flowers spill across the white background of the thick Persian carpet; picture windows are framed by yards of pleated cream-colored chiffon, draped and drawn back elegantly; glass chandeliers hang from the ceiling.

Antique and modern are tossed together with only ostentation unifying them. A large black-framed television set rests on an antique dresser with carved legs. Atop the television is an antique clock in a domed casing of gold filigree. And everywhere there is so much gold that the room evokes Versailles: from the statue of Jesus hung with gold chains to the golden cupids perched in the corners.

As Reili and I sit in the living room, Hugo's teenage daughter enters the room with a tray of coffee cups. She is large-framed and sultry, with long, flowing dark hair and sloe eyes rimmed with black eyeliner. Dressed in a sexy black see-through top and tight blue jeans, she's a startling contrast to the women in Rosa's conservative household who abide by the traditional Sinti mandate to wear long skirts that hide their legs. Everywhere I go on this trip, the past and the present seem to be colliding.

Gratefully, I take a cup of coffee and sip from it as Hugo comes back into the room with his paper and begins to read.

chapter *thirteen*

# *I cannot talk*

ତ୍ୟ

He heard whispers of the things that had happened in Ravensbrück. Something that a doctor did to his sister. Again his mother wept, long after even she thought she had no more tears. And then at Mauthausen, he heard the Nazis screaming at them to hurry, hurry, then the shots ringing out, splitting the air, and people falling to the ground. Now they were transferred again, to another camp in the northwest of Germany. Bergen-Belsen, it was called.

*The worst camp.*

Thirty other families – mothers, children – in a barrack built to house a fraction of their number. No food but rotten beets, one time a day. Oh, for bread, a little bread that his mother had gotten somehow, had saved in her pocket and divided among the children. Every minute of the day, the hunger raged.

And lice, lice, lice – they nibbled at you day and night. They said the lice could eat you alive. More often they brought typhus. His mother was sick with the typhus, so weak she couldn't walk. She was sent to the hospital block – and no one ever seemed to return from there. A mother could not protect her children here, but still – what if he lost her?

There were sick people everywhere, sick people among the dead people. Moaning, crying out in thirst, burning with fevers and delusions, unable to control their bowels. The stench. People dying in the night, their bodies cold in the morning. At Auschwitz, he had seldom seen a dead body.

Here, the corpses were everywhere, piled outside the barracks. Naked – someone always needed their clothes. Rats, giant rats tore into the bodies, devouring them. Their eyes. The eyes of the rats, glittering. The eyes of the dead as they stared up, at nothing.

*Bergen-Belsen was the worst camp.*

∾

Tens of thousands of new prisoners straggled into Bergen-Belsen. As the war neared its end, Nazis consolidated the concentration camps, causing massive overcrowding in the German camps. The camp administration disintegrated into chaos. Routines, such as the roll call, were abandoned. The food supply was shut off and starving prisoners were desperate. "Typhus and diarrhea raged unchecked, corpses rotted in barracks and on dung heaps," writes historian Raul Hilberg. "Rats attacked living inmates, and the bodies of the dead were eaten by starving prisoners."

"Dying was the order of the day in Bergen-Belsen," recalled survivor Rachel van Amerongen-Frankfoorder, who was in Bergen-Belsen with Anne Frank when she died. "Probably fewer people died there than in Birkenau but it was more visible. In Birkenau, entire groups would simply disappear – the entire Gypsy camp disappeared. There wasn't even any mourning. In Bergen-Belsen, you didn't say goodbye, you died slowly, from illness, exhaustion, cold, most of them from hunger. But you don't learn to live with death… Although you often fell over dead bodies, every time it happened it was again a shock. I couldn't get used to it."

∾

"In Bergen-Belsen, you didn't say goodbye." Too many people had died here, and you saw it. Hugo saw it; all the children saw it. This is the curse of memory, the images burned into a childhood memory – of lice and sickness, of rats and piles of corpses. He was still young and so were his brothers and sisters and his cousins, those who would survive – they were young, they still had a chance at a life. But they could not erase the memory, the childhood memory.

∾

Spring 1945. The British arrived to liberate the camp. Physicians came into the camps wearing gas masks because of the stench. Prisoners had died in their own excrement and mounds of bodies lay everywhere; no one had the strength to bury them. The dead had to be buried quickly and so the British brought in bulldozers and buried them in mass graves. It had to be done.

The British soldiers told the prisoners that they'd have to stay until they were all registered.

Stay! For Hugo and his family, it was out of the question. Hugo had found a little wagon somewhere – the weakest among them could ride while the others walked. His mother and the youngest child riding in the wagon, the family took off, making it as far as nearby Hanover, where they located relatives who took them the rest of the way back to Munich. His father and his brother Manfred arrived a couple weeks later.

But how do you return?

"None of us will return," writes Charlotte Delbo. "None of us should have returned."

Back in Munich, the family discovered that their house was occupied by strangers and they had to take shelter with Hugo's aunt and uncle, Eduard and Dina, Shukar's parents. Only after persistent haggling was their house finally returned.

And Hugo – he was now eleven years old, twelve by the time he went back to school, more than two years behind in his studies.

Hugo's grandparents, Johann Baptist andEmilie
(Mettbach) Höllenreiner, 1920s
(*Private family collection, print courtesy of Ludwig Eiber*)

*I was a big guy and didn't know anything. The kids teased me
and gave me a hard time.*

The children taunted him, humiliated him. How could he
respond? Could he explain that he was behind because he had
spent the last two years in Auschwitz, Ravensbrück, Mauthausen and Bergen-Belsen? Could he say that it wasn't his
fault, that he wasn't stupid or a slow learner, that he'd simply
been torn from his old life, ordered from his home by Munich
policemen, shoved into a cattle car bound for Poland, starved
and beaten into submission? Could he tell them that he'd
watched his relatives broken and beaten, that he'd seen his
mother naked, sick and starving, that he'd heard the weeping
and the whispers about brutal operations on his sister, brother,

and father? Could he tell his classmates that he'd been in death camps, to nightmare places beyond their imagination? That he'd seen rats feeding on piles of naked corpses?

No, there was nothing he could say, nothing. He was silent, embarrassed and ashamed. When his teacher made him talk, he struggled. Stammered. He had lost all ease with words.

~

Now Hugo reads the statement at the end of his paper. His face is strained with emotion as he pushes down his rage, struggling to submerge it. His voice is strong and bitter.

*To this day, I still don't understand why they did that to us.*

*We were, and we are, German citizens. I have a family tree that shows we've lived for 500 years in Germany. We always had decent homes and jobs and we lived like any other citizens.*

*I was a Munich boy, but it didn't count. I was a Gypsy.*

~

"Did that help you?" Hugo asks me.

"Yes – it was very good. But if you don't mind, could I ask you a few more questions?"

He agrees. But I've lost the organically ordered flow of a full interview where questions crop up naturally in response to a continuing narrative. The questions I ask now seem isolated and out of context. Hugo answers them briefly and then there is an awkward silence before I can think of the next question to ask.

"Did you have any friends in Auschwitz?" I ask, groping.

*Yes.* There is a tension in his voice that is palpable; the strands of anger seem to knot together and rise perilously near the surface.

*Yes, I had a friend named Albert Kaisen. And he made a rag ball and he was playing with it. And the ball came a little close to the fence and he ran after it. And the overseer, the SS, saw him running toward the fence and shot him.*

*All his intestines ran out. He held his intestines and ran to his father. An hour later, he was dead.*

Hugo's powerful voice comes to a sharp halt. Silence. I am shaken. I have asked for this story, a story he did not even mention in his paper, but now I wonder if I should have asked. What right have I to ask him to reveal such anguish? What can anyone gain from these revelations, from the searing pain of opening the never-healed wound? For a while, I sit in stunned silence, unable to ask another question for fear that anything I say will only trivialize the effect of the terrible vignette he's just told.

I try to remind myself of my purpose here. Remind myself that Hugo has agreed to this, that maybe there is some value in others listening to this terrible story. Remind myself that the unacknowledged pain is the worst. But I am not sure what I believe anymore. Finally, just to break the uneasy silence, I ask him if he can describe the transport from Auschwitz to Ravensbrück. Aware of how fatuous and probing I must sound, I make my request in a barely audible mumble.

*Auschwitz was an extermination camp and Ravensbrück was a concentration camp,* he answers, ignoring my question. *My brother Manfred was twelve years old, and he and my sister, Frieda, were sterilized.*

*The worst camp was Bergen-Belsen.*

He tells me about one of his relatives in the barrack whose daughter was very sick with typhus and finally died. Her body was thrown outside the barracks and soon the rats came to feed upon it. Hugo saw all this as he stood next to his aunt, the girl's mother. Tears streamed down her face as she watched helplessly.

*The mother was crying, "Ach, My child is dead, my child is dead!"*

*So the people came and threw her out on the ground and the child was entirely eaten up by rats. We saw all that.*

Hugo pauses. His anger is like groundwater, seeping into every word he speaks.

"When I got married and had my first child, I saw all that. It all came back to me, what happened to that child."

He turns to Reili. "The next three, four days I am finished. I cannot talk."

ॐ

Superficially – before he talked to me – Hugo seemed so successful. He has it all: a close extended family, a fine house, a lucrative job as an antique dealer and all that ostentatiously displayed wealth. But he's clearly tormented by his childhood experiences, by his memories. The last five years, since neo-Nazis began attacking Gypsy refugees, and firebombing their housing, as happened in Rostock, Germany in August 1992, he's been particularly uneasy, he says.

"I break out in a sweat. The incident at Rostock brings it right back. I see that child lying on the ground. It could happen again."

"Hugo is very insecure," Reili tells me in the car as we drive away. "That's why he wears all that gold." Then she explains why he wanted to read his paper rather than talk spontaneously. When he returned from the concentration camps after the war and went back to school, he was so humiliated by his ignorance that when he had to talk about an emotional topic, he stammered – a problem that was caused him intense embarrassment. She says she could tell he was afraid that he might stammer when he talked to me and that's why he ran to get the paper so that he could read from it.

"I couldn't tell you in there," she says. "That's why I give you the look."

ॐ

"I cannot talk," Hugo had said. Yet listening to him had given me a glimmer of the meaning of the Porajmos, the Great Devouring. It is there in Hugo's memory of the rats devouring his young cousin. And it is there in the devouring of the survivor, the child who lives with the memory, the adult who sees the image in his own child's face, the survivor who has lost even the language to tell it. The Holocaust is the raging wildfire destroying everything in its path. The Shoah is the devastating ruin scraping the earth into a parched wasteland. The Porajmos is the violently insatiable beast devouring humanity. The survivors of catastrophe are victims along with the dead, no matter what follows.

"The fear is there and never goes away," Hugo said to me, just before I said goodbye. "They all say you're doing well and all, but there's a fear there – you never get rid of it."

# chapter *fourteen*

## *Mano, the boy who was lost*

ɷ

*"Who are you? What is your name? Where are you from? Where is your family?"*

A barrage of questions and the rough grasp of hands roused the frail boy from his stupor. All of his bones ached. He saw the brown hollow of dirt around him and the scowling faces of strangers above him. He heard the foreign voices, the questioning, angry tone – and he said nothing. Was he German? Was he Gypsy? For as long as he could remember, outsiders had regarded his identity as vile – so vile as to merit slave labor and near-starvation and branding of skin and concentration camps. Where were his people? Where were the Nazis? Where was he?

Exhausted and afraid, Mano decided it would be better not to risk saying who he was. Better to remain silent, mute.

Mano was ten years old when his family – his parents and sister – was deported to Auschwitz and then transferred to Ravensbrück. Then he was transported again, to Sachsenhausen. In April 1945, as the war was coming to an end, he was separated from his parents and other adults. Three hundred children, including Mano and his cousins, were rounded up and ordered to march in the direction of the Baltic Sea. Mano and two of his cousins decided they would try to escape. The three children ran through the woods, fearful that at any moment they would be shot by the SS guards. But instead of shooting, the guards took off their uniforms and ran too, fleeing the approaching Russian army.

Somewhere, perhaps near a village, the three boys found bicycles and pedaled along the road that they hoped would eventually lead toward home. But Mano was weak and malnourished, and he could not keep up. Far behind his cousins, he became so exhausted that he fell off his bicycle and collapsed into a ditch, losing consciousness.

Mano's rescuers were French prisoners of war, newly liberated, who had been traveling down a country road near Hamburg in a horse-drawn wagon at the beginning of May 1945. First they'd seen the bicycle by the road, then the thin body of a boy in the ditch.

"*He's German!*" one of them yelled, after Mano refused to identify himself. "*Let's cut off his legs! In return for what the Germans have done to us...*"

They spoke enough German to deliver the threat to Mano, so he could understand their intent. Did they brandish a knife as well? In any case, the threat threw a scare into him. If he did not tell them who he was, then...

"*All right then, you can come with us,*" they said, looking at his frightened face. They lifted him into the wagon and continued on the way to France.

❧

The Child Search and Registration Department in Munich later composed a chronology of Mano's whereabouts:

> *16 May 1945:* Mano comes to the reception station Pantin (near Paris) and meets Madame Fouquet. She is a Frenchwoman who knows a little German and she can converse with this child.

> *Early June 1945:* Mano's nerves are bad and he often behaves like an animal. He is admitted to the Sick Children Hospital and stays there for six weeks after being examined by Dr. Huier.

The *Kranken Kinder* which Mano was taken to was actually a

sanitorium for mentally ill children. Mano's lack of communication and wild behavior were undoubtedly the result of his confusion and fear on finding himself in a foreign country with strangers after spending more than a year and a half in concentration camps. Yet it took six weeks before another doctor checked him thoroughly and found him mentally sound – and noted at last his Auschwitz tattoo. Mano was transferred to a 'resettlement home' for children and, after his release in August of 1945, was sent to stay with Madame Fouquet. In late August and September, an organization called Assistance to the Deported sent Mano to a vacation camp in Chevreuse-Tal.

"He does not enjoy being with other children," noted the report.

I imagine Mano – like Hugo returning to school, only even more isolated – unable to speak of his experiences or his identity. How was he to know that his parents in Germany were searching desperately for him? His father had enlisted the help of the United Nations Relief and Rehabilitation Administration (UNRRA), an organization for locating relatives lost in the war.

"My son has a tattooed number on his arm, z-3526, just one number apart from my own," his father would have told them.

Meanwhile, in January 1946, the director of Assistance to the Deported, Madame Marcheix-Thouumyre, agreed to care for Mano until she could find a French family willing to adopt him. By March of that year, Mano was adopted by a wealthy French couple, Monsieur and Madame Chevier. He remained with the Cheviers for the duration of his time in France.

*They loved me, they treated me like a son*, Mano says of the Cheviers.

During the twenty months of his residence in France, Mano seldom spoke about his identity. The people who cared for him never knew his true surname or ethnicity – only that he had been in a concentration camp. At first, because Mano was silent about his past, the people who cared for him assumed that he had lost his memory and had forgotten his family.

*I never forgot them*, Mano insists, explaining that he was afraid to speak of them, especially in German. As he learned French, and his fear subsided, he began to talk about his parents.

The record says that Mano claimed his father was a tamer of wild animals in a circus.

"No, that's not true!" objects Reili when I ask her about it. She sounds appalled at the very idea. "He was a full-fledged Sinto; he wouldn't bother with animals. He bought wholesale and sold retail. I don't know why Mano would say that. Maybe he lied to them, just to tell them something."

In any case – probably because his parents were looking for him and because the French assistance organization had duly noted his tattoo – at last, in December 1946, Mano's parents received the good news that their son had been located in France. They had been searching for him for more than a year and a half. (Even half a year after he was found, the United Nations organization, having made inquiries in Britain, Switzerland and the Soviet Union, wrote to tell his parents, "It is very much regretted that up to this date it has not been possible to obtain any information concerning him." The letter is dated May 1947.)

"As Mano leaves us, I wish first to congratulate his parents for the many good qualities their son possesses," wrote Madame Marcheix-Thoumyre to Mano's parents. "Whatever he owed us has been paid totally because he's given us only satisfaction during the twenty months of his stay in France. You can be sure that he's been treated as a real son... materially, affectionately, morally, and concerning his education. In a word, all his life would have been happy if he hadn't had to know what had become of his people."

Mano says his adoptive parents may have loved him so much that they didn't try very hard to locate his real parents.

The line "all his life would have been happy if he hadn't had to know what had become of his people" suggests that Mano may be right.

Yet the letter from Madame Marchiex-Thoumyre also directly denies this attitude. "Since his arrival in France, we've never stopped looking for his family," she wrote.. "It's thanks to this perseverance that we have today the profound joy to see him leave to join you ... How happy our French heart is today to give all of you this great happiness of Mano's return to his own family. Dare I say that while entirely sharing your happiness, our heart is broken at the idea of not seeing him again for a long time."

∾

Mano lives just down the street from his mother, whose house is lavishly decorated with knick-knacks, framed photographs, lace doilies and shiny fabrics. His house could not be more different. Here, there are no embellishments at all, except for a framed copy of the ubiquitous crest given by a duke to the *Familie Höllenreiner* in 1439 which I've seen proudly displayed in every Höllenreiner household. Otherwise, there are only the rugs and the furniture reflecting Mano's occupation as an antiques dealer: lush, authentic Persian carpets and very elegant, exquisitely carved, perfectly preserved pieces of antique furniture. It is all immaculate, and – despite the warm notes of the wood and the rich colors of the wool – the effect is sterile. Cold perfection.

On the opposite side of the room from me, Mano sits in an antique leather armchair, wearing a crisp white cotton shirt with thin blue stripes. He looks tense and slightly suspicious. He's over six feet tall, has a solid build, narrow beady eyes and a thin mouth set in a square jaw. He glares at me icily from wide, tinted glasses, and answers my questions with abrupt impatient phrases.

*I was born in 1933, and went to the lager, Auschwitz, in 1943,*

Coat of arms given to the Höllenreiner family by a duke in 1439.

he says. *The same thing happened to me that happened to Hugo. But I was too weak to escape and was found by the French.*

He stops, and I wonder if that's all he has to say. My tape recorder has been running for less than a minute. Only with the help of Reili and Mano's wife, do I begin to reconstruct his story. And then, just minutes into the conversation, Mano leaves the room in search of his papers, just as Hugo did. When he returns, he tosses a sheaf of papers on the table in front of me.

*Here – this is my whole life story*, he says tersely.

I can't remember seeing a person in a more agitated state. Mano conveys his conflicts through small gestures: the

Mano Höllenreiner, 1993.

brusque quality of his voice, the chilling bite of his eyes, the tense rigidity of his posture. Even when he describes how his French adoptive parents cared for him, how he was sent to the best French schools, his voice strains with anger and antagonism – and I am uncertain how much of it is directed toward me for asking the questions. *My experience was terrible, terrible*, he repeats impatiently, as if I don't understand.

When I ask Mano, tentatively, for details about his experiences in Auschwitz or Sachsenhausen, he says he can't remember. *I was just a child*, he says. But Hugo, one year younger, remembered those experiences all too well. Maybe Mano doesn't want to re-open the scarred wounds, expose weakness to a stranger, puncture the tough demeanor that thinly masks the fear and isolation of his childhood. Maybe, I think, Mano the man doesn't want to acknowledge Mano the boy – the boy who was lost.

"Mano suffers from his childhood experiences," explains his wife, Else, who sits on the sofa between Reili and me, dressed in blue jeans, a silk shirt and a blazer. In sharp contrast to her husband, her manner is both calm and warm, and when Mano is involved in talking to another relative, she whispers to us confidentially: "That's why he is so nervous and high-strung. So aggressive."

Mano is the toughest person I will interview; his hostility and bitterness are palpable. But he is not unique. Most of the Sinti men I interview are either reticent or very angry, it seems – much less forthcoming than the women. I wonder if it's because their experiences as victims were not only dehumanizing but also emasculating. When I mention this theory later to Reili, she agrees. "Oh yes," she says. "The Sinto man is always ego – the Sinto men are ego-people; you know what I mean? They're always a little cocky. That's inbred. The women are more the workers. The women are stronger."

Reili says she wishes Mano could have received psychological help when he returned. But nobody considered that at the time, she adds. Now, most of the relatives attribute Mano's abrasive manner to his childhood trauma and they make allowances. So when Else explains why Mano is so *aggresiv*, Reili just nods her head in understanding.

*"Ja, ja,"* she says. *"Die Angst.* The angst."

chapter *fifteen*

# *Spiritually broken*

ॐ

*In 1943 we went to Auschwitz.*
At first, after every question I ask – Where were you born? Where did you live when you grew up? What did your parents do for a living? – Margrette answers with the date and event that overshadows everything: *In 1943 we went to Auschwitz.*

Margrette, Mano's mother, is eighty-one but her dark eyebrows and short, wavy silver hair give her a youthful look. Dressed in a long straight skirt and white sweater, with several gold necklaces and crosses around her neck, she has a slender elegance. She greets us with a firm handshake and invites us to sit with her on the living room sofa, while her daughter Lilly serves us coffee. The room is highly decorated: coffee tables draped with blue satin, velvet couches loaded with lace-edged pillows and every flat surface adorned with silver and gold-framed photographs or ceramic knick-knacks.

Her family? *One sister, my older sister, was gassed in Auschwitz, with her six children. And Mama. And my brother was killed in Dachau.*

Margrette is easy to talk to; she speaks clearly and without hesitation, looking directly in my eyes as she talks. It is, by now, a familiar story: the arrest in Munich, the period in jail, the loading into a cattle car, the secrecy about their destination.

*We were terrified. No bread, no water, nothing, nothing. Nothing for the children.*

At Auschwitz, the doors of the cattle car were flung open.

Lilly and Margrette Höllenreiner, 1993

*Shnell, schnell!! They beat us in the direction of the barracks. In all my life, I will never forget what I saw there. All the dead bodies, a pile as high as a house, all the dead, Jews and Gypsies, all lay there. I said to my husband: "We will never get out of here. We will die here."*

One morning, all the people from her barrack in the Gypsy camp were herded together. Their hair was shaved, they were deloused and they were ordered to strip naked in preparation for a shower. They knew what would happen next – they would be gassed. Terrified, they screamed and cried and hugged one another. But just as they were about to enter the gas chamber, the officer received an order from a higher authority and the group was sent back to the barracks.

She tells the story of her reprieve without pleasure. She knows of too many others who had no such reprieve. Friends. Relatives. Strangers, linked only by circumstance. Once, she watched a man who tried to climb the electric fence. He died instantly. A suicide? Once, the SS chose a Sinto man on her work detail as an example of the punishment that would be given to those who tried to escape. They whipped him brutally with fifty lashes that lacerated his kidneys. He died on the spot.

What else does she remember of Auschwitz? The SS came and took the young girls out of camp, to use for their pleasure, she says. Her niece was impregnated by an SS Sturmführer and she carried the child to birth.

*The child is still alive and now she must be* ... She consults with her daughter and with Reili to determine the child's age... *over forty years old.* As soon as the child was born the Nazis tattooed her with a prisoner number, most likely on her upper thigh.

*My brother's daughter was in Auschwitz. And she had three small children. And the SS said to her, "You can go on a transport – a work transport – but the children must stay here and be gassed." And she said, "If my children must stay here, then I want to go with my children in the gas chamber."*

*She died with her children in the gas chamber. Thirty-six of my relatives died in the gas chamber.*

*We went from Auschwitz to Ravensbrück,* she continues. *Then my husband was in the men's camp and I was in the women's camp. And my husband came out and I saw him and I ran over and wanted to kiss him. And the SS overseer came with a big dog and an SS man. And she hit me with a whip and beat me. She said, "Why are you still interested in your husband?"*

*Then Christmas came and everyone in the camp got a piece of bread and some watery soup. We were all together, Jews and Gypsies. Then the overseer came and told us to line up. We were cold and barefoot, and I was so weak that I fainted. I fell against Ducha (her sister-in-law). And the overseer came and beat me.*

*We went from Ravensbrück to Mauthausen. That was the death camp, the death march.*

The Mauthausen concentration camp was a huge operation, set among rolling hills on the north bank of the Danube near Linz, Austria. Although Mauthausen was not an extermination camp, it had the record for the largest number of officially recorded executions of any concentration camp (in many cases, these records were destroyed as the Allies moved in). Over half of the camp's nearly 200,000 inmates died, often through brutal overwork and beatings at Mauthausen's stone quarry. Prisoners had to haul large, heavy stones up the quarry's 186 steps known as 'the staircase of death.' A common saying at Mauthausen was: "Each rock cost the life of a man" because the enforced labor, along with the brutality of the guards, resulted in so many deaths. In one typical example, prisoners were made to carry stones weighing sixty pounds or more on their backs, and were beaten, kicked, and hit with bludgeons if they collapsed; most of these prisoners died. In another recorded instance, Jewish laborers were commanded to walk to the top of a nearby mountain and then run downhill. As they ran, guards opened fire on them from behind bushes and trees. This was a familiar form of 'execution' at Mauthausen. No wonder the prisoners often called the camp 'Mordhausen' – '*Mord*' meaning murder.

In March 1945, 447 Gypsies – Sinti and Romani women and children – arrived in Mauthausen from Ravensbrück. Margrette was among them and she describes what happened there – an incident which may have occurred either while they were working in the quarry or when they were climbing the steep hill to the concentration camp.

*Then the mothers and the small children who could not walk anymore... The SS took the machine guns ... R-r-r-r-r-r-r ...*

Margrette's face and body stiffen, and she takes short, rapid breaths.

"She has to relax a minute," says Reili. "She has to relax."

But Margrette continues with no further prompts, insistent on the telling.

*There were some women and small children. They couldn't walk anymore. 'RAUS!' R-r-r-r-r-r-r-r!!! And thank God, I had my Lilly, she could walk a little, and I had my nephew on my back. Thank God, I made it. It was so high. And on that trip, twenty or thirty women and children were shot.*

She is visibly agitated, as if she sees it all again, hears the sound of the machine gun exploding bullets, again and again: *R-r-r-r-r-r-r...*

∾

As her mother speaks, Lilly drifts in and out of the living room, listening sporadically but intently, without comment. She's in her mid-fifties. Dyed black hair, thick eyeliner and a heavy layer of mascara have all failed to revive her weary face. She wears a tee-shirt with wide black and white stripes and a short black skirt. Later, posing for a photograph, she holds her arm naturally next to her mother's so that their Auschwitz tattoos fall into place, aligned one on top of the other: z-3969, z-3970.

*We were in the barracks for eight days,* says Margrette. *And then the train came and we went back to Bergen-Belsen.*

Accounts indicate that the Gypsies sent to Mauthausen in 1945 stayed two weeks. Those still alive were transferred to Bergen-Belsen, a process that took eight days. And Bergen-Belsen was even more wretched than Mauthausen.

*My child was hungry; there was nothing to eat. And a cart came by with turnips. And I went by it and took a turnip for my child. And the SS came and said, "Why did you take that?" "She is hungry," I said. "To the bureau office!" She took a whip and gave me twenty-five lashes.*

At Bergen-Belsen, Jews and Gypsies lived in the barracks together. The bunk next to Margrette was occupied by a Jewish woman, frail and sickly, and her daughter, who was little older than a baby. One morning when Margrette woke and looked over at the bunk, she saw that the mother had died in the night.

*The mother was already dead. And the child cried and kissed her: "Mama, Mama." I took her with me. I kept her with me, in my arms.*

Margrette fed the toddler pieces of bread from her own ration, bit by bit as if she were a baby bird. She would have kept the child, as if it were her own, but three Jewish women came to talk to her. *The orphan is of a Jewish mother*, they told her, *so we should care for her.* Reluctantly, Margrette gave up the little girl. Afterwards, the women would come to visit her in the camp, she says, so she could see the child on whom she'd lavished so much affection.

*R-r-r-r-r-r-r!* Margrette makes the staccato sound of the machine gun again. Just before the camp was liberated, she says, the SS told the prisoners to come to the kitchen to eat. Whoever came was shot down. *R-r-r-r-r-r-r!*

∾

Liberation. Margrette was still strong enough and coherent enough to welcome liberation. Exuberantly, she climbed atop the British tanks and hugged every soldier she saw. Many of the other prisoners were not so hardy. Some, she remembers, were too weak to withstand the combination of excitement and rich food; they died soon after the camp was liberated.

Now, for a brief time, the prisoners were vindicated, their roles reversed as they taunted and spat at the captured SS guards imprisoned behind barbed wire. The former prisoners were warned not to eat the food the Nazi guards had left for them – it was poisoned. The survivors were sheltered in the comparatively luxurious quarters of their former oppressors and fed from the SS supplies. *Aahhh…* she sighs. *Fresh milk. White bread. Good butter… and all of it was quality.* How long had it been since they had tasted such things?

Margrette stayed with Lilly in Bergen-Belsen until her brother arrived in an old car and drove the two back to Munich. Now Margrette found that her former house was gone; all her possessions were gone.

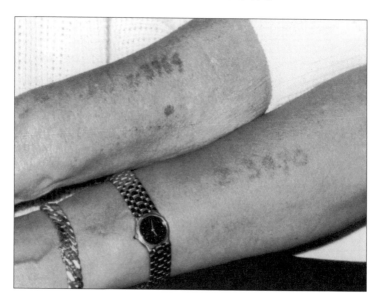

Mother and daughter Auschwitz tattoos

*Ah, nothing more there. Nothing more.*

But she refused to take this displacement meekly. She strode up to an apartment where a former SS officer lived and boldly knocked on the door. When a woman opened the door, Margrette grabbed her by the hair, beat her and threw her out of the apartment. *"RAUS!"* she yelled. "OUT!" She explains her action with a proud smile: *The Nazis had done the same thing to me.*

The woman went to the American soldiers to file a complaint and they came to investigate. When they learned that Margrette had been in a concentration camp, they declared that the SS woman had to go but Margrette could stay.

Her husband and son were still missing but her relatives came to the new apartment to celebrate her return. Margrette went to examine the cellar and found abundant supplies of food and champagne so they had a party. They all ate heartily, laughed, made music and toasted their liberation, drinking the SS-purchased champagne with a certain vindictive pleasure.

Months passed, then half a year. At last her husband, Johann, returned to Munich, but their son Mano was not with him. Was he even still alive? Over the next year and more they would try to locate him, but it was not until 1947, nearly four years since the family's arrest and deportation, that they were reunited with him. In the meantime, Margrette and Johann bought a small house, and began to reconstruct their lives in Germany.

But Margrette had nightmares, constant nightmares. *At first I couldn't sleep. Always SS shooting.* It took many, many years, she says, until she was 'normal' again.

*When I think back, I will never forget what I have been through. It never goes out of my mind.*

ᔕ

Reili is anxious to move on and urges me to finish up the interview. Before I leave, I ask one more question: What are the lasting effects of your experiences?

*Seelig kaputt,* she answers without hesitation. Spiritually, emotionally broken. *Nervous.* Exhausted. *Ganz seelig kaputt. Kaputt.*

## chapter *sixteen*

# *A piece of bread*

❧

There were the children who could not be children; there were also the mothers who could not be mothers.

"This is Hugo's mother," Reili says, introducing me to Sophie. "The beautiful one in the photograph who was in the lager and survived with all her children."

The 1941 studio photograph shows Sophie at thirty years old, surrounded by her six children. She is lovely, with smooth skin, deep-set soulful eyes and thick, wavy hair. Yet her expression is as grave and melancholy then as it is now, almost as if she could anticipate the pain that was about to overtake her family.

Fifty-two years later, Sophie sits in an antique leather armchair in the living room of her son's house in Ingolstadt. The down-turned corners of her mouth have deepened over the years and the lines of sadness are etched into her face.

"There's no point in talking about her experiences," Reili had told me, on the way to Sophie's house. "Anyway, it's the same story that happened to Hugo."

"But everyone's story is different," I protest. "Even if they experienced the same events, they'll have different memories of them. I'd like to talk to her. Please."

❧

Sophie's narrative *is* totally different in tone from Hugo's. Where her son was rigid and terse, she is spontaneous and

Sophie Höllenreiner with her children, in 1941. From the left:
Frieda (Emma), Rosemaria, Rigo, Hugo, Peter, and Manfred.
(*Private family collection, print courtesy of Ludwig Eiber*)

unselfconscious; where his voice was harsh and angry, hers is
soft and sad. Where he read from the printed page, she seems
to be reading from a script she creates to accompany the pic-
tures she sees on her internal screen. Her memories spill out
as fast as she can translate the images into language.

And then there are the silences – long passages when
Sophie is still watching the film, staring at images for which
she can find no words. These silences are not dead time while
she waits for another question. They are not indications that
she wants to stop the interview, halt the film. Her eyes – they
are looking at something, following a sequence that can't be
edited or spliced, a sequence with no dialogue or commentary.
Sometimes, after a long silence like this, she will sigh.

*Ach, ja,* she says quietly, her voice desiccated from a
drought of long-spent tears. *Lieber Gott.*

*Dear God.* Dear God, how brutality cast an evil shadow

Police station on the Ettstrasse in Munich, mid-1930s.
(*courtesy, Stadtarchiv, Munich*)

over this innocent family, a gloom which began when her husband was discharged from the army, after eighteen months
service. He was a Gypsy – therefore he could no longer serve.
He took a job with a trucking company. Sophie joined
German organizations, hoping this would improve their
status.

"It helped?" suggests Reili.

*Ja. But it was not enough. It went on like this for one year. And
then, early in the morning – I cannot say exactly, but I think
between five and six, we were arrested. And it was the ninth of
March, if I remember correctly. Nineteen-hundred and forty-three.*

*Yes, it was a transport. "Get ready! Get up! And take only the
necessities. You are going to be transferred, moved someplace
else...and you can live there the same as you live here, and, and..."*

They were taken to the prison on the Ettstrasse in Munich

and put in a communal cell with thirty people. *Then we had to sign that we would not leave the city. We were in prison for three or four days. It was warm – it was March – they gave us a piece of bread with some spread, a meat spread, and that was all, and that is how we all became sick. We wanted to save it so we wouldn't starve … in the train. And we all became sick. Oh, dear God!*

What did you think then was going to happen? I ask.

*We thought they were going to get rid of us!*

∞

Sophie's son, Rigo, was only five years old at the time but still remembers the experience. *We children knew less,* he says. He nods towards his mother. *But she knew it. And Papa knew it. And Manfred knew it. And Frieda knew it,* he says, speaking of his older brother and sister. *But we didn't.*

Sophie agrees, her voice shaking. *Nothing at all. Not until we had arrived at night. Then they drove us out like wild animals, as if we were worthless … And we were afraid. They beat us with the rifles. My brother-in-law was beaten with the gun …he died then.*

*We went out and immediately there was a huge barrack. There were fifteen hundred people in it – that I still know, because the next day they said. In one barrack. Fifteen hundred!*

Sophie held the youngest child, crying, in her arms. Overwhelmed by the viciousness of the guards, the grim reality of Auschwitz, Sophie's head reeled. *Because that was, that was unbelievable.* She lost consciousness and collapsed to the ground, the child still in her arms.

∞

*I can remember, partially,* Rigo says, in the lull that follows Sophie's description. *We had nothing to eat. And the sickness that we saw, and the dead people – that I can remember.*

He gives a specific memory of Auschwitz-Birkenau: *We*

Women on bunks soon after liberation at Auschwitz.
Barracks in the Gypsy camp at Auschwitz-Birkenau,
designed to hold 300 prisoners often
held 800 to 1,000 or more inmates.
(*Still photo from a Soviet film, courtesy of United States
Holocaust Memorial Museum Photo Archives*)

*always had to stand outside, early, for the roll call. And soon we
were frozen.*

The twice a day roll call was held to make a precise count
of the prisoners and match it up with the records of the dead.
Every inmate – no matter how sick or weak – had to line up
and stand outside while the officers counted them, until the
tally was complete and satisfactory. If the count of the dead
and the living did not match the supervisor's records, the roll
call could continue indefinitely. Frequently the officers
stopped the count, seemingly at random, to beat the prisoners
with cudgels.

"Not a small agony were the endless roll calls," remembered Sophie's husband Josef, in a testimony he gave before
his death. "Everybody had to be present, even the smallest
children."

"Roll call in the concentration camp was the horror of the day," writes Lucie Adelsberger in her book about her experiences as a Jewish prisoner-doctor in the Gypsy camp at Birkenau. "We were counted again and again, often by calling out every single number, and the prisoners had to stand, not only hours on end, but days, nights … Many prisoners have stood twenty-four and forty-eight hours in the broiling sun, in pouring rain, in frigid, sub-zero weather with howling winds… They stood in threadbare shreds of garments, in wooden clogs or worn-out and split remnants of what once had been leather shoes, their hands wrapped in a few rags. And they stood still, for they were not allowed to move."

*We often had to go and stand early in the morning,* says Sophie. *At four o'clock, sometimes until noon. In thirty degree cold. In thirty degree cold, we had to stand for five or six hours.*

*As children,* says Rigo, *we had to go through an alkaline solution. We all had to be treated for lice. Lice were also on the whole body. That I can remember. I had to go through three, four times. Today, I still can't forget that.*

The more the children cried, the more they were pushed around, treated brutally. A push from a guard and a child could fall into the caustic solution – and burn.

*If you were unlucky, you were dead,* says Rigo. *I didn't even have any lice but it was the same for me.*

ॐ

*My husband was beaten very much, very much,* says Sophie. *For nothing. Only because they wanted to make a joke. And the others too – for ridicule. They ridiculed for pleasure.*

On the way to Rigo's house, Reili had warned me that Sophie might not want to talk. But there is no evidence of reluctance as she speaks, almost in a reverie, as if she is watching the film as it threads through the spools.

She worked in the kitchen at Birkenau, she says. *The daily meal had to be fetched from the kitchen in heavy 'excavator' buck-*

*ets, almost heavier than the meal contained in them.*

Weak, sickly and hungry, the prisoners had hardly the strength to drag these buckets, so frequently some of the soup was spilled. *As punishment for it, 'Sport' was called.*

In Auschwitz terminology 'doing Sport' meant that the Nazis demanded various degrading exercises of the prisoners and beat them mercilessly in the process. Sometimes, they demanded hours of push-ups from the prisoners; whoever collapsed was beaten. Other times they demanded an even more debasing 'Sport' to alleviate their boredom. Prisoners were harnessed and made to run like horses, while the SS whipped them until they collapsed.

*The SS came there, with their long coats and with the boots. And everyone was outside. And then the misery began. Everyone was harnessed like horses. And I was unlucky because I was on the outside.*

*And this 'fun' took a good two hours. A sport for them. After they were through, they counted the dead. Thirty-six had died immediately.*

Though Sophie never recovered full use of her knee after the 'Sport,' she couldn't receive reparations for it, she says. She might have had that condition before Auschwitz, the authorities told her. And of course, she had no proof otherwise.

*In one word, that was cruel.*

❧

*The worst was Bergen-Belsen.*

Along with some other members of her extended family, Sophie and her children were transferred from Auschwitz to Ravensbrück, then briefly to Mauthausen and finally to Bergen-Belsen. Here, toward the end of the war, a constant stream of inmates, half-dead with starvation and exhaustion, filtered into the camp from the death marches. An epidemic of typhus raged in the camp; people died in droves and many were left unburied.

"It is impossible for me to express the scene that was before me: piles of bodies already decomposing, in fact about a mile of bodies," recalled a survivor who arrived in Bergen-Belsen at about the same time as Sophie. "Many people talk about Auschwitz, it was a horrible camp; but Belsen, no words can describe it... we were just put in there with no food, no water, no anything, eaten by lice."

Hunger was ever-present – an incessant craving, a searing pain that never went away.

*Every day – it was three months there – every day, red beets in water. And that only one time a day. No bread! Never any meat. Only red beets, one time. They came in with one barrel – and so many people...*

One day, Sophie and her oldest daughter waited and waited in the kitchen area so they could be first in line for the watery soup. They stood at the window where the soup was distributed, next to a large barrel of rotten beets. Behind them, the emaciated prisoners, all of them starving, and many suffering from typhus and malaria as well, jostled against them, trying to push their way up to the front of the line.

Suddenly, shots rang out.

*We were praying. And he shot. And our hands became moist and sweaty, and our faces looked shaken. And he saw us, and continued shooting. My friend also was shot. The whole thing lasted maybe twenty minutes. But it was like twenty-four hours.*

The guards then piled up the bodies of those who had been shot – dead or living, Sophie says, and shoved them into the scum-covered vat of rotten beets. Then they yelled: *Now, eat as much as you like until you are filled!*

*Ja, ja.* Another lapse, a long silence.

❧

Somehow, in Bergen-Belsen, she had managed to 'organize' a piece of bread. In concentration-camp terminology, 'to organize' meant to manipulate, negotiate – often through unsavory means – in order to get more than one's share. But in Sophie's case, it was not for herself but for her children.

The piece of bread was small, and it had taken a lot of trouble to obtain it, but she imagined that it would see her children through another day, strengthen them. How could children survive, much less grow, with only this thin soup made of beets? For herself it didn't matter, but for the children…

She slipped the bread into a deep pocket of her skirt and patted her skirt with her hand, assuring herself that it was safe. She would give it to the children tomorrow, keeping it one day just so she could prolong the joy it would bring them all, mother and children, when she gave each of them a piece of this life-sustaining substance. Every minute the piece of bread was in her pocket, she magnified its importance, its power to save them.

That evening, as she held her youngest child close, hugging him to her, the boy smelled the bread in the pocket of her skirt and began to cry, begging her for some. *Not now, not yet,* she said, but he kept crying, crying with his desperate hunger, his tears falling on her ragged skirt until she knew it was useless to try to save the bread for the morning. She called her children together, tore the bread carefully into equal pieces and gave each of them a piece. She watched as they devoured the little pieces of bread rapidly. With this bread she had done everything she could – but too quickly, it seemed, it vanished.

And still the children had the raging hunger of starvation and their hunger gnawed at her, a far greater pain than her own hunger, for she had done what she could, everything a mother could do in this God-forsaken place, and it was nothing, this piece of bread she had managed to get – it could not save them.

∾

Another day. Sophie collapsed again. She had succumbed to typhus, the killer disease that raged in the crowded unsanitary conditions of concentration camps like Auschwitz and Bergen-Belsen. Lice spread typhus, as the Nazis well knew. "One louse – your death!" proclaimed the bold letters of warning signs in the concentration camps. Yet the camps themselves, with their deplorably filthy conditions, led to the uncontrolled spread of lice, and with them, the scourge of epidemic typhus.

A person with typhus suffers from a high fever and chills, extreme apathy and weakness, delirium accompanied by intense thirst and a severe headache. Though typhus patients can often recover under appropriate medical attention, in the concentration camps typhus usually meant death. In Bergen-Belsen's last months, most prisoners were doomed to die of starvation or typhus.

*At the last moment, I got typhus. I went into a coma, and I wasn't here anymore. So they laid me down, and I lay six days without consciousness.*

Another of the women prisoners in Bergen-Belsen who suffered with typhus described the effects: "Now the illness took me over entirely; my head was bursting, my body trembling, my intestines and stomach were agony and I had the most abominable dysentery. I was just a sick animal lying in its own excrement." Such was the state of the concentration camp that victims of starvation and typhus, scarcely able to move, could barely be distinguished from the corpses that lay beside them.

But Sophie, for all her misfortune, had a rare stroke of luck. When she regained consciousness, she was in the infirmary, where a friendly prisoner-doctor attended to her, secretly adding medication to her food. Slowly, almost miraculously, she recovered. But she worried constantly about her children. What would happen to them now, left to the mercy of the Nazis without even their mother to protect them? Sophie hated being separated from them. Perhaps they would think that she had died, she thought anxiously.

She tried to persuade the doctor to let her go to the children, just to tell them that she was still alive. No, he said, she was still too weak to walk. Still, she decided, she had to try. If she could just walk through the gate and into the other part of the camp, she would be all right.

Dizzy and weak, she began to walk. Her vision blurred: she was seeing double. Then she collapsed, falling to her knees behind some bushes. She hid there for a while – minutes or hours? – until at last she felt she had the strength to go on. Sometimes walking, sometimes crawling, she made it through the gate, and her children saw her, ran to greet her.

∾

Nearing the end of the war, with the camp administration at Bergen-Belsen in such chaos, it may well have been that nobody took notice of Sophie as she returned from the infirmary. Eight days later, on 15 April 1945, the camp was liberated by British troops. They were shocked and appalled by what they encountered. Ten thousand unburied bodies, victims of starvation and disease. The horrified soldiers took photographs of what they saw at Bergen-Belsen and these photos presented the public with the first concrete evidence of the Nazis' mass murder.

Even after the arrival of the British, the dying did not stop. The inmates of Bergen-Belsen were so sickly and skeletal that they died at the rate of 300 a day, resulting in a stunning overall figure of 14,000 deaths *after* liberation. "There had been no food or water for five days preceding the British entry," reported a British army review. "... Their clothes were in rags, teeming with lice, and both inside and outside the huts was an almost continuous carpet of dead bodies, human excreta, rags and filth." A British soldier who helped liberate the camp said of the inmates: "I have never seen people looking so ill, so wretched and so near death."

Was it a dream, or were they really, finally free? They wouldn't stay around while the British buried the dead in huge pits. Sophie's children found a little wagon and bundled Sophie, still too weak to walk far, inside. The children pulled the wagon out of the camp.

∾

Sophie's account is dry and unsentimental but it envelops her. She seems unaware of her audience – Reili, Rigo, and me – and totally oblivious to the noise and chaos surrounding her.

As we talk in the living room, the other adults drink coffee in the kitchen, with a clatter of coffee cups and dishes, peals of laughter. Just behind the chair where Sophie is sitting, teenagers drift through the hallway, giggling and exchanging flirtatious comments. Younger children race back and forth through the hall and up and down a nearby stairway. They yell at each other and shoot raucous toy machine guns. *Rat-a-tat-tat. Rat-a-tat-tat.* I can barely hear Sophie's soft voice. But she goes on, oblivious.

∾

*"What was your worst experience?"* asked the official, years later, when Sophie went to apply for reparations.

She answered without hesitation. It was the time she had hidden the piece of bread in her pocket and her child had cried for it. The time she had torn the bread into pieces and given it to her children but it had disappeared in an instant, like their tears, accomplishing nothing.

*To this day,* Sophie says, *I still think of the piece of bread in my pocket.*

This, then, is her worst experience. Not the brutality, the beatings. Not the pain and humiliation of being harnessed like an animal to a cart for the pleasure of the SS guard. Not the cold-blooded murders of her relatives, her friends. No, her worst experience is her own utter helplessness in the face of her children's hunger and starvation. The pain of the mother unable to nourish her children, unable to mother.

*Oh, ja.* She sighs. *The children were so young. The youngest was only four years. He can still remember bits and pieces.*

Deafening staccato cracks from the toy machine guns. A boy stands directly behind Sophie, aims his gun into the living room and shoots. *Rat-a-tat-tat.* Sophie doesn't seem to notice.

*I often think, if they would have been bigger, what they would have suffered,* she muses.

*Rat-a-tat-tat.*

The two older children, Manfred and Frieda, were subjected to sterilization experiments, she says.

*For years, every night I would think about what happened, and cry.*

"I think she's reached her limit now," Reili says to me.

"Should I stop?" I ask, reaching for my recorder.

"I would."

But Sophie, swept into a current of ugly memories, doesn't want to stop. *It's always the same things! They whipped them to death, beat them to death, and electrocuted them, beat them to death on the street … or trapped them in a hole without a second thought.*

*I had a little crucifix. I had that every evening, in front of my eyes.* Every night she prayed to God: *"If You wish us to suffer and be hungry, as You wish – but bring us out of here …"*

"And you did come out, with your children," Reili says, trying to calm her.

*But I still have a great sorrow,* Sophie insists. *Manfred.*

## chapter seventeen

# *In the rain one sees no tears*

∾

*A great sorrow.* Sophie speaks of Manfred, her eldest son, who was sterilized when he was twelve years old.

Reili tries to console her. "He could have died," she says, implying that there are things worse than sterilization.

*Then I would have already forgotten*, Sophie says.

∾

When Sophie and her husband, Josef, and their six children were still in Auschwitz, Nazis announced that ex-soldiers who chose to be sterilized would subsequently be freed. It was not much of a choice; the alternative was the gas chamber. And in some camps, such as Buchenwald, specially trained attack dogs were turned upon Gypsy prisoners who refused to submit to sterilization.

These veterans were not sterilized in Auschwitz but were sent to Ravensbrück along with their families. Forty Gypsy veterans were said to have been sterilized by Dr. Franz Lucas, in late 1944 or early 1945. And, of course, they were not freed. After the operation they were transferred to Sachsenhausen. One witness who later testified at the Auschwitz trial said that six persons were sterilized daily; another recounted that he was sterilized without anesthetic and, when he screamed in pain, Dr. Lucas shouted, "Be quiet, you swine!" After the operation, the man had to spend six weeks in the hospital barracks.

Manfred's experiences also must have been wretched. He was just twelve, the age at which the Nazis required Gypsies to be sterilized. Though he had come to Ravensbrück with his father, who was also sterilized, it's doubtful that his father could have been by his side while he endured not just one, but four separate operations.

"Many died from the poor care," Josef recounted. "My twelve-year-old son had to undergo four of these operations." Josef's brother, who was also sterilized at Auschwitz, said, "They spared me nothing."

*The doctors came from Berlin,* Sophie says of Manfred's operation. *They were standing by laughing and joking. Three times he almost died. What I have been through, I cannot tell you.*

∽

Forced sterilization, which was intended as delayed genocide, was profoundly painful for every victim. It destroyed lives, caused severe psychological and social problems.

But why does Sophie not speak equally of Frieda's sorrow? Frieda, Sophie's eldest daughter, was also sterilized in Ravensbrück. I look at the lovely, smiling girl in the photograph. She was only fourteen years old at the time.

Nazi racial policy determined that people unworthy of procreation – Jews, Gypsies and Slavs – should be subject to sterilization. But the traditional method of surgical sterilization, especially for women, was too labor-intensive and too expensive for the Nazis' use. SS Chief Heinrich Himmler, in particular, was interested in cheap, efficient mass sterilization, and enthusiastically accepted a proposal by Dr. Carl Clauberg, a leading German gynecologist, for a method of "sterilization without operation … on women unworthy of propagation." Himmler gave Clauberg facilities and subjects at Auschwitz and financial support to carry out his experiments for rapid sterilization.

Clauberg's method was to give women intra-uterine injections of corrosive liquids that would obstruct their fallopian tubes. The procedure was done without anesthesia, in three stages over a period of months, and often caused infections of the ovaries and high fevers. Young Jewish girls from Greece, mutilated by such experiments in Block 10 in Auschwitz, were then sent to the gas chambers. The women prisoners at Auschwitz were so terrified of Dr. Clauberg that when they heard he was coming to the barracks, they would hide in corners, crying out hysterically: "The obese butcher is coming! The revolting rooster is here!"

After a year of experimentation, Dr. Clauberg sent a report of his work to Himmler, claiming that an experienced doctor could sterilize hundreds, perhaps thousands, of women a day. It's unlikely that sterilization ever took place on such a large scale but Clauberg would later draw on his work at Auschwitz to perform mass sterilization operations on young Gypsy women at Ravensbrück.

Another Nazi doctor working to find the most efficient method of sterilizing prisoners was Dr. Horst Schumann, the former director of an extermination center. He used X-rays to castrate men and sterilize women and surgically removed women's ovaries to determine whether the X-rays had effectively destroyed the tissue. Victims fell ill with infections that resulted in fever, severe pain and vomiting; others developed fatal complications. Schumann's experiments in sterilization by X-ray, which Gypsy women in Auschwitz were also subjected to, had to be abandoned. Most of the subjects died shortly afterward in great agony.

Clauberg fled to Ravensbrück in the beginning of 1945, as Russian troops approached Auschwitz – although he did arrange for some of his Auschwitz victims to be sent to Ravensbrück as well. Here he performed his experiments on Gypsy women, sterilizing 120–140 Gypsy girls who had been brought to the camp from Auschwitz.

Dr. Schumann also victimized Gypsy girls in Ravensbrück with sterilization experiments. One of Sophie's relatives, who was also interned at the camp, heard that seventy-two women had been sterilized there in just two hours. Reportedly, mothers of the girls signed consent forms after being promised release – but again, the conditions under which signatures were obtained are highly suspect.

Sterilization at Ravensbrück was most likely done by an injection into the uterus. Girls were taken away and brought back on a cart. "Like pigs," remembers a survivor who was in Ravensbrück at the time, looking after a girl named Resi whose parents had been murdered in Auschwitz. "And Resi (lay) on top dead, the others too, and a couple more were still twitching underneath them. It lasted less than two hours and then they too went cold."

Another Sinti survivor of Ravensbrück described the scene: "It was then said: 'The Sinti are all sterilized, so that there will be no offspring.' From girls of twelve up to forty-five year olds, I will never forget it," she said. "Without anesthetic, without anything …Then they took the children out in wheelbarrows when they had been sterilized and just threw them back in the block, twelve-year-olds!" One twelve-year-old girl whose abdominal wound was not even sewn up after surgery died after several days of agony.

Even girls as young as eight and ten years old were victims of these brutal procedures. A Czech prisoner-doctor who worked in the hospital barracks testified after the war that most of the sterilizations were performed without anesthesia. "I tended children the whole night after the operation," she said. "All these girls were bleeding from between their legs and in such pain that I had to secretly give them painkiller."

Those who survived the operation were not freed but were sent to other camps. The sterilization was irreversible; many of the girls were permanently damaged.

"For those women who were the victims of these operations there was no liberation in 1945," writes historian Karola Fings, noting that the German government never punished Dr. Clauberg for his crimes. "In view of the significance of the

Sophie's sister-in-law, Alma "Notschga" Höllenreiner, who died at
Auschwitz. Her children were sterilized at Ravensbrück.
(*private family collection, print courtesy of Ludwig Eiber*)

family in Romany culture and the fact that most of the
women could not speak about what had been done to them
because of the existing taboos, these women in particular still
suffer today."

Finally, Sophie does talk briefly about what Frieda went
through after liberation.

*Frieda – nine times she had to have operations. Had to! Other-
wise, she would have died. Everything was deformed.*

I cannot talk to Frieda, but I imagine that she would echo
the words of a survivor who wrote about the effects of this
experience: The physical and psychic damage cannot be calculated.

∞

*But Manfred, he became unhealthy, unlucky.*

Sophie continues to focus more on Manfred's suffering. Perhaps it's because the taboo against talking about this procedure is more powerful with women than men. Or perhaps it's because Frieda, though unable to bear children of her own, later adopted some of her sister's children to raise as her own, while Manfred's wife left him and he was never able to have or to raise children.

For a while after the war, the family hoped that Manfred's sterilization could be reversed.

*There was a doctor who took a great interest in Manfred. He gave him two operations. But he couldn't fix it.*

*The boy still suffers from it,* Sophie says.

She calls Manfred *"der Junge"* – the boy – as if she has utterly forgotten the passage of time.

*He's sixty-two years old,* she acknowledges. *But I can never forget. Because he has no family. He has terrible problems. You cannot speak with Manfred about it. He doesn't want pity or sympathy. There is no consolation. None at all.*

"She cannot mother him," says Reili, in her own translation of Sophie's words.

∾

Sophie sighs again. *I think I could talk for three more weeks and still not be finished. Tonight, I cannot sleep. So much has happened. And then I think of the children. How small they were when these awful things happened. Ach, lieber gute Gottes.*

"We sympathize with you, *Tante,*" Reili says. She's noticed that my eyes are damp. "She cries with you, *Tante.* She has children too."

Despite my intention not to become emotional during the interviews, this one has really struck me. Reili can see it in my face.

"It is emotional," Reili says to me, kindly. "Naturally, you get involvement. I mean, you can't help it."

*After so many years ... you have cried and cried,* continues Sophie. *One can cry no more. It comes sometimes. Now and again. But otherwise, you are already drained out. Ach, lieber Gott. But it breaks my heart. How terrible that was, one cannot say. One can say nothing. One cannot explain!*

Tears edge over the rims of my eyes. Reili gives me a knowing nod. "Now you get emotionally involved," she says. "I get that too. I have to fight that back. I get too emotional and I'm lost."

*It breaks my heart,* Sophie says again. *They cannot have children. And he recently told me, he said: "Mama, it is a grief! In the rain, one sees no tears."*

Her voice cracks. *My heart broke. He said, "Every time, if I hear ..."*

"Hallo!" We hear a booming voice in the hallway and Sophie breaks off, mid-sentence. A tall, husky man with auburn hair and a bushy mustache greets Reili and Sophie heartily. Reili rises to embrace him.

It is Manfred – the boy who does not want sympathy, the broken, inconsolable man.

"Now we must stop," Sophie commands me. "Turn off the tape."

I shut off the recorder.

∾

"No one can talk about the Nazis or the concentration camps when Manfred is around," Reili explains to me, as soon as Manfred leaves the room, still unaware that he was the subject of our conversation. "He goes crazy."

Now I remember Reili's stories about her cousin – Manfred – who was emotionally damaged from his experience, who suffered from severe bouts of depression and alcohol abuse, but never received any kind of psychological help. "In those days, nobody went to a psychologist or a therapist," Reili had told me.

Sophie repeats Reili's warning. "We cannot talk about this when Manfred is around," she says, with an abrupt note of finality.

*In the rain one sees no tears,* I think. So much grief that one person's tears are as nothing. Manfred's suffering, and Frieda's, are only drops in the deluge, hardly worthy of notice. Somehow the image only intensifies the sadness. *There is no consolation,* as Sophie said. *None at all.*

Sophie and Reili both leave the living room and go to join the other relatives in the kitchen. I hear silverware clinking against dishes; the lilt of conversation and laughter drifts down the hallway.

I stay behind, alone, rewinding the tapes, and packing up my equipment again, in silence.

chapter *eighteen*

# *Their ways and our ways*

Ro̤sa and Shukar don't seem to agree on anything. They argue so vehemently that Reili feels compelled to reassure me: "They're not arguing; they're talking."

Shukar comes over nearly every day to see Reili while she's visiting. He sits in the big leather armchair by the sofa, sips coffee and eats the day's offerings. Usually Rosa has prepared some kind of potatoes – fried or dumplings or potato salad – and she serves them with pork or sausages, sauerkraut, dark bread, cheese, coffee and pastries. Then she sits down and, as she nibbles on a bit of a pastry and Shukar eats heartily from his plateful, they bicker. Rosa complains incessantly about the younger generation while Shukar says she is wrong to be so intolerant.

Reili usually just listens and explains the discussion to me. She also has strong opinions but is more reserved in expressing them. "I'm like Switzerland – I'm neutral," she says, when caught in the crossfire of an argument. She doesn't want to be aligned with any one faction among her relatives but hopes to stay on good terms with them all.

But all three of them agree passionately on one point: they reject the Roma, absolutely.

Groups of Gypsies use different names to designate themselves and often these names refer to linguistic groups. The Roma, the largest Gypsy group in Europe, speaks Romanes, while the name Sinti derives from the language originating in the Sind region of India. In pre-war Germany, the Sinti was the largest group of the very small Gypsy minority, while in pre-war Austria, the Roma were more numerous than the Sinti.

"Those Gypsies who arrived in Germany in the beginning of the fifteenth century call themselves Sinti, derived from the river Indus. Those Gypsies who arrived later, in the nineteenth and twentieth century, call themselves Roma," explains German historian Wolfgang Wippermann. "There are difficulties because they were divided for more than 400 years."

Some have likened the hostility between these two groups of Gypsies, the Roma and the Sinti, to the feelings between Ashkenazi and Sephardi Jews, the two ethnic communities of Jews defined mainly by a common region or country of origin. Though both Ashkenazi and Sephardi communities share common histories and beliefs, there are differences in language (only the Ashkenazi spoke Yiddish), customs and life style. And when Ashkenazim and Sephardim have been thrown into close contact – as in the 1600s when Ashkenazi Jews from Poland and Germany clashed with Sephardi Jews from Spain and Portugal or in modern-day Israel, where Jews from around the world live together – the pressures of inter-ethnic difference boil to the surface. Rivalry and antagonism is strongest between kin, it is said. Yet in times of crisis, some point out, the Ashkenazim and Sephardim have pulled together.

Similarly, when all Gypsies were in trouble – when the Nazis abolished distinctions and labeled all Gypsies carriers of *Artfremdes Blut* – alien blood – the Roma and Sinti often did help each other. Reili's own stories bear testimony to that: Roma helped her family when they were fugitives in Romania, Bulgaria and Yugoslavia. The Roma helped her Sinti family find places to live and hide; they made the connections for them so they could sell their gold and buy food; they advised them in foreign lands.

*We didn't agree with a lot of things they did, they probably didn't agree with a lot of things we did, but we stuck together, they helped out,* Reili told me. The two groups formed a practical bond based on recognition and resistance.

But the clasp formed by the commonality of suffering unfastened under the strain of the post-war years. Since the fall of communism in Eastern Europe, the Roma, now the largest sub-class of Gypsies in Europe, have been fleeing to Western Europe, seeking refuge from prejudice and outbreaks of mob violence against them. Originally many of them came to Germany in particular because of Germany's liberal laws toward asylum seekers, created post-war to show the world their new tolerance. But neo-Nazi attacks on Roma and other foreigners to Germany followed their arrival. Local officials, supporting the public outcry against foreigners and even the public sympathy for the attacks, called for the expulsion of Roma in towns throughout the country. Finally, in 1992, the German government ordered the deportation of refugees from Romania. The majority of these were Roma. The attitude of the post-war government toward Gypsies, whether Roma or Sinti, has never been welcoming.

༄

Naively, I'd expected that the Sinti would be supportive of the Romani refugees from Eastern Europe. But I was completely mistaken. Even Rosa, a native of Austria where the Roma have traditionally outnumbered the Sinti, is adamant.

"I don't like the Roma," she insists. "Don't call us Roma – it's an insult. We're Sinti. The Roma have no pride. The Sinti won't have nothing to do with them."

The Sinti, who have been in northern Europe since the 1400s, now number at least 60,000 in Germany. They are generally established economically and have stable residence; they are accustomed to being the dominant Gypsy culture here. Despite – or perhaps because of – their treatment at the hands of the Nazis, the German Sinti feel they have full rights to partake in all the benefits of German citizenship.

In contrast, the impoverished Roma on the streets in Germany have no long-established residence or economic niche. The most visible of the Eastern European refugees are the beggars and they incite the most antagonism from the Sinti. Many Roma regard begging as a legitimate form of economic activity for women. To the Sinti, however, begging is wrong; Sinti women make money by selling lace or other goods door to door. The Sinti fear that these Romani beggars will only sully their own reputation, causing non-Gypsies to lump Sinti and Roma together under the same roof: no-good Gypsies.

"My family has been in Germany for over 500 years," Shukar says. "You cannot compare the Sinti with Roma from Poland, Romania and Yugoslavia. Their ways and our ways are very different."

But it is Reili who surprises me the most with her prejudice. The Roma are dirty and disgusting, she says. "Some of them even make their living handling bears." She shudders.

Both Reili and Shukar tell me stories about Roma who make money begging on the streets and then drive away in fancy cars. "I don't want to be compared with them," Reili says. "We are not prejudiced but through the Roma we get a bad name. They don't want to work, they don't want to send their kids to school."

It's interesting that Reili feels so strongly that education equals superiority. She is careful to point out to me that Sinti value education highly. Her grandmother insisted that all her seven children went to school, she says, and she was "150 percent Sinto."

I wonder if these attitudes contribute to Reili's embarrassment at not finishing school, since the years spent in hiding and in a concentration camp caused her to miss out on her own education. But she still holds a strong sense of inter-ethnic superiority. The Roma people are different, she insists, as she repeats one of the oldest discriminatory myths about

Gypsies. "They are not like us. Some of them even steal children."

I'm startled – and saddened – to hear these prejudices from my Sinti friends. They sound so much like the classic *gaje* stereotypes of Gypsies that it makes me uneasy. Don't they realize how few non-Gypsies distinguish between Sinti and Roma, between Gypsy street beggars and Gypsy professors, between Gypsies who travel in caravans and those who are settled house-dwellers? Don't they realize that they have been cast with the same stone that they seem so ready to throw at their Romani brethren?

Worldwide, the Gypsies are striving for political unity, strengthening the movement for self-determination. But if the conversation in this living room is any indication, the Sinti and the Roma in Germany don't seem about to join efforts anytime soon. A friend who works with an organization for Gypsy self-determination in Holland told me that if either the name 'Sinti' or 'Roma' were used in an organization, the other group would refuse to join. But perhaps it's the Sinti who are the most prejudiced, since one organization that risks having both names in its title, the Rom and Cinti Union in Hamburg, reportedly has a higher percentage of Romani members.

The Sinti seem to forget their own recent past under the Nazis when they blame the Roma for the prejudice of their non-Gypsy neighbors. Is it the amnesia of the new prosperity that causes them to argue that the Romani beggars reinforce the worst stereotypes of Gypsies? Or is it a fear that the past will recur and that the Roma will somehow have a part in the blame?

"The Roma ruin it for us," Shukar says, shaking his head.

"On this, Shukar and I agree 100 percent," says Reili.

Another thread pulled from the fabric of my frayed idealism. But it's useless to argue. I didn't come to their home in Germany to try to convince them of anything, I remind myself. I came here just to listen. To respect. And to record.

chapter *nineteen*

# Homeland

∾

Reminders are everywhere in Germany; you cannot avoid them. Even the landscape is tainted. As Reili and I ride from Munich to Neumarkt, about 150 kilometers to the north, with her cousin, Stramsee, at the wheel, I marvel at the impossibly picturesque countryside. Rolling hills, dotted with ancient castles and steepled churches, thick curving stands of trees with leaves turning red and gold, cows grazing in lush pastures, stone houses with balconies, shuttered windows, bright flowers overflowing from window boxes, white geese flapping their wings in a yard …

Before a bend on the tree-lined country road, Stramsee slows the car and pulls up beside a stone wall. "This is the spot where Nazis murdered nearly 400 prisoners who worked in a munitions factory," he says. "They were shot on a death march just before the Allies arrived to liberate the labor camp."

On either side of the stone wall entry is a memorial plaque to the victims of National Socialism; beyond the wall is a wooded cemetery where the prisoners are buried. We read the plaques silently, then drive on.

∾

My father left Germany in 1939 and did not return until he and my mother came for a visit in October 1968. When my parents got off the plane they were greeted by a German customs agent. "Good day," the agent said in English to my mother. "Have a pleasant trip."

Then, noting that my father had been born in Germany, he turned toward my father and greeted him in German. "*Willkommen, Herr Sonneman,*" he said, with a certain emphasis on the word. *Welcome*, Mr. Sonneman.

My father turned away, flushed with anger. As soon as they were out of earshot, he started fuming about the official's rude behavior.

"What's the matter?" my mother asked. "Why are you so upset? It was a perfectly friendly greeting."

"Oh, Edith, you don't understand. Friendly? You have to have grown up in a country to understand the nuances of the language. *Der Ton macht die Musik.* The tone makes the music."

For beneath the simple greeting, my father insisted, there were other implications: *Why have you come back?* and *Where were you the whole time?*

"And still more," my father tries to explain, as he recounts the story to me. "Can you understand that, Toby?"

"Now all that happened is already half a century ago, and my best customer last year lives in Hainburg, close to Frankfurt, and we have a great kind of communication, an understanding. Nevertheless, my aunts, my uncle and cousin were all wiped out, killed without grounds, and only because they were Jews ..."

He pauses as he searches for the English words to explain his feeling. "I have no animosity," he says. "No hate whatever. All that happened is already years ago. In German one says, *die Zeit heilt* – time heals. Deep within me, I am simply sensitive and can't help remembering the past – but without reproaching that on the sons and the daughters of the current generation. Can you understand this, Toby?"

∾

When I first met Reili, she told me about a conversation she'd had with an American Jewish woman. "It's time to forget the Holocaust and go on," the woman had told Reili.

Reili felt her blood, hot, rise to her cheeks. "No!" she protested, surprising the woman with the force of her anger. "We should NEVER forget about it!"

∾

Rosa asks me to accompany her to the grocery store on a Saturday afternoon, shortly before it closes for the weekend. She buys meat, cream, fresh rolls, cheese and bottled malt drink. Long lines of customers wait in the check-out lanes, crammed into the front of the little store. Everyone is anxious to buy their supplies for the weekend since no stores around here are open on Sunday. In the crush, the woman behind us rolls her shopping cart too close and the wheels bump into Rosa's heels. Rosa spins around and admonishes the woman. I can't understand her words but I can hear the sharp acidity of her tone.

"Did you see?" she asks me angrily, when we carry our groceries outside the store. "That Nazi woman pushed the cart right onto my feet!" She curses.

Could it have been a mistake? I suggest. In the store, I had assumed it was but now I realize that I don't really know for certain.

Rosa disputes my interpretation bitterly. "No! She saw that I wasn't a German, that I was a *Zigeuner*, and that's why she did that."

How do I know what happened? A stranger to the language and the customs, I might have missed the more subtle signs of discrimination that Rosa perceived. Even if it were an innocent mistake, would it make any difference to Rosa? For her, there are no innocent mistakes, no innocent Germans. The past seeps into the present, blood staining the thin cloth. Rosa, a proud Sinti, spits at the ghosts of the Nazis, dead or alive.

"I don't like the Germans," she reiterates, as we walk home from the grocery store. She must think it's essential to tell me again. "Nazis! Nazis!"

∽

My father's visit to Germany in 1968 was a difficult one. As he walked Frankfurt's *Sonnemann Strasse* – the boulevard named for his great-uncle who founded one of Germany's finest progressive newspapers, *Die Frankfurter Zeitung*, started a workers' party, and served in the German Parliament – as he visited the parks and cafes of Mannheim where he'd grown up, and talked with the widow of his boyhood friend who had joined the Nazi youth, he was overwhelmed with memories.

One warm day, as my father was walking, stabbing pains struck his chest. He gasped for breath and nearly collapsed. My mother was alarmed: suspecting a heart attack, she rushed him to a hospital where he was tested thoroughly. The doctors could find no physical cause for the attack. Emotional stress, they concluded. "Coming back, after such a long time – and with all that had happened…"

"*Ja*," my father says, telling me about it nearly thirty years later. "And on top of that, it ended up costing me $500 for the examinations!" And he laughs.

∽

My father describes his Uncle Leo, his father's brother, as "thoroughly patriotic."

"He was 100 percent German,' my father says. "Or, I should say, 99 percent German and 1 percent Jewish."

Leo served as an officer in the First World War and received the highest honor, an Iron Cross First Class. He immigrated to the United States, with his wife, Emily, only when anti-Jewish regulations began to damage his textile business. But rather than blaming the German government for his troubles, he seemed to resent even more the fact of his own Jewishness.

"Uncle Leo was not inclined to be a Jew," explains my father. "As a matter of fact, I think of him as a person who really hated the fact that he was born Jewish."

"Emily, on the other hand, came from a very positive Jewish family in Berlin and they constantly bickered and fought about the fact that she felt what was going on in Germany was just awful."

Leo, suffering from an acute case of homesickness, blamed the country's ills on Hitler and the war but was anxious to return.

"He scarcely could wait until Germany would be free of Nazis and he took the first ship the first summer in order to spend his vacation in his beloved Germany. Year after year, every summer he went back to his beloved homeland."

But Leo went without his wife, Emmy. She would have no part in it. Her parents had died in Auschwitz; she did not want to even set foot in Germany ever again. Yet Leo persisted, trying to persuade her.

After twelve years of solo summer vacations to Germany, "Leo begged Emmy to try, one time... to see that the times were changed, that all was changed." She must at least come for a visit to Germany, he said. And if she still felt so bitter about Germany, they would have to divorce. They could not go on this way, he insisted. Finally, Emmy caved in.

On board the ship, in the middle of the Atlantic Ocean, Leo suddenly took ill, perhaps from a diabetic attack, and died. Emmy told the German captain about Leo's life, about his homesickness for Germany and also about her own revulsion toward the country. On hearing all of this, the captain said, "We will bury your husband early in the morning, exactly in the middle of the Atlantic ocean."

So Leo was buried at sea and the German ship continued on to Hamburg. Emmy never disembarked, never stepped off the ship onto German soil. She stayed on board while the ship

The Herrmann family and friends in the courtyard in Freudental,
1932. Sidonie and Moritz and Adolf Herrmann are sitting
at the table on the right; Lina Herrmann is standing, far right.
Julius Herrmann is standing, second from the left.
(*print courtesy of Ludwig Bez, Pädagogisch-Kulturelles
Centrum, Freudental*)

sat in the harbor then made its return voyage to New York
City. "Back to *her* homeland."

"Homesickness," my father says. "The sickness that
changed the lives of two wonderful people ... until death set
them free."

∾

In 1994, my father and other Jewish survivors from Mannheim
were invited back to Mannheim, all expenses paid, by the
Bürgermeister, the mayor. Many cities in Germany have

extended these sorts of offers to Jewish survivors in an attempt, perhaps, to come to terms with the country's shameful past.

Since they were already in Mannheim anyway, my father decided that he and my mother should take a side trip to visit Freudental, the village where he'd spent boyhood summers at his mother's childhood home, visiting his grandparents and working on his uncle's farm.

The former synagogue still stands in Freudental. It was scheduled for demolition in the 1960s, like so many other unused synagogues, but thanks to the efforts of a remarkable man, Ludwig Bez, who was then a schoolteacher in nearby Stuttgart, the synagogue was saved, the building restored and turned into a cultural center and place of study.

So this simple village synagogue, once a common sight in Germany, is now extraordinary, simply because it still exists. It stands in the center of the village and next to it is the house where my grandmother grew up.

It is a traditional German village-style house, a two-storied, half-timbered house of white stucco, with brown shuttered windows and a steep, red-tiled roof. In the late 1930s, my grandmother's brother, Moritz Herrmann, lived in the house, with his wife, Sidonie, and their youngest son, Adolf. Along with the Herrmann family, two other people lived in the house: the shammas, who took care of the synagogue and prepared it for services, and the teacher of the Jewish school.

During the summers, when my father visited, he rose at dawn to work in the fields all day for his Uncle Moritz, a farmer who trained young Zionists from all over Germany for work in the kibbutzim of Palestine. My father fed and groomed and milked cows in the barn next to the house. It still stands, a heavily weathered building with a tiled roof, its plaster worn away to reveal the original stone work and supporting timbers. My father worked a long, full day in this barn and in the pastures, returning to the house at sundown to

Passport for Adolf Herrmann, with a large "J" for "Jew," 1939
(*print courtesy of Ludwig Bez, Freudental*)

devour the hearty meal that his Aunt Sidonie had prepared for the family. Then he would fall into bed, exhausted, to sleep for just a few short hours before Moritz pounded on the door to wake him for another day's work. "If you think it's hard here, wait until you work in Israel," Moritz used to tell the young people who worked for him. "Then you will wish you could be back in Freudental."

"There is a story about this house in Freudental," my father tells me. After Kristallnacht, even though the synagogue had not been burned, the Jewish community decided to remove the precious Torah from the building, so that it would not be vulnerable. They hid the Torah in the homes of the synagogue's members. As Jewish families were arrested and deported, one after another, they passed the Torah from one house to the next, so that whoever stayed behind could guard it for safekeeping.

Moritz Herrmann and his family were the last Jews left in Freudental. Their oldest son, Julius, had left for America in 1937. Their daughter, Lina, had departed for the Netherlands in 1939. And also in 1939, Moritz and Sidonie had decided to send their sixteen-year-old son, Adolf, to live with an aunt in Belgium, hoping that he would be safer there, as they made plans to immigrate to Argentina.

The Herrmann family, it's said, were so respected in town that even the Bürgermeister had tried to help them escape the Nazis, writing a letter to officials in Argentina recommending them as good citizens. The letter was carried by the Belgian underground, and everything seemed in order – except the money for the passage. Moritz tried to raise the money by selling his house – but in Nazi Germany this was an impossible task for a Jew. It was all too late: Moritz and Sidonie were arrested in Freudental in August 1942 and deported to Theresienstadt. Later they were sent to Auschwitz where they were gassed. And in Belgium, their son, Adolf, had already been captured by the Nazis and deported to Auschwitz, where he too died, after first being subjected to Dr. Mengele's gruesome experiments.

"So," my father tells me, "Moritz and Sidonie were the last Jews in Freudental, and as the story goes, the Torah must be hidden somewhere in his house."

In October 1993, after my visits with the Sinti families, I traveled to Freudental to see the synagogue and the house. My parents visited Freudental the next summer, in June 1994. Our experiences were identical. Ludwig Bez, the director of the synagogue/cultural center in Freudental, accompanied my father, as he accompanied me, and knocked on the door of the house. An old woman opened the door halfway and peered out.

"This is Eric Sonneman," said Mr. Bez politely. "He is the nephew of Moritz Herrmann. The Herrmanns who used to live here. He would like to see the house, if you don't mind."

The old woman eyed my father suspiciously. "*Ja, Ja,*" she

said. "*Die Juden.*" She gripped her hand firmly on the door, and did not open it wider.

∾

"I couldn't have found the Torah, of course," my father told me later, when we compared our experiences and found them remarkably similar. "But wouldn't it have been nice if she had let me come in, look around, see how things have changed?"

Later, my parents realized that the old woman might have been afraid that my parents (and I) had come – more than fifty years after our ancestors had been forced to leave their home – to evict her and reclaim the house that was rightfully theirs. My father still wondered whether the Torah was hidden in some secret place in the house. But, for whatever reason, neither of us had the chance to look inside.

"*Die Juden haben hier gewohnt,*" the old woman said. "The Jews lived here."

And with that, she shut the door, in my father's face.

chapter *twenty*

# *Primitive people*

∾

There are stories that cannot be told, stories that violate the sense of the self too profoundly. Stories that, if told honestly, would disintegrate boundaries of culture, of individual integrity … of humanity.

Manfred and Frieda, Sophie's children who were subjected to brutal sterilization at Ravensbrück, will not talk about their experiences. And this, I think, must be what Lawrence Langer calls "humiliated memory," that which "records those moments when history failed the individual." Memory which allows no expression of affirmation in the past or hope for the future, but rather "crushes the spirit and frustrates the incentive to renewal."

Stramsee, Reili's cousin, was never in a concentration camp but was subjected to enforced sterilization.

"He was only twelve when they sterilized him," Reili had told me before our trip to Germany. Once, Stramsee's wife, Otillia, had described the grim details to her and this is how Reili remembered it:

"They lined up the boys, and made them lie on a wooden table with straw underneath to soak up the blood. Then they sent them on. If they lived, okay. If they got infections, they just threw them away."

When Reili told me we'd be going to visit Stramsee and Otillia, she was quick to caution me against asking any questions about the sterilization. Talking about it would violate strict rules regarding sexuality, she told me.

"Stramsee...," she began, and then her voice trailed off. "I cannot ask him that, in person."

Living in the United States, Reili had adopted a slightly more relaxed code of propriety than she grew up with, but she still abided by traditional Sinti rules when in Germany.

"There are rules that even I cannot break. Even for me it's taboo."

∾

Sterilization of 'inferior' people was one of the first measures Nazis proposed in order to improve the 'race' through selective breeding. Precedent for such 'negative selection' had been applied in the United States in 1899, when a prison doctor developed the vasectomy and used the procedure on prisoners. Nazis proposed sterilization as early as the 1920s but it was not until Hitler took power that a compulsory sterilization law was issued, on 14 July 1933. The law ordered sterilization of all those suffering from hereditary illnesses – and such dubious characteristics as 'feeblemindedness' and chronic alcoholism were attributed to heredity.

For the handicapped, the sterilization program led to the euphemistically entitled Euthanasia Program, a systematic campaign of extermination that legalized the murder of some 72,000 people. It was officially ended only in 1941, after pressure from public protests. But sterilization was still being proposed as a way to stop procreation of inferior races – notably, Jews and Gypsies.

It was only a short step from the sterilization of those with 'hereditary illness' to the sterilization of Gypsies. Although sterilization for racial reasons was illegal, it was simple enough to classify the victims as 'feebleminded,' a category defined more by social criteria than by medical formulations – and it was also useful to classify people as criminal. So, in 1939, when Dr. Johannes Behrendt of the Office of Racial Hygiene wrote an article entitled "The Truth about the Gypsies," reporting that Gypsies were "criminal and asocial and … impossible to educate," he claimed that they "should therefore be treated as hereditarily sick." This logic led quite naturally to his conclusion: "The aim should therefore be *elimination without hesitation* of this characteristically defective element in the population. This should be done by locking them all up and sterilizing them."

The task of giving 'scientific' validity to such sentiments had been given to Dr. Robert Ritter, the racial scientist who headed the research institute (under the Reich Security Main Office) assigned to locate and classify all Gypsies in Germany and Austria. Though Ritter recognized that Gypsies had originated from India and were thus pure Aryans, he argued that most of them had mingled with inferior races during their migration to Europe and had lost their pure Aryan characteristics. Some 90 percent of Gypsies were of this impure 'mixed blood,' or *Mischlinge*, Ritter concluded.

Besides just classifying Gypsies, Ritter conducted a systematic study of what was termed 'the Gypsy problem' in order to make recommendations for policies and legislation. Ritter subscribed to the biology of criminality, the popular theory of the time which held that criminality was hereditary and, since criminals could not be rehabilitated, those with inherited criminality must be locked up or sterilized. Thus his recommendation – that "asocial and good-for-nothing Gypsy individuals of mixed blood" should be sent to labor camps or sterilized – came as no surprise. The "Gypsy question" would be settled, Ritter posited, only "when the further breeding of this population of mixed blood is stopped once and for all."

Ritter's chief assistant and protégé, Eva Justin, also recommended the sterilization of Gypsies, even more strongly than her mentor. Along with Ritter, Justin was the most well known of the racial scientists who researched the Gypsy population for the Nazis. In 1933 she had visited Gypsy settlements, posing as a missionary, and Gypsies had affectionately given her the name 'Loli Tschai' or red-haired girl. Later, they

Eva Justin measures a Gypsy woman's head.
(*courtesy, Bundesarchiv, Koblenz*)

were startled when they saw her behind the interrogation table in the police headquarters where they'd been brought for questioning. Her personality had changed as well. Sometimes she hit them or threatened to cut off their hair if they didn't tell the truth, remembered some of the Gypsy survivors.

Justin's research, which she later used toward her doctoral dissertation in anthropology at the University of Berlin, studied the history of 148 children brought up in orphanages or in foster homes by non-Gypsy adults. She concluded that Gypsies could not be integrated because they were racially inferior. They had a *primitive* way of thinking, she said. She did not draw the line at those who had been classified as 'asocial,' as did Ritter, but instead recommended strongly that "all educated Gypsies and part-Gypsies of predominantly Gypsy blood, whether socially assimilated or asocial and criminal, should, as a general rule be sterilized."

In May of 1944, thirty-nine Gypsy children from the Catholic orphanage where Justin had done her research were deported to Auschwitz. Only four survived. By the date of the deportation, Eva Justin had already completed her dissertation.

∽

Stramsee is about sixty, with warm eyes, olive skin, black hair and a salt-and-pepper beard. He dresses casually in a plaid cowboy shirt, grey checked trousers and a cotton baseball jacket. He is self-effacing, quiet, perhaps shy. Sitting next to Mano at the dinner table, he seems like Mano's temperamental antithesis. Stramsee is soft-spoken, calm, undisturbed – while Mano continues to look agitated throughout the dinner conversation.

Besides Mano and his wife, and Reili and me, Bluma and Willie have also come to Stramsee and Otilia's house for supper. Bluma is Reili's cousin, a Mettbach. She was married at a young age to Manfred Höllenreiner but left him and ran away with Willie, causing a bitter rift between her family, the Mettbachs, and some of the Höllenreiners. But the atmosphere seems peaceable enough today between Bluma and Mano's family.

Stramsee's wife, Otilia, who looks like a typical German *Frau* with her light skin, blond hair and short, rather stout physique, has a way of making everyone comfortable. She is certainly the cheeriest person I've met here: warm and generous, bursting with *joie de vivre*. She proudly gives us a tour around their Bavarian-style home which is crammed with exuberant collections of everything from framed antlers and

Stramsee (Helmut) Schönberger, 1993

glass hummingbirds to old copper pots, seashells and dolls. Stramsee and Otilia are dealers in furniture and carpets, and every floor in the house (including the kitchen and the surprisingly modern exercise room) is covered with gorgeous Persian carpets. But Otilia is most proud of her modern kitchen with its large double-door refrigerator, a real luxury in Europe where refrigeration is usually more modest..

"Time to eat," Otilia says, guiding us toward a table laden with food. It is all home-cooked, and it is all delicious: a rich chicken soup with noodles, potato salad with greens and dark gravy, and a creamy pudding topped with a purple syrup which Otilia made from elderberries. She is rightly proud of her cooking but she insists that we show our appreciation by overeating. Just when I think the mid-day meal has ended, Otilia brings out a pot of fresh coffee and a swirling fluted mound of *Gugelhopf*, a rich pound cake filled with golden raisins.

The setting and the meal are delightful – but even after all the relatives leave, the scene is not at all conducive to the subject of the interview. Yet despite Stramsee's reticence and Reili's warnings not to ask inappropriate questions, Stramsee does tell me something about the unspeakable thing that happened to him when he was twelve, when his father was serving in the German army and his mother received a summons.

᷒

"We do not know exactly how many Gypsies were sterilized," notes historian Henry Friedlander, "but we do know that the numbers were large enough to support the conclusion that sterilization of Gypsies was a calculated policy." In 1938, drawing on the recommendations of Dr. Ritter, SS Chief Heinrich Himmler had ordered that all Gypsies over the age of twelve were to be sterilized. The policy was carried out not only on prisoners but also on those exempted from the concentration camps.

Himmler's order to send the Gypsies to Auschwitz in 1943 had excluded those still serving in the military or soldiers who had been wounded or released with decorations. The application of this order was erratic, however, and many servicemen, like the fathers of Hugo and Mano, showed up in Auschwitz, some even wearing uniforms with war decorations. Shortly before the liquidation of the Gypsy camp at Auschwitz-Birkenau, officials announced that veterans who volunteered to be sterilized would then be freed. The offer was false, of course; they were not freed after sterilization. But because these ex-soldiers – like Josef and Johann – and their families were transferred from Auschwitz to Ravensbrück before the mass murder, the arrangement spared their lives.

Yet other Gypsy soldiers, like the fathers of Shukar and

Stramsee, were exempted with their families as the law provided. But, for most of them, there was one stipulation: They must submit to sterilization.

The Nazis were careful to extract a document from the victims saying that they voluntarily chose to be sterilized. Yet they also made it clear that if a person refused to submit to sterilization, they would be sent to a concentration camp. This threat nearly always brought about a consent. "I had to sign a paper that I submitted voluntarily to sterilization," said Eichwald Rose, a witness at the Nuremburg Trial. "If I had not done this they would have sent me back to a concentration camp."

∾

At first, the situation was simply that of a family during wartime. Stramsee's mother and the three children had been evacuated from their home in Munich in 1944 because the city was under threat of bombing. Since Stramsee's father was a soldier in Germany's war, the family was moved to the country for their own protection. Housing was scarce in this small town outside Munich, so they had to live in a bunkhouse for farm workers. But really, life was not so bad. Stramsee was twelve and he attended school just like the other children. Of course, the other children teased and ridiculed the Sinti children and teachers simply ignored them but this was not unexpected. Stramsee knew that Germans regarded Gypsies as inferior; that the other children talked about him behind his back. That was normal. Gypsies had never fitted into German society and Gypsy children never socialized as equals with German children. And naturally Stramsee had heard talk of concentration camps – everyone had – but they were never associated with anyone he knew. Even when his relatives in Munich had mysteriously disappeared one night, everyone said they'd gone to a labor camp and Stramsee imagined them all at work, perhaps on some project to help with the war.

Then Stamsee's world collapsed. His mother received an official summons to report to the hospital, with her son. Under coercion, she signed the papers and Stramsee was sterilized. It was *involuntary*, despite any documents to the contrary. Stramsee didn't even understand what it all meant.

Stramsee's mother was pregnant and thus escaped sterilization – that time. If not for his father's status in the army, perhaps the Nazis would have killed the baby, Stramsee says. And it was only a temporary reprieve. After the baby was born, his mother had to report to the hospital again. This time, she too was sterilized.

*At least the young doctor who sterilized me was human,* Stramsee says. Possibly the surgery could even have been reversed, he adds. I imagine that this means the operation was a vasectomy. But a couple months later, Stramsee was summoned again, for what was euphemistically termed a 'checkup.' This turned out to be a second, permanent sterilization, most likely the terrible castration scene that Reili had described: *They made them lie on a wooden table with straw underneath to soak up the blood.*

*This doctor was an animal,* Stramsee says.

In the midst of the brutal procedure, his mind reeling with pain, Stramsee began to rage and swear against the Nazis. His mother rushed to his side to calm him. *If it hadn't been for her,* Stramsee says, *I would have been in serious trouble.* And trouble, as everyone then knew, meant a concentration camp.

The incident was violent, bloody and tortuous. Yet nobody explained to Stramsee the consequences of the operation, much less why it had been 'necessary' at all. Why did his mother have to sign those papers? Why was this cruelty committed? He didn't even know *that* he'd been sterilized, much less *why.*

Later, when Stramsee did discover the effects of his trauma, what further damage did it cause him? Gypsies place great value on children, attaching the highest importance on an adult's ability to procreate. The social status of both men and women depends on their having children. When did Stramsee realize that his personal pain would continue? When did he realize that Nazis had intended not only cruelty to him but also the delayed genocide of his people?

∾

"Did you ever try to get compensation?" I ask.
*Yes. Fifteen years later.*
"Why so much later?"
He shrugs, explains that he was put off by the paperwork, the requests for check-ups and more check-ups. I imagine the daunting process of putting in a claim for compensation: submitting to the indignity of endless examinations and interrogations by government authorities. How could Stramsee, then a young man of twenty-seven, have endured this further humiliation?

But perhaps Stramsee had heard that the federal government had determined that those who were sterilized were not entitled to compensation, since their ability to earn a living was not diminished. Not until 1980 did the government approve a one-time payment of 5,000 marks for those who had been subjected to compulsory sterilization. Then, finally, Stramsee received a lump payment for his loss.

∾

And what happened to those racial scientists and researchers who had recommended sterilization or concentration camps as a solution to Germany's 'Gypsy problem'? After most of the German Gypsies had been deported, sterilized, or killed, Dr. Robert Ritter (still director of the research institute) turned his attention to investigating 'asocial' adolescents interned in a 'police youth custody camp.' Ritter intended to show through such research that whole families with 'criminal-biological' tendencies could be subjected to sterilization or concentration

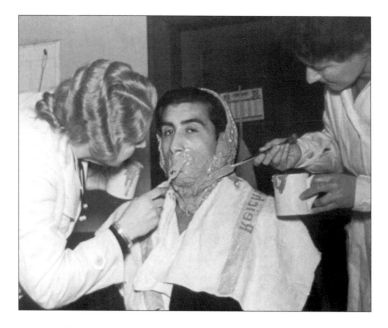

Sophie Ehrhardt paints the face of a Gypsy woman
(with a plaster-like substance) as part of a racial examination.
Circa 1936–40. (*courtesy, Bundesarchiv, Koblenz*)

camps, just as the Sinti and Roma had been.

And after the war, during denazification trials, the Federal Republic's leading academic advisor on Sinti and Roma prepared reports based on Ritter's research and testified that Ritter had a "profound appreciation for the situation of Gypsies." On the basis of such testimony, Ritter was allowed to resume work as a child psychiatrist. Eventually, Ritter was the subject of an inquiry that lasted nearly two years but the public prosecutor closed the case on the grounds that there was not enough evidence to indict him. He committed suicide in 1951, less than a year after the decision. His files, along with 24,000 'racial testimonies' were sent to the newly-formed Travelers' Office of the Bavarian Criminal Police in 1953.

Ritter's assistant, Eva Justin, found employment after 1945

as a social worker in Frankfurt/Main. An investigation of her activities with Ritter's research institute did not begin until 1959, when the public prosecutor of Frankfurt/Main responded to accusations by several Gypsies who claimed Justin had ordered the compulsory sterilization and deportation of Gypsies. But when the investigation ended in 1960, Justin was absolved of the charges.

Other investigations of Ritter's assistants, Sophie Ehrhardt and Adolf Würth, similarly ended without indictments. Dr. Sophie Ehrhardt became a professor at the University of Tübingen and continued to work on material she had gathered from the East Prussian Gypsies who came, dying, to Auschwitz from Bialystok. Though the Gypsies she studied were dead, in 1966 Ehrhardt was awarded a grant from the federal government to support her work for "population studies on Gypsies."

ॐ

I ask Stramsee if he still thinks there's prejudice against the Sinti.

"Oh, ja, ja." He sighs deeply. "The Sinti will never be on the inside. They will always be on the outside."

"Did you ever want to leave Germany?"

"Ja – I wanted to go to Australia. But my mother tore up the papers (the application for immigration). If I had been younger, I would have gone to the United States."

We are both silent for a while. Then I ask him if he has anything else he wants to say.

"I don't like the German people," he says quietly. His eyes look sad, not angry. "Always the same. The hate. The neo-Nazis – they are very primitive people."

chapter *twenty one*

# The question of complicity

 ‿

The concentration camp at Dachau is just ten miles from Munich, an easy day trip by bus. It's somewhat of a tourist attraction for foreign visitors but not particularly popular with Germans who are more interested in visiting the castle nearby. At the tourist office in Munich, I find no mention of the former concentration camp. When I ask for information about it, the woman at the counter cringes slightly and wordlessly hands me a scrap of paper with directions. I suppose that the City of Munich is not particularly proud of this site but I have another day between interviews and I'm curious, so I decide to go.

The village of Dachau is a lovely little hillside town, immaculate and picturesque with its requisite castle and its hardy bicycle-riding citizens. In the old high German 'Dachau,' meant 'loam' and 'meadow,' and its proximity to Munich made it a popular spot in the country for city dwellers. When my father was a boy he often came to spend the summer holidays with his grandparents in Munich and on Sundays he would join his cousin Lilly for long bicycle rides.

"We would go to the mountains or to the nearby vacation spots," he told me. "And believe it or not, one of the spots we went to several times was Dachau. Because it was a very nice little town, and just a half-day bicycle ride from Munich."

Dachau was the first concentration camp established by the National Socialists in 1933, just months after Hitler seized power. Because Munich was the center of the Nazi movement at the time it was built close to the city, on the site of an abandoned munitions factory from the First World War. Heinrich Himmler, then Munich's new Chief of Police, placed Dachau under the command of Theodore Eicke who made the camp a supply of slave laborers, and a training ground for concentration camp administrators, including Rudolf Höss, the commandant of Auschwitz. Dachau became a prototype for the whole Nazi concentration camp system.

At first the camp was used to incarcerate Communists and other political prisoners – as well as Bavarian Gypsies from 1936 – but by 1939, Dachau's prison population was a microcosm of the diverse groups targeted by the Nazis: political opponents, criminals, Jehovah's Witnesses, homosexuals, Jews, Gypsies, clergymen and resistance fighters.

With this ready supply of human guinea pigs, the camp became a favored site for human experimentation, which the Nazis called 'research.' Dr. Siegmund Rascher, who is said to have obtained bodies of prisoners for the collection of human skin, led some of the most gruesome experiments at Dachau, which were enthusiastically supported by Heinrich Himmler. Rascher used the Air Force's decompression chamber to subject prisoners to high-altitude air pressure until they went mad and finally stopped breathing.

Then there were the freezing experiments that began immediately after the high-altitude experiments, to test how much cold a human being could endure. The purpose was to find the most effective way of re-warming German pilots who were shot down into icy water. Rascher forced prisoners, naked or dressed in pilot uniforms, into vats of ice water until they lost consciousness and died. Other prisoners were ordered to lie naked outside all night in the winter. (Rascher once tried to convince Himmler that Auschwitz was more suitable than Dachau for these experiments, since it was both colder and larger, more isolated. "The subjects cry out when they are freezing," he noted.) Prisoners were re-warmed in various ways, including hot baths. In September 1942, Himmler personally ordered attempts at re-warming by exposure to human warmth. Four Gypsy women were sent from Ravensbrück and rewarming was attempted by placing the frozen victim between two naked women.

Most of these experiments failed and many subjects died. The brother of Julia Lentini, a Sinti survivor from Germany, was a victim of one of these experiments. "They were testing the frostbite for the soldiers in Russia, to see how much cold they could take and how they could get them out and keep them alive," she says. "They experimented on him and, when my brother came out, he was never right. He died."

∾

Some people tried to rationalize incarceration at Dachau, claiming it was just punishment for traitors, political dissidents and criminals. Yet judges routinely meted out punishment that far exceeded the crimes, and the notion of 'criminal tendencies' became hopelessly entangled with the concept of race and racial inferiority.

Reili's Uncle Eduard (not the same Eduard as Shukar's father) was one of the victims of the Nazi judicial system. Since 1937, police and judges had been ordered to especially crack down on young criminals. Eduard was a frail young man who had been forced to do heavy labor at a hardware factory. Because of a special tax on Gypsies, he received only a small payment. Finally, unable to handle the strains of the work or the situation, he ran away and hid. But he needed food to survive, so he stole some items from a grocery store. He was caught.

The judge noted that Eduard was a *"Zigeunermischling"* (a 'half-blood' Gypsy) and of an "inferior race." According to Dr. Ritter and his colleagues, whose systematic studies of the Gypsies for the Nazis had resulted in racial classifications, the *Zigeunermischlinge* were asocials, and had inherited criminal tendencies. The judge sentenced eighteen-year old Eduard to death. He was executed in 1942, in Dachau.

ॐ

Now little of the original camp remains to remind visitors of these horrors. The site is manicured and almost devoid of evidence. The thirty-four barracks that housed prisoners were torn down after the war. In 1955, German officials decreed that the crematorium at Dachau should be torn down as well but a decree signed between France and Germany spared the building, guaranteeing the inviolability of all sites of former concentration camps.

Still, it is difficult to imagine what once existed here. The former prisoners' kitchens and showers now house a modern museum. The original barracks are gone and only two long, grey, tin-roofed buildings, reproductions of the barracks, stand at the edge of the vast expanse that once held rows of such buildings. These simulated barracks with wooden bunks, eating areas and washrooms are all new, clean and sterile – and they fail to evoke the harsh realities of the concentration camp. In 1944 the barracks at Dachau, designed to house fifty men, were jammed with as many as 800 lice-ridden, emaciated prisoners, and four people had to sleep together in one narrow bunk. Now, as an Israeli friend told me after a trip here, "it looks like a camp – a summer camp."

ॐ

Looking away in the face of wrong – is this complicity? If so, then Dachau must be its physical manifestation. For Dachau is not Auschwitz – with its unfathomable expanse and its vast machinery of slave labor and mass murder, well hidden from public view. No – Dachau is very local, almost a neighborhood concentration camp: trees and tidy grassy areas and flower beds near the crematorium; only low walls and insignificant

Crematorium at Dachau

looking hedges and barbed wire separating the compound from the village beyond.

But I can't imagine that Dachau ever looked like a summer camp to the neighbors who saw the guard tower from their windows or watched the 206,000 prisoners file through the main gate. (It was the first such gate erected by the Nazi regime, its wrought iron inscription, *Arbeit Macht Frei*, now forged in the collective memory as a symbol of all the deceit and terror of the concentration camp.) I wonder if Dachau residents could hear Dr. Rascher's subjects crying out as they froze to death naked on the cold ground, or if they could hear the floggings of prisoners who could not stand during the unbearably long roll calls, sometimes as long as twenty-four hours in the bitter cold. Did they smell the smoke from the crematorium, a low red-brick building with four large incinerators and meat hooks nearby to hang the bodies?

The neighbors probably would never have seen the large grey windowless building beneath a cluster of pine trees, the fully equipped gas chamber that supposedly was never used. But did they hear the shots or the screams as prisoners like Eduard were executed on a grassy spot, their bodies toppling into the ditch? Under the Night and Fog decree, people were taken from their homes at night and shot in front of the Dachau crematoria to speed up the process of obliteration. This is where "we turn them into fog," the Germans said. When the crematoria were operating, the heating gas in nearby homes was noticeably reduced, it's said, and a flurry of ashes from the crematoria's chimneys peppered the area for miles around. People said they had no idea where the ashes came from.

ॐ

The site of the former concentration camp of Dachau is not just sterile but almost shockingly pretty. The grass is trimmed, there are tree-lined paths, and roses and violets grow in flower beds near the crematorium. I try to imagine what happened here to young Eduard, shot in Dachau as punishment for a petty crime. But I cannot imagine. The setting is so tranquil, so neat, so placid that it's unsettling. It's a sedative for indignation, not to mention rage.

Houses just twenty feet from the prison walls, with windows that look over into the concentration camp. Yes, these are newer houses; in 1933 or 1945 there may not have been any houses so close to the site. But the impression of innocence is misleading here. I read that a former pastry chef – who would think? – worked at Dachau and killed 20,000 people – all by his own hand.

Still... the people of Dachau – the elderly ones – look so harmless when I see them in town, with their ruddy cheeks and their bicycles and their muslin bags of groceries and their tidy houses and their window boxes full of bright flowers. Still ... for twelve years this concentration camp existed in their back yard. How could they not have known?

∾

In Heidelberg, where my father was once employed as a photo technician, I meet the parents of a German-American friend, Anne. They are gracious, inviting me to their home for coffee and sandwiches, and expressing great interest in my work with Gypsy survivors. I tell them that I am Jewish, that my father grew up in nearby Mannheim and once worked in Heidelberg. "The war was horrible, terrible," they say. "Hitler was a dictator."

Anne's father had been drafted into the service when he was sixteen, and shortly thereafter was captured and taken to a prison labor camp in Belgium. Anne's mother tells me how she watched the city of Mannheim burning after the bombs were dropped, how she shook with fear for all her friends who lived there.

Anne's father offers to show me around Heidelberg, and he takes me on a walking tour of the *Philosophenweg* park, to a beautiful view of the old Heidelberg, with its ancient ruined castle, churches and old bridge. He helps me negotiate the post office, where he used to work, and the schedules and tickets at the train station; then he treats me to coffee and cheesecake at a café. He is truly a lovely gentleman and again my stereotypes fall away. How can I judge his actions of more than fifty years ago when he was only sixteen? Gypsies, too, had been drafted into the army, and had served. Shukar's father, Hugo's father, Rosa's husband – all of them had been in the army. Perhaps no German who was an adult at the time of Hitler could claim innocence – except the victims.

I know that Germans supported Hitler too, that on these terms he could not really be called a dictator. But after talking to Anne's parents, I am unable to judge. I imagine myself in their place: teenagers who grew up in a world dominated by Hitler, who were drafted into service, who saw their friends and family suffer from war. Jews? Gypsies? Perhaps they were

Gypsies are forced to march through the streets of Asperg
on their way to the train station in May 1940.
There they boarded deportation trains bound for
the General Government in Poland.
(*courtesy, Bundesarchiv, Koblenz*)

aware, but how many of them were personally touched by
their disappearance, much less believed they had the power to
do anything about it? How many were simply caught in this
dreadful time and place, this escalating madness, without the
vision or the resources to resist?

The very existence of the concentration camps served to
intimidate the population. Beginning with Dachau, Himmler
recognized that the purpose of the concentration camp was
not only to punish the enemies of the National Socialists, but
also to inspire fear among the people, to suppress any resistance to Nazi rule. They "cast a pall of terror over the entire
population," writes historian Leni Yahill, "and were an effective deterrent to disobedience of the government's orders, to
resistance of any kind, and even to criticism."

The threat of the concentration camp may have been in

the minds of the villagers of my grandmother's hometown, Freudental, as they heard the SS pounding on the doors of the Jewish homes and peeked from behind their curtains as their neighbors were taken away. The threat of the concentration camp may have been in the minds of the villagers of nearby Asperg in 1940 when they watched silently from the windows as long columns of Gypsies, hundreds of them, from towns around Stuttgart, were herded toward the ominous stone fortress of Hohenasperg prison to await deportation to Poland. The threat of the concentration camp may have been in the minds of the Munich citizens who watched as the local police arrested Hugo's family and their other Gypsy neighbors in 1943.

But these reasons only go so far in explaining the past. What about the citizens of Dachau who lived just on the other side of the wall? Are they innocent or sinister? I am unable to decide. The very word 'complicity' comes from the same root as the word 'complicated,' meaning to fold together. So does the question of complicity seem infinitely folded and complicated.

∾

"If we can see the present clearly enough, we shall ask the right questions of the past," writes John Berger in *Ways of Seeing*. But for me, the two are so entangled in Germany – the past and the present folded together inextricably.

*It seems to me that with age and experience, life does not sort out, resolve, or become more clear,* I write in my journal after visiting Dachau. *But only becomes more complex, muddied, and muddled.*

chapter *twenty two*

# *R*un and run

∾

*Then, I run again.*

Rosa is ready to talk again. Two weeks after being sent to Ravensbrück, she tells me, she was taken to another labor camp. *Wolkenburg a.d. Mulde* was a camp housed in a factory building, near Zwickau in the eastern part of Germany. Gypsy, Russian and Polish women prisoners worked twelve-hour shifts making airplane parts. They slept on the third floor of the building. Though the building was surrounded with armed guards and barbed wire, the ordinary windows made it possible to escape. For three or four weeks, Rosa and another Sinti woman carefully tracked the movements of the guards at night. One night, when the area below was unguarded, the two women slid down the drain pipe outside their third story window, hit the ground and ran as fast as they could in their crude wooden prisoner shoes.

*The whole night, run and run and run.*

Finally they stopped near the town of Zwickau and hid in a barn until daylight.

Dressed in the simple, rough cloth dresses of the *lager*, their hands raw and bloodied from scraping against the metal drainpipe, the girls unwisely ventured into town in the morning to try to find some other clothing. The townspeople, instantly recognizing that they were escaped prisoners, surrounded them and called the police.

"*I was stealing,*" Rosa tried to convince the police, but the townspeople knew otherwise.

*Everybody say, "No, no, you no steal nothing."*

The police accused the girls of escaping from a concentration camp but they met each accusation with an adamant denial. Finally, they were taken to the jail in Zwickau, where they were held for weeks.

*I'd rather be in jail than in the lager.* Rosa smiles, remembering the food and the beds. *That was good – it was like a hotel.*

But all too soon this holiday was over. When SS officers came to interrogate the two prisoners, the police asked that the girls be taken back to the camp so the SS could do "what they had to do" to them there; the police officers did not want to witness it.

And so Rosa was brought back to the forced labor camp at the end of November 1944. Her long hair was cut off and little knives were poked into her shaved head, she says. Women prisoners were brought into the big room and instructed to beat her with their wooden shoes until the blood poured from her skull. A female SS officer lifted a metal pipe to beat her with, and as she brought it down to strike Rosa's head, Rosa raised her arm to block the blow. The pipe cracked against her arm and broke the bone. Rosa shows me the jutting bones in her elbow as evidence: the bones have never healed.

Bleeding, naked, Rosa was taken to an underground cement bunker so narrow that she couldn't lie down but could only stand or kneel. There was a bucket for her wastes, and that was all. The darkness swallowed her.

*There was no day.* Time stretched endlessly in the void of the black hole, not even a glimmer of light to mark the passage of night into day. Interminable silence, darkness, fear. She drifted in and out of consciousness, fitful sleep, wondering if she had been left to starve to death. She called out but there was no answer. She would go mad, starve, die here, alone and in darkness, she thought. She had almost given up when she saw the irregular gleam of a flashlight. "Are you still alive?" a guard called out. He shoved a lump of bread and a small pitcher of water at her but did not change the bucket. The door was locked again, burying Rosa in the darkness and isolation and silence and stench of her cell.

"How did you manage to keep yourself alive?" I ask her. She shrugs, gropes for the words to describe her vanished will, the annihilation of her spirit and the fluke of nature that allowed her physical body to survive.

*I couldn't care less. If I live, I live, if I die . . . you know? My feet and hands were all swollen, and my hand swollen from the broken bones. And I had so much pain, I really wasn't sane any more, you know?*

*Four weeks I do that. Four weeks.*

Day and night were indistinguishable in this burial chamber but when Rosa was released, on Christmas Eve, she realized how much time had passed. On her return she was given rough clothing and wooden shoes like the other prisoners, and each one of the Polish women prisoners put a spoonful of their ration in a bowl for her as a gift to welcome her back. Now even the normal prison routine itself was a gift: the watery hot turnip soup and the ersatz coffee warmed her, and she cherished the pale light that filtered through the prison windows.

ॐ

"*Can you read?*" one of the female guards asked her. The guard held out a postcard that Rosa had received in her absence.

"*No*," Rosa answered. She could tell only that Hamlet had sent it.

"*Then I'm going to read it to you,*" the guard offered. When she read the name at the bottom she repeated it thoughtfully: "*Hamlet… Hamlet… I think I know him.*"

The guard, Sonia, had formerly been a waitress in a Munich nightclub and remembered Hamlet, the generous customer who had frequented the club. Thus began an unusual friendship between Rosa, the Sinti prisoner, and Sonia, the SS guard.

But Rosa's troubles were far from over. Bent on making an example of her, prison officials continued to punish her for the attempted escape. She was given twenty-five lashes which caused her skin to crack open again, inflicting such searing pain that sleep was impossible. A red piece of cloth was sewn to the back of her uniform so that everyone would know she was a runaway. And she was given a nickname, "The Runner." While other prisoners were called by their number, Rosa was always called by her nickname.

She was too weak and her arm too badly damaged to go back to work immediately, and so, incredibly, she was sent to the infirmary to recover. *I felt like I had the best thing going.* Her face lights up with a big smile, remembering. *For one week, I'm a king. I had a straw bed – and two blankets. And that's a luxury!*

After eight days in the infirmary, Rosa returned to the main camp. Sonia, the guard who had known Hamlet, took a special interest in her, taking the time to talk to her and even, on occasion, giving her a rare, special treat: a cigarette.

But after Rosa returned to her work at the factory, her supervisor there took an instant dislike to her. *The mean guard,* Rosa calls her, unable to remember her name. Rosa was still too weak then to lift the heaviest pieces of equipment and a male foreman – who happened to be the "mean guard's" boyfriend – took pity on the prisoner and helped her. This enraged the female guard and she turned her jealous wrath on Rosa.

"*The Gypsy puts a lot of make-up on her eyes!*" she yelled accusingly.

Rosa's friend, Sonia, came to the rescue. To save Rosa from a beating, she pretended to be in agreement with the jealous guard. "*Why don't you take your white handkerchief and wipe it off?*" she asked her. The "mean guard" rubbed at Rosa's eyes so hard that she gave her a black eye but, of course, nothing came off.

Meanwhile, the foreman had watched his girlfriend's jealous behavior with growing dismay. "*You can tell that she has no make-up on, really,"* he said. *"Where's she supposed to get it from?"*

Rosa turns to Reili. *He was a mensch, Reili, a good man. He had no designs on me, he was just sympathetic.* But the incident caused the foreman to cool toward his vicious girlfriend and the supervisor never stopped blaming Rosa. Every day Rosa had to walk past her frequently – and each time, the jealous woman kicked her.

As she tells us this story, Rosa leaps up in order to physically act out the motions of Sonia and the jealous supervisor, rubbing at the imaginary make-up on her eyes. She's surprisingly agile even in her aged, unhealthy state, and it's not difficult to imagine her in the prime of her youthful beauty. Still, it's hard to believe that she inspired such jealousy as a prisoner in a concentration camp, skeletal and weak after her ordeal in solitary confinement, a white kerchief covering her shaved head.

*I had dark, thick eyebrows and eyelashes, then,* Rosa explains. *Not like now.*

∾

"I need a cigarette," Rosa says, reaching for the pack. We pause in her story while Reili goes to find an ashtray for her.

"I no can…" she begins, trying to find the English words for what she wants to tell me. "I have *too* much troubles. Lots of them."

She takes a puff from her cigarette, then twists in a spasm of coughing. As her hacking subsides, eerie strains of organ music drift from the television set in the next room.

"I have so much headaches," she says when she recovers. "Some people have lots of trouble … and some people have *nothing.*"

She spits out the last word like a bitter seed: *nothing.*

"I have lots of trouble. All my people died. All of them. I'm the only one."

# $\mathcal{N}$o trust nobody no more

~

March 1945. Three o'clock in the morning. Everyone in camp is jolted awake, summoned outside to prepare for a transport. Sonia finds Rosa and whispers to her: "*The Russians are not more than 100 kilometers away. They're going to take you to Dachau.*"

The prisoners are ordered into formation. Those too weak to walk are instructed to climb aboard big trucks. Rosa starts toward the truck but Sonia pulls her back. "*You can walk,*" she insists. Sonia has information that those who ride in the truck will not survive. "*Hang on,*" she tells Rosa. "*It'll be over soon.*"

In a whisper Sonia confides her plans to run away, escaping in the chaos of the Allied advance and hasty evacuation of the camp. The two friends, prisoner and guard, look at each other a last time, silently wishing each other farewell.

For two days Rosa walks with the other prisoners, stopping only for the night in a local prison. Rosa remembers the big kettle at the prison kitchen, from which the prisoners were served potatoes with a little salt. *That was the best dinner,* she says, with a broad smile.

At the town of Weiden, about 150 kilometers south of the camp, the prisoners are marched to a train yard and forced inside a cattle car. The door is closed shut, bolted. Inside, the frightened women listen to bombs exploding all around the train.

No stranger to risk, Rosa decides once again to crawl out

the small window of the train car. As soon as she falls to the ground outside, all of her fellow prisoners call to her, begging her to let them out too. She pushes open the steel bolt on the outside door, and it bursts open as the prisoners stream out.

Quickly the SS guards appear, beating everyone back into the train – but in the confusion Rosa slips underneath the train and lies down on the axle. *Nobody sees me.* She sees two other young women, prisoners she doesn't know, lie down on the axle as well.

The guards slam the door of the cattle car shut again and Rosa sprints off on the opposite side of the train, running as fast as she can. In front of her, a German soldier looms into her sight. An ordinary soldier, not an SS. He sees her prison uniform and pushes her to the ground to protect her as a bomb explodes near them. Then he leads her to his home in Weiden where he lives with his wife and several other families. They give her a room in the basement. And the soldier hands Rosa that ubiquitous, always desired, item – a cigarette. The soldier's wife brings her bread and a little bit of sugar. Someone else brings her a dress but she keeps her prison jacket over it to ward off the cold.

Hungry and desperate, Rosa wolfs down the food as quickly as she receives it, rarely pausing to converse with her benefactors even though she appreciates their efforts.

*The people didn't have nothing themselves. The Hitlers were all over, but these people were good people.*

Yet, not surprisingly, Rosa's faith in humanity is too shattered to reclaim. The couple offers to keep her safely in hiding but she refuses to stay.

*I didn't trust.*

She intends to walk all the way back to Munich, almost 200 kilometers to the south. Before she leaves, the couple gives her some bread, some cigarettes and a package of matches.

Walking through the streets of Weiden, she has not gone

far before she comes across two women she recognizes – the two other prisoners who had hidden with her under the train's axle. The train's engine was bombed, they tell her, and the train cannot move. *"What shall we do? Shall we go back?"*

Rosa is unhesitating. *"You can go back. I'm taking off."*

The two women decide to follow her and the three set off for the woods. They tear Rosa's bread into three pieces and consume it hungrily but then there is nothing left to eat. They are ravenous and when they pass a house with chickens in the yard, they lose no time in stealing one. Nearby, they find a discarded metal can that will serve them as a cooking pot. With Rosa's matches, they can make a fire.

But hungry as they are, her companions are still fussy. Now they want salt for the chicken. They must have it. They beg Rosa to go to the house to ask for some. *"You must go, please – you have the lightest skin,"* they say. Finally she gives in. The old woman of the house, never suspecting that Rosa has just stolen one of her chickens, not only gives her the salt but a couple of potatoes as well. The three women fetch water from the river and build a fire so they can cook the chicken soup in their makeshift pot. Rosa's two companions are so hungry, they burn their mouths eating the hot soup. How long has it been since any of them have eaten such a meal?

The war is almost at an end and chaos reigns. Hungarian SS officers converge in the woods, their horses running wildly about as the women, trembling with fear, somehow manage to slip past them unseen.

Farther on, American soldiers surround the women in a town and Rosa startles with fear at the black soldiers – the first blacks she's ever seen. A soldier who speaks German notices the prison dresses of Rosa's companions and asks the women if they've been in a concentration camp. Rosa shows them the Auschwitz tattoo on her forearm and the soldiers shower the women with food from their rations. *Coffee, tea, chocolate, cocoa. Cigarettes.*

*"Stay here, in this area, where you are safe,"* the soldiers tell

them. But Rosa, afraid that the soldiers might bring them back to the concentration camp, wants to keep moving.

*No trust nobody no more, you know?*

# $\mathcal{N}$obody comes back from my people

$\infty$

$W$alking, walking, walking, heading south. Back to her family, if there is still a family. To the baby she left a year and a half ago, to the husband. If there is still a baby, still a husband. Perhaps to find the mother, if she is not really dead, or the sister, the father, the brother, the nieces and nephews she's last seen in a cattle car headed for Poland. Back to the home she left in Munich, the home she left in Vienna. If there is a home. If one is not killed first. If one can survive. But better not to think, only to walk, walk and walk.

Afraid to sleep outside near the houses, Rosa hatches a new plan. She pulls off her prison jacket, walks up to the front door of a house and brazenly tells the residents that she is working for the German government, recording statistics, and needs a place to stay overnight. She can stay in the barn, in the hayloft, they tell her. Rosa calls to the other two women, hiding in the woods, and leads them into the barn. As her eyes adjust to the dim light, she sees a miraculous vision.

"*Women, look up there and see what's hanging!*" she calls out, her dry lips cracking into a smile.

The hungry women cry with joy as they see the plump hams and sausages hanging from the rafters. "*Be careful,*" Rosa advises. She knows that malnourished people can die from consuming too much rich food too quickly.

But the women don't heed her advice. *The whole night they eat and eat their way through the hams and sausages. I never – just a little bit.* The greasy salty meat tastes so good to the hungry women. But the next day the two women are sick with diarrhea and stomach cramps and the trio has to wait two more days before they are able to move on.

Walking southward, they pass through towns and villages in turmoil as the German military fights its final battles with the Allies. Villagers try to escape the bombing, looting the destroyed stores as they flee. The women come across a bombed-out train car full of fabric. Muslin, percales, linens – "Ours for the taking!" cry Rosa's companions. But Rosa is not interested – there are no ready-made dresses here, only bolts of fabric. The two other women load themselves down with the materials. Walking on, their arms heavy with bundles of fabric, they beg Rosa to help them carry the goods. She refuses. "*No, no. If you want it, you carry it yourself.*" *Stupid women!* she thinks.

Besides some money she finds on the street, there is only one item that Rosa considers worth the burden of carrying. Cigarettes. She walks into a bombed-out tobacco shop, finds a big knapsack and fills it with packs of cigarettes. *Just the cigarettes – that's all I want.*

She continues, alone now, making her way to Munich where she waits on the outskirts of town for the Allies to come. Finally, she hears the news she's been waiting for: "*Munich has fallen.*"

∾

At last, she has made her way back to her old home in Munich – only to find that it is now occupied by Polish and Russian refugees. But they welcome her, having been told that the former residents were in a concentration camp. They notify her relatives and they come – Hamlet, her husband and all of her other relatives through marriage. They hug her, embrace her and dance around her, weeping tears of joy. She sees her baby once again, the baby her mother-in-law has cared for. The six-week old baby she'd had to leave behind is now a nineteen-month-old toddler, a stranger in her arms. And Rosa, seeing all these people alive and well, begins to nourish a small seed, a tiny bud of hope as she thinks of the family she left behind in Austria when she was still a girl.

"*I want to see, maybe some of my people come back too,*" she tells Hamlet.

∾

The motion that propels her story dies as ominously as the wind subsiding before the dead calm of doldrums; her voice drains away. She traveled to Austria as soon as she could, she says. She couldn't reach Vienna the first time, but in Linz the Sinti told her the news.

*Nobody comes back from Litzmannstadt. Nobody. Nobody comes back from my people. Lots of Sintis, but not from Litzmannstadt. Nobody. Nobody comes.*

Her voice is parched, thick with choked grief. *I go back to Munich. I cried. I couldn't understand.*

Later, when she could reach Vienna, she went to inquire again. Perhaps there was a mistake. Perhaps this really was only a story and the ending could be changed, the text rewritten. But no. The officials in Vienna confirmed it: everyone in her family was dead.

Hearing this news was the worst thing that ever happened to her, she says. Worse than the torture, the brutality of the concentration camp, the fears of her escapes. Far worse.

*I cry, I think a year long. When I think back, I cry again. I no can do nothing.*

chapter *twenty five*

---

# *Thorns in the garden*

ෆ

Breathless, heart pounding, I climb the narrow, winding staircase of St. Peter's Church to the bell tower – up and up and up – and at the top, step outside to join the other tourists squeezed around the tiny platform overlooking the city. From this height, you can see the Alps in the distance to the south, the church steeples like giant thorns puncturing the sky, and all the curving, sloping red tile rooftops of the old city, coppery in the glint of fading sunlight. A beer garden perches on a roof below, holding tables and chairs, waiters and patrons in a miniature Bavarian tableau. Tiny figures cluster in the square far below, bathed in golden light, faces turned upward toward the minuscule metallic dancers of the Glockenspiel. Wispy, rose-colored clouds in the crystalline blue. As I turn back inside the dark tower to descend the staircase, the church bells rend the air, a deep melodic bellow resonating beneath my skin.

Outside, the waning afternoon light casts widening fingers of shadow over the cobbled streets and the outdoor tables of cafés and *Biergartens*. An inviting warmth seems to radiate from the open doorways of the indoor beer halls, pubs, and restaurants; the clattering of dishes and clinking of beer glasses mingles with laughter and conversation in a lively, encompassing sociability. I could partake of this too, I tell myself. I'm here for the purpose of work, it's true, but right now there's no reason why I can't simply treat myself to a beer and a meal, meanwhile basking in the charming conviviality of a Bavarian pub.

So I enter, walking through the open door of one of the city's historic beer halls. Wooden barrels of beer, vaulted ceilings, brightly painted designs on the walls – I admire these as I walk through the oversized room and up the stairs, where I choose a small table next to the rail, overlooking the downstairs. After I order beer and big crusty yeast pretzels and a bowl of soup, I gaze down, over the rail. The long tables below are full of tourists and hearty Bavarians, raising their enormous glasses of beer with gusto. And I think again of my father, my father as a young man, perhaps in 1930, when he would have been twenty years old. Visiting Munich in the summertime, he would have gone to a place like this to enjoy a beer with his companions, feeling at home in this jovial atmosphere.

And then a stocky blond woman in classic Bavarian costume – the puffy white embroidered blouse, the full-skirted bibbed dress – appears with an accordion and begins to play oom-pah music. And all at once it is all too much for me. This Bavaria – the Bavaria of the jovial beer halls and accordion players, of charming winding streets and red-tiled roofs and steepled churches and views of the Alps – this careless, lusty Bavaria slams violently into everything I know from my history and everything I've heard in the past few days. This Bavaria did not belong to my father, did not belong to Rosa, does not belong to me. Tears spill from my eyes and soak into the white tablecloth with dismaying suddenness. Under the din of the accordion, I hear a silent litany: *The German soil is soaked with the blood of my people. The German soil is soaked with the blood of my people.*

In 1930, when my father was twenty, Adolf Hitler would also have been in Munich, the city he came to in 1913 and used as his headquarters to plot the rise of the Nazi movement. Rudolf Hess, Heinrich Himmler, Hermann Göring – all were from Munich or other towns in Bavaria. But so was my great-aunt, Else Sonnemann, the one who was shot by the Einsatzkommando. And so was Hugo Höllenreiner. *I was a Munich boy, but it didn't count. I was a Gypsy,* he had said. He hadn't even been born yet when Hitler lived in Munich and developed the theories of racial inferiority that would shape his destiny.

"I no like the Germans," Rosa had told me the other day. "Why they kill the Sintis?" When she shook her fist angrily, like she had that day, you could see the pale blue numbers of the Auschwitz tattoo on her forearm. When I asked her if she had ever thought of leaving Germany, she just shrugged. "I hate it, I don't like it," she answered. "Where can I go? I'm old too. I have nobody."

The salty taste of the pretzel mingles with the salty brine of my tears, choking my voice as I ask the waiter for the check. I am awash with memories that are not my own. I keep hearing Rosa's voice describing her return to Austria to search for her family. *Nobody comes back from my people. Nobody. Nobody comes.* All that was left from her family was a collection of photos pasted in the album, fading paper ghosts from a world that had been eradicated. Mother, sisters, children. *Tot, tot, tot.* Dead, dead, dead.

∾

In Germany, when I am lost, it is the old women that I turn to for help. I search for them, scanning the street until one appears, then blurting out my question in a crude approximation of German. Their faces are pale and floury, lined with wrinkles, and I think that age has stripped dry their power, that they can hold no threat.

I don't want to ask help of the younger people. With their certain strides and determined faces – who knows what neo-Nazi sentiments might lurk within? One recent demonstration of neo-Nazis in Munich brought a mob of 6,000. Of course, it's easy to exaggerate that element: I know there are more humanitarian and anti-racist youth than there are neo-Nazis. Ten thousand anti-fascists protested that same demonstration of neo-Nazis. German youth have held candlelight vigils to protest racial violence against foreigners. So many young Germans have genuinely acknowledged and repudiated their country's Nazi past – it isn't fair to judge them by their forbears.

Still … as irrational as it may be, I feel safer approaching an older person. But not an older man. The old men – well, of course they might have been in the army, might have been Nazis. I am reminded of my great-aunt, Emmy, the one who fled Germany to live in the United States and never wanted to go back to visit after the war. "How would I know that the person serving my food hadn't killed my parents in Auschwitz?" she asked.

In Germany, perhaps it is forgivable for even the daughters and sons of survivors and refugees to ask such questions. Did this old man kill Else, Adolf or Frieda? Did he kill Rosa's family? Though I try not to think like this, these kinds of questions rise unbidden.

Yet why do I imagine that the women, the old women who smile kindly and give me directions, are not also complicit? Didn't they feed and love and support their Nazi husbands and sons, join Nazi organizations themselves, enroll their children in the Nazi youth organizations?

In the village of Freudental, where my father's mother grew up and where more than one-third of the town's population had been Jewish before Hitler, the villagers ransacked the synagogue in 1938, and took their Jewish neighbors to the sports field where they made them dance around a bonfire of their prayer books and holy objects. After the war, with the synagogue still standing (it was not burned, probably because it was in the center of town) the townspeople stole the wooden prayer benches from the building when the deported Jews did not return. Some of the villagers put the benches in their gardens.

It would have been women who coveted these benches, and they would not have been old women then, in 1945 or 1950, but middle-aged women, like me. I can imagine them walking down the narrow cobbled streets of Freudental with their scavenged treasures. Now, after the war, the town was *Judenfrei*. Perhaps they thought: Why not use these lovely benches? They'd be so nice in the garden, bright colors to set them off, vines winding and curling about their legs. No point in letting them go to waste – no one here will use them anyway. The Jews? From where they went, they won't be coming back.

But my father did come back to Freudental, to see his mother's hometown. And when he saw the prayer benches in the gardens of his mother's neighbors, he was outraged.

∾

A friend of mine recently took a Jewish Heritage tour of Europe with his father. "The Tour of Vanishing Jewry," he called it, with a bitter laugh. As the tour progressed, through cemeteries, concentration camps, museums and abandoned synagogues, the group reeled with the magnitude of loss, and grief began to transform to vengeful anger. "Everyone would have been completely fulfilled if only they could have killed a Nazi," my friend reported. He was joking, of course. Or was he?

∾

I used to hold such deep prejudice against Germans that I couldn't even recognize it, could only cringe with horror and disgust when I heard the German language. But then I met someone who happened to be German and who became my friend. For me it was an astounding breakthrough, not without its agony. Did I betray my father to befriend a German? Could the sound of the German language actually be pleasing when spoken by a friend, a person of character and sensitivity? As foolish as it seems, I wrestled with such questions as I formed my first friendship with a German – and these were questions I had never asked about any other nationality, race or ethnicity. I knew that it was prejudice and I knew that it was wrong.

Yet even after I thought I had resolved the conflict, even after I supposed that my emotions agreed with my logic, I felt the primal prejudices spring to life again when I was in Germany. After a day of sightseeing in Munich, I wrote in my journal: *I really do have a distaste for all that is German. The language is as harsh as the people.*

Of course, I knew better, knew that there were Germans – older ones, too – who did not believe in the Nazi cause, who were not perpetrators or even sympathizers. There were even those who stood by the Jews or the Gypsies. Nearly every survivor tells you of someone who helped. Still, they were few, too few.

## chapter *twenty six*

# *Friedhof / Judenfriedhof*

∾

All week we have been talking of going to the cemetery, *der Friedhof.* Rosa says she wants to show me Hamlet's gravesite. "Do you want to see it?" she asks. Yes.

European cemeteries interest me in general, but in particular I'm aware of how important this is for Rosa. She likes to go frequently to maintain the gravesite and to pay her respects. Reili tells me that when Hamlet fell ill and died three years before, Rosa sold all her valuable possessions to pay for his medical expenses, burial and the gravestone. The stone is so ornate, Reili says, that passers-by must think he was someone famous. Rosa shows me photographs of Hamlet and herself reunited after the war, camping in Switzerland in the summer. They were a handsome pair, and it seems remarkable that Rosa could look so happy after her terrible experiences. Hamlet, together with the baby, had to take the place of Rosa's entire original family. He became her strongest bond, all her relatives rolled into one. No wonder she wants to go to the cemetery so often.

Still, other things keep getting in the way of our visit. Gypsies are not noted for planning or scheduling events, making the cemetery visit especially difficult. The *Friedhof* is some distance away from Rosa's apartment so we have to take a bus. And the grounds close promptly at five o'clock when the gates are locked. Every day there is some delay – we have to wait for Velda to show up, or Rosa is making chicken soup, or other relatives come by – and then it is too late to go.

On one of the days we plan to go to the *Friedhof,* Shukar comes over in the late morning. Rosa serves him *Weisswurst,* Bavaria's renowned sausage, and dark bread and cheese, and we talk while Rosa disappears into the kitchen. A couple hours later she emerges, producing an enormous and delicious meal: *Suppe,* a rich chicken soup with homemade noodles, *Kartoffelsalat,* a warm salad of potatoes and greens in vinagrette, and chicken with garlic. She insists that we all sample the food, though she hardly eats anything herself. By the time everyone has finished eating and we have washed the dishes and bundled up Velda's children, it is – of course – too late to go to the cemetery. We end up walking to a nearby shopping center instead. And, at the children's insistence, we go to a McDonald's where they order Chicken McNuggets.

"We go to the *Friedhof* another day," Rosa says that evening as she chain-smokes Kent Lights and the television issues a German-dubbed Western. "Maybe tomorrow."

But it is several days before the visit comes about. One day Hamlet's brother and his wife (a German non-Gypsy) come by to visit. Again the food emerges: bread and sausage and cheese and sliced meats spread out on big platters covering the coffee table (there is no dining table so we eat on the chairs and couches in the living room). Rosa and the couple smoke continually, and the warm air in the apartment becomes thick and hazy, stinging my eyes. The conversation is loud and animated. We drink cups and cups of coffee until somehow it is decided that we will all go to the cemetery. This makes the venture quite a bit easier, since they have a car.

We emerge from the smoke-clouded apartment to discover a clear sunny October afternoon, fresh after a rain the night before.

∾

The *Friedhof* is a lovely place really. It is spacious and forested, with tree-lined paths winding alongside the graves. All the graves are so well-tended and so orderly; it's clear that relatives come often to keep the plants on the sites healthy, to offer fresh flowers and candles of commemoration. On the way here, Rosa stopped to buy a bouquet of flowers and several 'everlasting' candles in red glasses, and now she places them in front of Hamlet's gravestone and draws the sign of the cross over her heart. She pulls up a few stray weeds on the gravesite, fussing until it is perfectly trim and orderly. The headstone on Hamlet's grave is large and curvaceous, rather like a scroll, with a large relief figure of Jesus carved into the middle. As Reili observes, it is regal compared to the gravestones of the relatives. Especially the rival ones – the Höllenreiners.

The Mettbach family – which includes Reili's mother and Rosa, through her late husband – and the Höllenreiners maintain an element of hostility, although (or perhaps because) there's a lot of intermarriage between the two families. It's a little hard for me to keep them straight since Reili is connected with both families – her mother's sister and her grandmother's sister, of the Mettbach *Familie,* both married men from the Höllenreiner side. I have to ask Reili to help me draw a family tree to understand all the relationships. Since Reili maintains ties with both families, when we visit with her cousins, they may be either Mettbachs or Höllenreiners.

But Rosa identifies solely with the Mettbachs, because of her husband. She is fond of Reili, who claims to be neutral in any inter-family squabbles. And she tolerates Shukar, although he bears the Höllenreiner name, because his mother (Reili's aunt) was a Mettbach. But she hardly bothers to disguise her scorn for others of the Höllenreiner clan. When Reili and I return from talking to members of the Höllenreiner family in Ingolstadt, Rosa says she doesn't like Ingolstadt, that the people are too snobby and "they don't eat anything."

"Did they feed you anything ?" she asks suspiciously, and when I answer yes, she doesn't look convinced. She asks me how I liked one of the Höllenreiner women I talked with. "Well, she seemed quite nice," I say hesitantly. Rosa hisses under her breath in German, and Reili translates for me: "She's a snake!"

The Höllenreiners are buried in this cemetery too, but they have a simple tablet headstone with a small relief of a tree, and ten family names listed below. Hamlet's gravestone, on the other hand, names him alone.

Reili's mother is also buried here. I remember a story Reili told me about her mother's burial which illustrates the Mettbach-Höllenreiner feud. Reili had come from the United States for the funeral and the whole extended family was there, including of course, many of the Höllenreiners. But one young woman, who came to pay her respects, hid behind the bushes, terrified that a Höllenreiner would see her. She was Bluma, one of Reili's Mettbach cousins, the woman I met at Stramsee and Otilia's house.

Reili told me the story that led up to this drama. When Bluma was only fifteen, an older Sinti girl convinced her to dress more fashionably, to cut off her traditional long thick braid and wear her hair in the latest bobbed style. Then the older girl provided a front so that Bluma could go out with Manfred Höllenreiner, Sophie's son who had been sterilized in a concentration camp. Manfred was much older than Bluma – twenty-six or twenty-seven – and he fell in love with her but didn't dare ask to marry her. He knew her parents would say no. "The Mettbachs regarded themselves as superior to the Höllenreiners," Reili says.

To pressure the parents into agreeing, the two disappeared one night and didn't come back until morning. According to Reili, this action "soiled their daughter's reputation" so they couldn't refuse.

The two were married and now Bluma had to act older than her age, dressing in a sophisticated manner to please Manfred – growing up too fast, Reili says. Of course, the couple couldn't have children, and periodically Manfred would go on three-day drinking binges. He was out of control, Reili says – still tortured by his sufferings under the Nazis. In any case, the marriage had problems.

Then, when Bluma was thirty-two, she fell in love with another man, also a Sinto, and once again disappeared for the night. This time the action was not just youthful impetuousness, though: it was adultery. Manfred and his family were ready to kill the other man if they saw him.

When Reili's mother was buried, all of this had just occurred, and the tensions were high. The Sinti expect, even require, that all the friends and relatives attend a funeral, but Bluma wasn't among the crowd that day, even though she had always been close to her aunt, Reili's mother. Later, she told Reili that she had come to pay her respects but had hidden behind a bush. "She came at the risk of her life," Reili said. "If they'd seen her, they would have killed her."

It seems that even here in *der Friedhof*, the peace yard, there is no peace.

ও

The main *Friedhof* of Mannheim, across the bridge over the Neckar River, is similarly well-kept. Like the cemetery I visited in Munich, it is a vast expanse of parkland enclosed by a fence. Meticulous, neatly planted plots dot the tree-lined paths; the gravestones look as if they've been scrubbed. Many of the plots have small rail fences around them. As in Munich, there are many visitors here, pulling weeds and placing fresh flowers on the graves, maintaining the gravesites. And groundskeepers keep the paths clean of debris and the grass freshly mowed, all as orderly as a park.

I walk and walk – it seems for miles – through the paths of the enormous graveyard, and still I can't locate the Jewish section, the *Judenfriedhof*. No one seems to know where it is. When I stop people to ask them for directions, they are politely confused – as if it has been a very long time since

anyone has inquired about the Jewish cemetery. Finally someone explains to me that I must go back the way I came, all the
way out of the main cemetery gate and around to the other
side of the ten-foot fence. Again, I walk and walk.

Outside the cemetery walls, there is a public city garden,
with dozens of little huts and plots filled with fruit trees, vegetables and fall flowers. An old man leans on his rake.

*"Judenfriedhof?"* I ask him. He smiles and points toward a
gate on the side of the main cemetery.

∾

When my father was a young man in Mannheim, his girlfriend's father was the caretaker of the Jewish cemetery. The
whole family lived in a house on the grounds. Now it seems
that no one takes care of it, except to lock the gate in the
evening and open it again the next day. I am all alone here. It
looks as though nobody has been here for a very long time.
Ancient neglected stones, gracefully encircled with winding
vines of ivy. Pathways blanketed with yellow leaves. Dried
leaves, yellow and ochre, scattered everywhere, a hollow whisper in the soft October gusts.

It is calm here – silent but for the rustling leaves – and
more beautiful, with its haphazard growth of neglect, than the
main cemetery with its rigid order. Yet despite the beauty,
there is something so sad here, and it too is born of neglect.
No families come to visit these graves, to look after them, to
lay stones of remembrance on the gravestones. No one cares
for these graves anymore. There is no one left here to care for
them.

Few of the Mannheim Jews of my father's generation are
buried here, for a simple reason. There were those like my
father and his family, lucky enough and persistent enough to
have obtained visas so they could escape. The others – more
than half the Jewish population of Mannheim – were
deported to concentration camps. Their graves are elsewhere.

∾

My father has fond memories of his boyhood in Mannheim. Hikes and bicycle rides and ice skating with friends and relatives, trips to the nearby asparagus festival in the spring. His family was not well off but they considered themselves very cultured. His father was a published poet and a music and theater critic for the Mannheim newspaper and he let my father accompany him to concerts and operas. My father still remembers going out to late dinners after performances, with his father and stars like dancer Anna Pavlova, conductor Arturo Toscanini, and renowned theatrical director Max Reinhardt. It was a civilized life, and one in which Jews and non-Jews were equal.

*As Jews, we tried everything to be just the same as the non-Jews,* my father says. *We went to public schools, paid the same taxes, lived among them in the same houses, the same apartments, dressed the same, went with them to parties, theater, concerts. There wasn't much of a dividing line then.*

In the 1930s, when my father was in his early twenties, he continued to live with his parents, but enjoyed the company of friends and girlfriends, the social and gastronomic and cultural offerings of European society. A photograph of him from the time shows him looking dapper and elegant, almost a dandy. He leans against a patterned wall – is it a dance hall? – dressed in a dark suit and polished shoes. A crisp white shirt and pocket handkerchief, a dark bow tie. It looks remarkably similar to the way he still dresses today, at age ninety-one – always a classy suit and starched shirt, expensive shoes and characteristic wildly patterned silk bow tie. In the 1930s photo, his dense black hair rises from his forehead like a seawall; his eyes are thick over intense dark eyes and his long hooked nose. There is no hiding his ethnicity: he is decidedly not an Aryan.

Eric Sonneman, Mannheim, mid-1930s.

∾

My father was a leader of a Jewish youth group but some of his friends, including his best friend Karl Auper, had joined the Hitler Youth, *die Hitler Jugend.* It seemed the thing to do at the time; many young people were joining organizations. The Hitler Youth trained boys for the military while the League of German Girls, *der Bund Deutscher Mädel,* trained girls for motherhood. Even my father's cousin, Rhea (whose mother was Jewish and father was Christian), wanted to join the League of German Girls – but her parents told her that she would not be accepted because she was Jewish. She cried.

Karl, my father's friend, was well aware of the anti-Semitism that accompanied the organization's emphasis on health and physical activity. He tried to warn my father. *Karl would say, "Eric, you'd better get out of Germany. We're going to bury the Jews."*

Once Karl even took my father to hear Hitler speak, in Mannheim.

*Yes, Adolf Hitler. I think about 1929 or 30. I must have been the only Jew in the assembly. He had everybody spellbound against Jews. They were the evil of everything that was wrong with Germany. We didn't have the other side of the Rhineland. That's the fault of the Jews. The Jews brought us into the war. We lost our money in inflation, that was the fault of the Jewish bankers and the Jewish businessmen. And then on and on and on and on. Raving. And of course everyone yells "Sieg Heil" and salutes him.*

*Then the election came up in 1933 and I was one of the very few people who went and voted against him. Others wouldn't dare to do that... Why?*

In 1933, the year that Hitler came to power, the interior of the main synagogue in Mannheim was demolished, alerting all the Jews to the intentions of the new regime. A Nazi law was passed throughout Germany to fire all teachers who were Jews or political opponents, and hundreds of textbooks were replaced by Nazi-written materials. Eugenics, the study of hereditary improvement of a race by genetic control, was introduced at the universities. Boycotts of Jewish shopkeepers, doctors and lawyers took place all over Germany, and Jewish businesses were 'Aryanized,' as Nazis enforced the sale of property and fired all Jewish personnel.

In 1933, my father was twenty-two and working for a pharmaceutical company, training for a promising career. In 1936, he was fired – his boss had been ordered to dismiss all Jewish employees. Ironically – in one of those odd paradoxes of Nazi policy – my father drew unemployment insurance from the same government that had ordered his dismissal. He wanted then to leave Germany, to go to the United States but he couldn't meet the requirements. *I had no means to leave Germany. You couldn't leave* (to the United States) *unless you had a sponsor, and I had no sponsor.* The Jewish community helped retrain my father to work in photography and he worked for a small subsistence wage as a laboratory assistant in a store in nearby Heidelberg. Still, as much as he still loved his *Heimat*, his homeland, he wanted desperately to leave – to go to America.

*Well, comes 1938. You have to realize the pressure you are under with all that's happening. Stores being closed, the stores marked 'Jew' on the window, don't buy there, and all that.*

My father was not alone in his desire to leave. Long before the synagogue was burned during Kristallnacht in 1938, Jews crowded into the American Consulate in Stuttgart. On an average day in 1938 the line flowed down from the second floor offices to the street and wound another two blocks around the building. But everyone knew you needed more than desire to get a visa. Before you could even apply, you had to have a guarantor, an American citizen who was related to you and who would agree to support you on arrival so you wouldn't become a burden to the American taxpayers.

*"Think,"* my father begged his parents. *"Isn't there anyone who can be a guarantor so I can get out of here?"*

His parents racked their brains. There was a brother who had immigrated to America long ago and disappeared. Another brother who had gone there, with help from the banking family, the Warburgs, but he was not an American citizen and couldn't act as a guarantor. Relatives who were American citizens? No, they couldn't think of anyone.

And then – like in a fairy tale – my father's mother woke up one morning in a state of great excitement. She'd had a dream, she said, and in the dream was a woman, a woman from America who had once visited her mother when she was a child. She didn't know her name but she was quite sure she was related.

*Who was she? My mother doesn't know who. So she had a friend in St. Louis who had been with my mother in school, Frieda Trapp, she was a member of the Quakers. And I wrote Frieda in English and my mother wrote in German. "We are trying to get out of Germany," we told her, "and my mother had this dream. Do you remember who it is?" Two weeks later we got a letter from Frieda Trapp and she said, "I sure know who it is. Her name is Loveman and they are very well-to-do people in Nashville, Tennesee."*

Immediately, my father composed a second letter. *"We are from the Herrmann family,"* he wrote in his best English, invoking his mother's maiden name. *"You once visited my mother's mother. I am trying to get out of Germany, to come to America. Can you do anything to help me?"*

∾

Standing on a leaf-strewn path in the Mannheim cemetery, I remember my father's story about the dream… *If my mother, your grandmother, had not had that dream, I would not be alive today,* my father told me, countless times throughout my childhood and long into my adulthood. *And you would never have been born.*

But I remember also that Rosa and the others in Reili's

family, Mettbachs and Höllenreiners alike, had no one in America to dream of, no one to write for help. My father and his family were lucky: they had Mrs. Loveman of Nashville. Without any further questions or correspondence, she sent an affidavit attesting that my father was related to her and that she had adequate funds to support him if necessary. My father took the affidavit to the consulate and they gave him the number.

*The number I think I had was something like 7,250. And this was the beginning of 1938, so it was going to take almost a year before I would get an appointment.*

∾

The date of the appointment – 10 November 1938 – drew near. My father and his parents had moved to a new apartment in a different section of Mannheim. On 8 November, Karl Auper, my father's friend who had joined the Hitler Youth, came to visit my father and his parents.

*"Frau Sonnemann," he said. "I'm sorry what I have to tell you, but tomorrow the party is going to try to take everything that you have, all your valuables, and take your husband and Eric and Max into a concentration camp. My advice to you is that you hide in the attic. Please give me all the gold and silver that you have in your possession so I can hide it for you…"*

*So my mother took off her ring and gave it to Karl. My father took off his gold watch and his ring, my brother brought the silver candlesticks from Friday evenings. And we gave him a beautiful silver breadbasket and lots of stuff that we had in the house. And Karl left, saying, "Good luck, don't forget to hide tomorrow."*

Since my grandmother died, and I inherited her gold wedding band, this story has become even more tangible. I twist the ring around my finger as I listen to my father.

*So we were hiding in the attic and we looked out and saw that the Nazis came and threw the furniture of the neighbors from their third floor apartments into the streets and took the men away to the concentration camps, and it was a pretty shaking event. They didn't find us because they didn't know we'd moved in. In Germany, within ten days after you move, you have to register with the police. But we hadn't done that yet – so they went to the old address and they didn't find us.*

The night that my father hid with his brother and parents in the attic of their Mannheim apartment was 9 November 1938, the infamous night of *Kristallnacht,* the night of broken glass. But the very next morning, while dense clouds of smoke hung over the city, he had to get to Stuttgart to keep his appointment with the American Consulate. Later he heard that 1,200 men had been arrested and sent to concentration camps that previous night. How could he escape notice today of all days, when no Jewish man dared show his face?

He knew that the SS always checked the express trains and so he decided to take a series of local trains to Stuttgart. But first he had to walk through the streets of Mannheim, the streets I have walked along on the way to this cemetery. I imagine him walking the morning after the pogrom, through streets littered with shards of broken glass and smoldering rubble. Past the burnt out synagogue and the desecrated Torahs scattered on the ground. He finds one Torah intact and hides it before he continues on his way.

*I go by the synagogue where I was made bar mitzvah. Destroyed by goons. But I see the youth center, where I was youth leader and I had a key. There was one torn Torah and I put it in the closet, I was hiding it.*

My father walked to the train station, past the SS guards and boarded a local train to Heidelberg. Then one to another small town, and another to Stuttgart. The American Consulate was not jammed with people this day – in fact, it was ominously empty, except for two SS guards in black uniforms, standing by the entrance. But my father strode bravely past them for his appointment with the consul.

And though this story continues with setbacks along the way – the consul told him that he must have an operation for

Frieda Herrmann Berger. She was deported from Mannheim to
Gurs concentration camp in France in 1940, and from Gurs to the
gas chambers of Auschwitz in 1942.

a hernia before he could receive the visa – the end result was
that my father eventually succeeded in obtaining his visa. He
did come to America, and he succeeded, with the help of the
Lovemans, in getting visas for his brother, Max, and for his
parents.

And so this is a story of luck, of success. But not only that.
My father also tried to get a visa for his aunt Frieda, who had
lived with his family in Mannheim. But it was too late.

In October 1940, 2,000 of the remaining 3,000 Jews in Mannheim were arrested, along with over 4,500 Jews from other cites in Baden-Württemburg (Karlsruhe, Heidelberg, Freiburg/Breisgau, and Konstanz). They were packed into seven special trains and sent to France. To Gurs, a concentration camp in the Pyrenees, in the unoccupied zone. Many died of starvation or disease in the miserable conditions of Gurs. In August 1942, Vichy officials handed over most of the remaining prisoners to the Germans who deported them to Auschwitz. They were gassed on arrival.

"We have very tragic news for you," began the letter to my father and his parents from the American Friends Service Committee, dated 16 October 1942. " – that Frieda Berger has 'DEPARTED UNKNOWN DESTINATION.'" When I read the letter, fifty-eight years later, the words are still chilling.

∞

Thus the last generations of Mannheim Jews have been buried in the cemetery in Gurs, cremated in Auschwitz, or with luck, buried in true peace-yards in Israel or America, England, Canada, Chile, Argentina, China, South Africa or any of the countries that offered them refuge. But there are few Jews left in Mannheim to maintain the cemetery. There is a sparkling new Jewish Center here but it is attended mostly by Jews from Eastern Europe and the Soviet Union who, ironically, see Germany as a place of greater freedom and opportunity.

When my father, along with other Jewish refugees and survivors, was invited to come to Mannheim in 1994 as the guest of the mayor, he was treated royally. He wrote to the mayor after the trip, thanking him profusely for his generosity, saying that the experience had helped to "somewhat lessen the terrible hurt and pains of the past ... maybe, in part, helped the healing of it."

Yet when my father describes his visit to me, another note creeps in. "He's a very nice man," my father says of the mayor. "But he doesn't understand what it was like. How can he understand? He was only a few years old when Hitler was in power."

"You can't blame someone for when they were born," I admonish my father, self-righteously. He shakes his head at my failure to understand. And maybe he's right, after all. All Holocaust victims, whether concentration camp survivors or refugees, despair of ever conveying the experience to anyone who hasn't lived it. The more I talk with survivors, the more I realize this.

And I feel my father's sadness also about the lack of continuum. The Mannheim of today is not only devoid of historic buildings – most of the city was demolished by bombing during the war – but also of its historical Jewish population, which had been a part of the city since the middle of the sixteenth century. The Jews who live in Mannheim today have no ancestors in this cemetery with its weathered gravestones in the clutch of ivy, its clutter of weeds and fallen leaves.

It begins to drizzle, a light mist that dampens the leaves and darkens the stones. But I am reluctant to leave just yet. I read the names on the graves. Kahn, Dreyfuss, Marx, Maier... These are not my ancestors but I place stones on them nevertheless. Who else will come here to place stones? Then I sit on a stone bench in the middle of the leaves, looking at the Hebrew letters engraved in the stone tablets. There is such a silence here, a peacefulness that chills rather than comforts. Involuntarily, and without fully understanding why, I weep.

*Epilogue*

---

# *A spool of thread*

∾

On the windowsill, next to my desk, there's a spool of thread. It's a tall wooden spool, and the thin layer of thread on it is light brown and very fine, with a lustrous sheen. My father brought the thread with him from Germany when he came to America in 1939. *Take some thread and needles,* his mother had urged, knowing that my father would likely have no money to buy new clothes in America. *You can sew your clothes when they need repair.*

My father came to New York and searched for a job, knocking on the doors of every photography shop, and hearing over and over again that there was no work. He would soon be needing the thread, it seemed. But when the wealthy relatives in Nashville learned that he was unemployed, they insisted that he come to stay with them. When they saw the spool of thread, they laughed at him. "Did you think we wouldn't have any thread in America?" they asked.

∾

It is 1999, the end of the century, and I am standing at the door of an old house in Freudental, Germany, with Aviva, my thirteen-year-old daughter. Ludwig Bez, who has devoted several decades of his life to restoring the former synagogue and turning it into a thriving cultural and educational center, has brought us to this house, just as he did when I was here six years before. This is the house where my great-grandparents lived, where my grandmother grew up, where my great-uncle lived with his wife and family. Now the old lady who lived here when I visited before – the one who shut the door in my face – has moved to the nursing home and sold the home to an Italian family. They are very open to letting us visit our relatives' former home and they invite us in to look around.

I have a notebook with instructions from my father that read like a treasure hunt: Go upstairs. Turn right. Go to last room on the left. Go into the closet. That's the secret room.

My father hopes that somehow, in this secret room, I'll find the Torah that may have been hidden here, perhaps in the walls, some seventy years ago, before my grandmother's brother and his wife were arrested and deported. We walk upstairs and it is all just as my father said – through the doors, we see what looks like a door to a closet. When we open this door, we emerge into the hidden room – a small room, like a large walk-in closet, with a window. The original window has been replaced with a modern window, but in 1942, when Moritz and Sidonie Herrmann still lived here, it was a thick glass tile, planted in the red tile roof.

Ludwig has already searched the house thoroughly before the Italian family moved in, and he could find no trace of the Torah. "I've thought about this for a long time," he tells us, "and I spent many hours in this room, imagining how the Jews left in Freudental would gather here to pray. After the synagogue was ransacked in 1938, they came to this room to pray because it is hidden, with a window that faces east to Jerusalem. See how the window is hidden from the street?"

Ludwig shows us the marks left on the door post of the room, where he found a mezuzah (parchment inscribed with biblical passages, which is rolled into a small container and fixed to the door frame of a Jewish household). Since a mezuzah is usually placed on the main door to the house, its placement here was yet another indication of their need for secrecy. We stand at the window and try to think what it must have been like for them to pray here, holding the small Torah they had rescued from the synagogue. Even in mid-day, the room is quite dark but golden sunlight falls through the window, just as it must have fallen onto the ancient scroll.

∾

"They must have been really cold-hearted," says my daughter, after she listens to Ludwig's wife, Marlis, explain how the villagers of Freudental turned against their Jewish neighbors, burning their holy books and forcing them to dance around the bonfire as they beat them with sticks. Not everyone was so cruel, says Marlis. The postmaster helped many Jews, including Moritz, my great-uncle, helping them make telephone calls around the world as they looked for refuge. The postmaster's daughter, who still lives in Freudental, says that many of the older villagers won't speak to her, Marlis tells us, because her family helped the Jews.

∾

"I can forgive but I can never, ever forget," Reili once said. Maybe she'd heard the saying "forgive and forget" once too often. "I had to work to get the hate out of me," she told me. "I used to see them all as Nazis —even young Germans who had no part in the war. Most of my relatives who survived the concentration camp have emotional hang-ups and nightmares that never quit. It slows down, but it's always there. People don't realize what we went through, what it did to us emotionally."

Reading Reili's words years later makes me think of Gitta Sereny's words in *Into that Darkness*: "To achieve the extermination of these millions of men, women, and children, the Nazis committed not only physical but spiritual murder: on those they killed, on those who did the killing, on those who knew the killing was being done, and also, to some extent, for evermore, on all of us, who were alive and thinking beings at that time."

∾

In Freudental one evening, I take a walk alone. The walking and bicycle path is a country lane through a landscape of gently rolling hills. Small fields planted with wheat, asparagus and corn, spliced with pocket-sized apple orchards. Here is a tiny orchard surrounded by a wire fence, a rustic bench under one of the trees. All of this land used to belong to Moritz, who raised cattle and grew hay here. The land is so beautiful, the sun slanting across it like a length of golden velvet. It feels like home here, I think, tears springing once again to my eyes.

"It could have been *our* land," said my cousin Henry Hoppe, the grandson of Moritz Herrmann, when I talked to him at his home in the Hague. His mother, Lina, had gone to the Netherlands, leaving her home in Freudental. After the war, there was nothing to return to. Jews had lived in this valley for 400 years but they had been wiped out in a mere twelve years of Hitler's regime. Looking at this countryside, I feel the loss sharply, as if this land had once belonged also to me.

∾

I want to visit Rosa again, want my daughter to meet her. So we take the subway to the outskirts of Munich, and walk the streets of a nondescript neighborhood until we find Rosa's building. I am pleasantly surprised to find that she is still alive. Sophie has since died, and Reili is ill, incapacitated. It's something of a miracle that Rosa keeps going. She says she doesn't feel well and she is dressed in her robe, with an apron tied around the waist, but she welcomes us into her home, giving us fruit and orange juice and pastries.

I sit on the sofa next to her, as I did six years before, and

Rosa Mettbach and the author, 1999

she holds my hand and we smile at one another. I give her an
article I wrote about her, with photographs of her. And, as
Reili's husband has suggested, I give her a carton of American
cigarettes. In turn, she brings out all sorts of gifts for us: a
Bavarian embroidered shirt and a long, full, plaid silk skirt for
me; a gold ring for Aviva.

Then she hands me a bronze crucifix.

"This is for you," she says. "Take it."

I look a bit doubtful. "He's *Jewish*," she says, to assure me.
"He will bring you luck."

I smile and thank her. Without a translator, our conversation is restrained, but it's satisfying to see her nonetheless.

As we are about to go, Rosa notices that I'm wearing the
lovely silver necklace that she gave me six years ago. "You still
wear the necklace," she says, touching the delicate filigree.

"I never take it off," I tell her. "I love it. It makes me think
of you."

❧

Gravestones in Freudental, 1993

I stand in the cemetery in Freudental, where my ancestors are buried. They lived normal lives, died normal deaths, so the pain of this village does not reside here. Freudental means 'valley of joy' and standing here, overlooking this lovely rural valley with its gently rolling hills bathed in golden light, green fields and stands of trees, I can see why it was so named.

The cemetery itself is nearly 200 years old and almost all the gravestones (with the exception of a few former residents who chose Freudental as their burying place) are from before 1942, the date of the deportations. Jews from surrounding Stuttgart and other towns were also buried here. Now the gravestones are sinking into the earth and the sandstone writing is fading, so you can barely read some of them. On one side the writing is in Hebrew, the other side in German. And many of the stones bear designs – a broken rose to show a bloom that faded too soon, a vase to show that the vessel of life is easily broken. "Each of us is a shattered urn, grass that will wither, a flower that will fade…" says the Jewish prayer book.

Broken rose, gravestone, Freudental
(*print courtesy of Ludwig Bez, Freudental.*)

One part of the cemetery has no stones, just grass: this area had been reserved for the next generations of Jews in the village – but they were not to be.

∽

It is the year 2000, the beginning of the new century, the new millennium. I am visiting my ninety-three year old friend, Manfred Vernon, a Jewish survivor from Germany. I tell him I have been feeling depressed since I learned that Reili died.

The author with her father, about 1952

Though I'm happy that my book is being published after all these years, the pleasure is diminished now that I know she'll never see it. "It would have meant so much to her," I say.

"Does she have children?" he asks.

Yes, and grandchildren, too. I know what he will say before I hear his words: "It will be meaningful to them," he says. I hope so. I have children, too, and I often wonder what will be meaningful to them. Which threads will they follow, which will they discard?

∾

I notice that my father used most of the thread he brought with him to America. He kept the spool as a memento and gave it to me some sixty years later. When I look at it, I think of how this spool of thread tied him to his mother and his former homeland – unlike any thread he could have bought in America. The spool is an ordinary looking object, devoid of interest but for the story behind it, charging it with personal significance.

And another spool of thread, one in my imagination, unwinds slowly and unpredictably, sometimes fraying or tangling. It's a thin and delicate thread that leads me to the Gypsies, to Reili and to Rosa and the family that I meet in Germany, the country of so many tangled memories and emotions. And as I talk to them, and I listen, and as I follow the threads of their stories backwards in time, to the 1930s and 40s and before, their memories start to become mine as well. I carry their memories with me as my father carried a spool of thread to his new home – and I hope to pass these memories to the next generation, as my father passed the spool of thread to me.

∾

"Conscience is formed by memory," wrote the authors of the *Declaration of Repentance*, the 1997 statement of apology for the behavior of the Catholic church in France during the German occupation, "and no society can live in peace with itself on the basis of a false or repressed past any more than an individual can."

This statement stays with me, lodging in my mind, sustaining me during the times when I question the value of trying to retrieve these stories and pass them on, when I despair that after my own generation dies, no one will care. The Porajmos, the Shoah, the Holocaust were dark moments for all humanity, and we are compelled to examine them, to sift them over in our minds again and again, acknowledge them, look at them closely from every angle, ask difficult questions of others and of ourselves. For if memory is the thread to the next generation, then it's conscience that imbues it with strength, perhaps even the strength to repair cloth that has worn thin, to stitch together seams that have torn apart. There is power in recognizing our common sorrows, in listening to the stories of those who have suffered these appalling crimes, in making these memories our own.

*Conscience is formed by memory*, and these two strands must twist together into one. For memory is essential – but memory alone is not enough.

# *Acknowledgments*

ᕗ

All writers who write about other people know that they ultimately owe their work to those they write about. I am deeply grateful to those people.

First of all, I must thank my parents who gave me not only life and a sense of identity, but also a respect for the experiences of others and all the elements of conscience. Beyond the call of duty, they have patiently and good-naturedly answered my persistent and probing questions about my family history, and even translated German documents. I am indebted to them beyond measure.

The word 'gratitude' may be overused in author acknowledgments but I want to restore its significance to express the enormous and profound debt of gratitude I owe to Reili Mettbach Herchmer. I cannot find strong enough words to thank Reili, my friend and guide who inspired this project and made it possible. Although she is no longer alive to read these words, I wish to give my special thanks to her husband, Larry Herchmer, and to their children, who allowed Reili to be so generous to me, giving freely of her time, commitment and spirit.

I find it similarly difficult to express the magnitude of my debt to Reili's extended family in Germany who shared their painful stories with me. They trusted me – a total stranger – to listen to and to represent their intimate and often violating experiences, and they were willing to endure the suffering of reopening these shattering memories. I welcome this opportunity to give my warmest thanks to all of them for their trust, kindness, and generosity: Rosa Mettbach, who welcomed me and shared her home with me, Stramsee and Otilia Schönberger, and members of the Höllenreiner family: Sophie, Hugo and Rigo; Margot, Mano and Lilly; and Shukar. I also give my heartfelt thanks to two other survivors, Noemi Ban and Julia Lentini, who granted me interviews for this book.

Over the years, many people have helped me research the topic of Gypsies in the Holocaust, and I am indebted to all of them. They are too many to name here but I would especially like to thank Ian Hancock, Ludwig Eiber, Ludwig Bez, Benno Müller-Hill, Gabrielle Tyrnauer, Sanford Berman, Harry James Cargas, Sybil Milton, Christopher Browning, Donald Kenrick and Lani Silver. In the finishing stages of this book, I also received consistent and highly valuable help from the researchers and archivists at the United States Holocaust Memorial Museum, for which I would like to give thanks. A special thanks to Chris Sims of the United States Holocaust Memorial Museum Photo Archives, for prompt and helpful replies to my queries.

I gratefully acknowledge the financial support of the initial project from the Ella Lyman Cabot Trust in 1992, which enabled me to take the trip to Germany with Reili and obtain the testimonies. A grant from Western Washington University allowed me to conduct research at the United States Holocaust Memorial Museum in 1997. I also wish to thank my teachers and advisors at Western Washington University during the graduate school phase of this project who gave me valuable advice and feedback: Robin Hemley, Rosina Lippi, Mary Janell Metzger, Steve VanderStaay and Marc Geisler.

After many years of searching for a publisher, I was fortunate enough to find Bill Forster, editor of the University of Hertfordshire Press, who not only recognized the importance of this story but also allowed me the creative freedom, for the most part, to tell it in my own way. I am thankful for his steadfast support of this book. I also wish to thank book designer, Geoff Green, for his fine work and his flexibility in working with me.

This book has had a long journey and, along the way, I've found sustenance in the encouraging support of friends and family. I thank especially Jetske Mys, Nia Michaels, Freddie Yudin, Peggy Engel, Jennifer Wilke, Manfred Vernon, Paul Wilderson, Maggie and Scott McManus, Laurie Braunstein, Suzi Langton, Meta Chessin, Cathy Mihalik, Danny Levitas, Rick Steigmeyer, Milly Sonneman, Iris Gomez and Cathy Miller. A special thanks goes to Jetske Mys for leading me to the University of Hertfordshire Press and for offering her home and friendship in Amsterdam; to Paul Wilderson, for his long-term commitment to helping me find a publisher; and to Peggy Engel for translating from French those documents pertaining to Mano Höllenreiner.

I am enormously grateful to Steve Sanger who read and reread countless versions of this text and offered respectful and astute suggestions. I am especially indebted for his ongoing support of my work, which helped me to persevere.

Finally, I wish to thank my children, Aviva and Zakary Steigmeyer, for putting up with a mother who was often obsessed with a dark topic and especially for giving me a reason to write this book: the hope that this is a meaningful story for generations to come.

# End notes

∾

*1 – A bit of sweetness*

p 18. *Zigeuner, the German root for 'vagrant' or even 'criminal'*
German historian Wolfgang Wippermann explains the German
origin of this word and warns against using it, saying "It is impossi-
ble to call them (Sinti and Roma) *Zigeuner*." From 'Nazi Racial
Policy and the Roma and Sinti,' *Roma and Sinti: Under-studied
Victims of Nazism.* Center for Advanced Holocaust Studies, United
States Holocaust Memorial Museum. 21 September, 2000.

*2 – A bitter root*

p. 23. *There was Else Sonnemann*
For many years, my father's family believed that Else had been shot
in Dachau, but recently we discovered through the Munich State
Archive that Else Sonnemann was deported from Munich to
Kaunas, Lithuania on November 20, 1941. Together with 2,900
other Jews from Munich, Frankfurt, and Berlin, Else was shot in
Fort IX near Kaunas on November 25 1941, by German and
Lithuanian members of Einsatzkommando 3.

p. 25. *I had discovered only one full-length book in English*:
Now there are more books about Gypsies and the Holocaust, but at
that time, Kenrick and Puxon's book was the only authoritative text
on the subject. It is now out of print, but has been republished by
The University of Hertfordshire Press as *Gypsies Under the Swastika*.

p. 25. *Why was there such a dearth of personal memoirs from Gypsy
survivors?*
In *Gypsies and the Holocaust*, xx-xxii, Gabrielle Tyrnauer addresses
the question of why there is so little written about the subject
of Gypsies and the Holocaust; Sybil Milton also discusses this
question insightfully in "Reassessing the Racial Context of the
Holocaust," pp. 3-4.

# End notes

p. 27. *"The most urgent research now needed…"*
This paper was republished by the Montreal Institute for Genocide Studies as an introductory essay in *Gypsies and the Holocaust: A Bibliography and Introductory Essay.*

p. 31. *Gypsies, or Roma, arrived in Europe from India …*
Kenrick and Puxon give an excellent discussion of Gypsy history. Another especially valuable work on the subject is *The Pariah Syndrome* by Ian Hancock.

p. 32. *Soon after Gypsies migrated to northern and western Europe in the 1500s…*
Hancock, "The Roots of Anti-Gypsyism," pp. 5–8.

p. 32. *It is the treatment of Gypsies in Europe that is so similar to that of the Jews …*
Brearly, "The Roma/Gypsies of Europe: A Persecuted People."

p. 33. *Never were the fates of the Jews and the Gypsies more tragically intertwined…*
A most convincing argument for this view is made by Sybil Milton in "The Racial Context of the Holocaust," p. 106, and "Reassessing the Racial Context of the Holocaust"

p. 33. *Raul Hilberg says, "The fates of the two communities were inextricably linked."…*
From "Closing Remarks," *Roma and Sinti: Under-studied Victims of Nazism.* Center for Advanced Holocaust Studies, United States Holocaust Memorial Museum. 21 September, 2000.

p. 33. *As Benno Müller-Hill writes, this question is "inappropriately phrased."…*
In *Murderous Science: Elimination by Scientific Selection of Jews, Gypsies, and Others, Germany 1933–1945,* p. 97.

### 3 – The family photographs

p 39. *The systematic genealogical and genetic research on Germany's 30,000 Gypsies.…*
Because the Nazi's early criteria for racial persecution of Gypsies was opposite to that applied to Jews – 'pure' Jews were considered a greater danger than those of mixed ancestry – this subject has led to confusion and the idea that Nazi anti-Semitism was fundamentally different than Nazi anti-Gypsyism. Historian Sybil Milton, argues against this view. Since 90 percent of Gypsies were determined to be of mixed ancestry, she notes, the early policy simply included most of the population. Further, she argues that Nazis often spared Jews of mixed ancestry because they didn't want to lose support from Germans who were related to Jews; the German relatives of

most Gypsies, on the other hand, held low social status, so this was not a concern.

Milton's views are controversial, but I find them convincing. In my own family, one of my grandmother's sisters was allowed to live freely in Germany because she was married to a non-Jew from an important family, while another of her sisters was deported to Auschwitz and murdered. Similarly, Rosa was sent to Auschwitz while her husband was allowed to live openly in Munich, working in a slave-labor factory. And many of those 'pure' Gypsies who were originally slated to be spared the Nazi death machine, were registered, arrested, deported and killed. The Nazi racial theories that led to murder were never "rational or consistent," Milton says, but their results – "the relentless bureaucratic drive toward extermination" – were strikingly similar for Jews and Gypsies. This discussion is based primarily on the work of Dr. Sybil Milton's essay, "Holocaust: the Gypsies" anthologized in *Genocide in the Twentieth Century*. See especially pp. 220 and 228–9.

p. 45–7. *Litzmanstadt. Lodz...*
This description of the Gypsy camp in Lodz Ghetto is based on Ficowski's work in *Gypsies on Polish Roads*, pp.129–51, and *The Gypsies of Poland*, pp.44–5.

### 4 – Before and after

p. 49–50. *Eugenics, the idea that hereditary improvement of a race could be achieved by genetic control...*
This discussion of the eugenics movement is based on Barry Mehler's article "In Genes We Trust" and Jeremy Noakes' "Social Outcasts in Nazi Germany." A good discussion of the *Zigeunerlager* can be found in Sybil Milton's work.

p. 51–2. *Rosa was fourteen in 1938, a critical year for the Gypsies...*
See Novitch, p. 7 and Stojka, p. 8

p. 52–3. *Austria's 11,000 Gypsies were now to be treated the same as those in Germany....*
Kenrick and Puxon, *Destiny*, p. 94–5; Lewy, p. 56–62; Thurner
The description of the removal of Gypsy children from the schools is based on information from Lewy, pp. 60–1.

p. 53–7. *By the end of 1938, it was impossible for Gypsies to ignore the restrictions and persecution by the Nazi regime...*
Much of the following discussion on Gypsies in Austria and the Lackenbach camp (including the quote from a former prisoner, on page 55) is from Erika Thurner's research: "Gypsies in the Austrian Burgenland – the Camp at Lackenbach," collected in the book,

# End notes

*In the Shadow of the Holocaust: the Gypsies during the Second World War*, pp. 37–58. Thurner notes that altogether 4,000 Gypsies were interned in Lackenbach. "Over two thirds of the 11,000 Romanies and Sinti in Austria were murdered in the Nazi period," Thurner writes. "Many went to their death via Lackenbach." (58). Thurner also sees parallels between Nazi treatment of Jews and Gypsies in Austria. "Studies of anti-Semitism and the Nazi persecution of Jews in Vienna give clear parallels with the persecution of the Gypsies in Burgenland. ... The persecution of Gypsies and Jews under the Nazi Empire was a process that developed its own momentum and evolved as it went on. Although the general direction was established, the details, the timetable, the means and finally the intensity and brutality were not thought out in advance. The earlier 'mild' forms made the escalating drastic nature of the Holocaust possible. Carrying out orders from above was possible because ideological discrimination – in the case of the Gypsies as antisocials and racially inferior – had sunk deep into the population over the centuries." (58)

Another source I used for this description of Lackenbach is Donald Kenrick and Gratton Puxon's book, *The Destiny of Europe's Gypsies*, pp.170–3.

### 6 – The sky was grey

pp. 67–8. *Rosa was separated from the Jewish prisoners and sent to the Gypsy camp at Birkenau, the so-called 'family camp.'...*
This discussion of the differences of the 'family camp' and the possible reasons for them is based on Kenrick and Puxon, *The Destiny of Europe's Gypsies*, pp.151–61. See also Karola Fings' "Romanies and Sinti in the Concentration Camps," in "From Race Science to the Camps," pp. 71–107.

p. 68–9. *The Gypsy family camp was only 400 feet from the crematoria...*
The description of the camp is based on Lewy, pp. 153–4, and Michael Burleigh and Wolfgang Wipperman, *The Racial State: Germany 1933–45*, p. 126.

The camp was described as "extraordinarily filthy and unhygienic even for Auschwitz..."(pp. 68–9) by a German doctor interviewed by Robert Jay Lifton in *Nazi Doctors*, p. 323.

p. 69. *Over half the Gypsies deported to Auschwitz-Birkenau died as a result of the poor conditions...*
Fings, p. 103

pp. 69–71. *The infamous Josef Mengele...*
Robert J. Lifton's, *The Nazi Doctors*, is an excellent source on

Mengele, p. 185, and 337–83. Dr. Mengele's experiments and activities in the Gypsy camp are also described by Müller-Hill, in *Murderous Science*, pp. 70–2, and Lewy, pp. 158–62

p. 71. *Rosa tells a story that I've also read in other accounts, about a young Gypsy boy...*
The story about the Gypsy boy who was Mengele's 'favorite' is told in Sara Nomberg-Przytyk's *Auschwitz: True Tales from a Grotesque Land*, pp. 83–4.

p. 73. *But I wonder if her memories aren't fairly accurate, after all...*
Kenrick and Puxon, pp. 161–4

p. 74. *"In camp when a selection of people for work took place and families had to be separated..."*
Höss, Rudolf, p. 140

p. 74. *Although Mengele is said to have initially opposed the mass murder of the Gypsies...*
Lifton, Nazi Doctors, p. 186.

p. 75. *"The Gypsies knew what was in store for them..."*
Kenrick and Puxon, *Destiny*, p. 163.

p. 75. *"I did not see it," wrote Rudolf Höss in his memoir...*
Höss, Rudolf, p. 139–40

p. 75–7. *Some time after I spoke with Rosa, I talked to a Hungarian-Jewish survivor...*
I Interviewed Noemi Ban in Bellingham, Washington, 1997.

### 9 – I never was a child

pp. 92–4. *By 1938, the Nazi regime was ready to respond to the growing hostility toward Gypsies...*
The description of increasing anti-Gypsy agitation of the late 1930s is from Lewy, pp. 49–55

p. 95. *While the first wave of arrests, deportations, and confinement was taking place in Germany and Austria...*
An explanation of these 'waves' is given by Betty Alt and Silvia Folts in *Weeping Violins: the Gypsy Tragedy in Europe*, pp. 30–9

p. 96. *In Romania tens of thousands of Gypsies were deported to Transnistria...*
Kenrick and Puxon, *Gypsies Under the Swastika*, p.110. For a full description of these deportations see Michelle Kelso, "Gypsy Deportations from Romania to Transnstria," pp. 95–130, in *In the Shadow of the Swastika*.

p. 97. *The Roma and Sinti shared a cultural and linguistic core, but a historical separation caused distinct differences...*
A full description of this history is given by Ian Hancock in *The Pariah Syndrome*

# End notes

p. 97. *"By force of circumstance, their particular predisposition, and their mode of life…"*
Jan Yoors' book, *Crossing*, p. 62 and p. 96

p. 98. *Had Reili herself been caught helping the partisans, she too would have been shown no mercy…*
The example of children caught aiding the partisans in Transnistria is cited in Kenrick and Puxon, *Gypsies under the Swastika*, p. 110.

pp. 99–100. *They were sent to…a forced labor camp on the Yugoslavian border, near Marburg-an-der-Drau…*
This is also known as Maribor, and is in Slovenia. I was unable to find the name of the camp itself.

p. 101. *Giving testimony at the Nuremberg Trials, Marie Claude Vaillant-Couturier explained…*
Vaillant-Couturier's testimony was given on the forty-fourth day of the trial, 28 January, 1946. From the Avalon Project at the Yale Law School, http://www.yale.edu/lawweb/avalon/imt/proc/01–28–46.htm (accessed September 2000)

## 10 – Inconsistencies

p. 102. *Eduard had been a decorated soldier during the First World War…*
Information about Eduard is from Dr. Ludwig Eiber, from research for his book about Gypsies in Munich. Personal correspondence, 12 December 1994.

p. 105–6. *Bavaria had a history of especially harsh policies to persecute Gypsies*
In *The Destiny of Europe's Gypsies*, pp. 60–1 and 70–1, Kenrick and Puxon detail this information, as does Wolfgang Wipperman in "Christine Lehmann and Mazurka Rose: Two Gypsies in the Grip of German Bureaucracy, 1933–60." I also used information from Ludwig Eiber, author of *Ich wusste, es wird schlimm*, in personal correspondence, Munich, 12 December 1994.

p. 108. *Though Jews were excluded from military service…and Gypsies were officially excluded from the army from 1937…*
Military policies towards Gypsies are detailed in Kenrick and Puxon, *Destiny*, p. 82.

p. 109. *"The regulations governing their arrest were not drawn up with sufficient precision…"*
Höss, p. 138

p. 109. *And, as historian Raul Hilberg notes, some Gypsies served in the German army throughout the war…*
From "Closing Remarks," *Roma and Sinti: Under-studied Victims of Nazism*. Center for Advanced Holocaust Studies, United States Holocaust Memorial Museum. 21 September 2000.

### *11 – A matter of surviving*

p. 116–7. *In any case, the post-war German government routinely denied restitution payments to Gypsy survivors.*

Restitution policies towards Gypsy survivors are addressed by Sybil Milton, in "Holocaust: The Gypsies," and Burleigh and Wipperman in "The Persecution of Sinti and Roma," p. 127. Also, see Wolfgang Wipperman's stunning case study of how restitution payments were denied to a German Roma, Mazurka Rose, in "Christine Lehmann and Mazurka Rose: Two 'Gypsies' in the Grip of German Bureaucracy, 1933–60," pp. 112–23 in *Confronting the Past.* The quote by Wipperman on page 118 is in *Confronting the Past*, p. 123. An analysis of a negotiated fund for slave laborers, and the need to reach Gypsy survivors, can be found in the editorial, "Gypsies and the Holocaust," in the New York Times, 14 August 2000.

p. 118. *What these survivors faced was utter devastation...*

Yoors writes about this in *Crossing*, pp. 180–1

### *12 – Then I realized*

p. 125. *It was called a block, this long dark shed with no windows...*

Hugo's father's comments are contained in Ludwig Eiber's book, p.100.

The description of the crematoria and the smell of the smoke is from various sources, notably Sara Nomberg-przytyk's vivid description of "the sea of human blood" and the "sweet, choking odor" of the smell of burning human flesh, in *Auschwitz: True Tales from a Grotesque Land*, p. 81. Also in *The Story of Karl Stojka: A Childhood in Birkenau*, Stojka remembers that "one could see the fire day and night; it stank terribly. The main street of the Gypsy camp was in front of our barracks; we named it the highway to hell. My brother and I stood at the fence and saw the rows of people with yellow stars pass by on their way to the gas chamber." (p. 10)

p. 126. *The night of the arrival, Nazi guards beat Hugo's family and the others...*

Description of such an arrival is given by another Gypsy survivor, Elisabeth Guttenberger, in *From "Race Science" to the Camps*, p. 96. "The impression. It was awful," she writes. "The people sat motionless in their bunks and just stared at us. I thought, I am dreaming. I am in hell."

p.127. *For the women, especially, being forced to display their naked bodies to the SS was unbearably demeaning...*

After several women told me how profoundly shaming it was for them to have to be naked in front of men, I began to realize that this practice was as brutal as any physical violence for them. Karola Fings also describes the reaction of Romani and Sinti women in "Romanies and Sinti in the Concentration Camps," in the book *From "Race Science" to the Camps*, p. 89.

p. 128. *The so-called children's nursery had been instituted in the Gypsy camp for the purpose of propaganda...*
The description of the children's nursery and the conditions of Birkenau is based on the following sources: Kenrick and Puxon, *The Destiny of Europe's Gypsies*, pp 157–9; Guenter Lewy's *The Nazi Persecution of the Gypsies*, pp. 160–1; Lucie Adelsberger's *Aushwitz: A Doctor's Story*; and Rudolf Höss's *Commandant of Auschwitz*, p. 139. Yahill describes the drinking water in *The Holocaust*, p. 372.

p. 129. *Hugo's parents had already tried to resign themselves to their own death...*
Hugo's father, Josef Höllenreiner, tells this recollection in Eiber's book, p. 100.

### 13 – I cannot talk

p. 133–4. *Tens of thousands of new prisoners straggled into Bergen-Belsen...*
Raul Hilberg describes Bergen-Belsen in *The Destruction of the European Jews* (student edition), p. 256. A powerful first-person account of the camp by survivor Rachel van Amerongen-Frankfoorder's can be found in Willy Lindwer's, *The Last Seven Months of Anne Frank*.

p. 134. *"None of us will return..."*
The phrase is taken from the book of the same name by Charlotte Delbo.

p. 136. *To this day, I still don't understand why they did that to us...*
This statement is part of the document Hugo wrote, and read at Dachau, reprinted in Ludwig Eiber's *Ich wusste, es wird schlimm*.

### 14 – Mano, the boy who was lost

p. 141–4. *The Child Search and Registration Department in Munich later composed a chronology of Mano's whereabouts...*
Mano Höllenreiner gave me copies of this and other documents referred to here; my sincere thanks to Peggy Engel for translation of French documents.

### *15 – Spiritually broken*

p.150. *As soon as the child was born the Nazis tattooed her with a prisoner number, most likely on her upper thigh...*
According to a report by a prisoner in Kenrick and Puxon's, *Gypsies Under the Swastika*, p. 135, the only interest the Nazis took in newborns was to tattoo them immediately, on the upper thigh.

p. 150–1. *The Mauthausen concentration camp was a huge operation...*
The description of Mauthausen is based on Lewy, pp. 177–9

p. 151. *In March, 1945, 447 Gypsies –Sinti and Romani women and children – arrived at Mauthausan*
I researched similar incidents as reported in Shirer, p. 955 and 967; Hilberg, p. 255; Eiber, p. 99; and the United States Holocaust Memorial Museum display on Mauthausen.

### *16 – A piece of bread*

p. 159. *There were fifteen hundred people in it...in one barrack...*
The barracks were originally designed to sleep a few hundred prisoners, but at times held as many as 1,000, according to Lewy. Sophie's husband recalled about 800 prisoners in the barracks (as recorded in *Ich wusste, es wird schlimm)*. However, it is possible that the barracks held as many as 1,500; during the Nuremberg Trials, the reputable witness, Marie Claude Vaillant-Couturier, said that some of the barracks contained as many as 1,500 and in those barracks not everyone could lie down at night.

p. 159–61 . *The twice a day roll call was held to make a precise count...*
This description of the roll call, and the quote by Adelsberger on pages 160–1 are from Lucie Adelsberger's *Auschwitz: A Doctor's Story*, pages 46–8. The quote from Sophie's husband, Josef, on page 160, is recorded in Eiber's *ich wusste, es wird schlimm*, p 106.

p. 162. *In Auschwitz terminology, 'doing Sport'meant that the Nazis demanded various degrading exercises of the prisoners...*
Kenrick and Puxon, *Destiny of Europe's Gypsies*, pp. 159–60

p. 162. *It is impossible for me to express the scene that was before me...*
The survivor of Bergen-Belsen is quoted in Martin Gilbert's *The Holocaust*, p. 785

p.163. *Somehow in Bergen–Belsen, she had managed to ' organize' a piece of bread...*
In *Auschwitz: True Tales from a Grotesque Land*, Sara Nomberg-Przytyk defines the term: "'To organize' meant to improve your own situation, very often at someone else's expense by taking advantage of that person's ignorance or inexperience. 'To organize' meant to

procure for yourself, by any means, better clothing, lodging, or food." (p. 72)

p.165. *Another of the women prisoners in Bergen-Belsen who suffered with typhus...*
Fania Fenelon's testimony is recounted in Martin Gilbert's *The Holocaust*, p. 791

p. 166. *"There had been no food or water for five days preceding the British entry..."*
The British army review and the British soldier who helped liberate the camp are quoted in Gilbert's *The Holocaust*, p. 795. Other information on Bergen-Belsen is from Yahill's *The Holocaust*, p. 622.

### *17 – In the rain one sees no tears*

p. 169. *When Sophie and her husband, Josef, and their six children were still in Auschwitz, Nazis announced that ex-soldiers who chose to be sterilized...*
Kenrick and Puxon, *Destiny*, pp. 176–7; 180. The information about the attack dogs in Buchenwald is from Yahill, p. 536.

p. 169. *These veterans were not sterilized in Auschwitz but were sent to Ravensbrück...*
Kenrick and Puxon, *Destiny*, p. 176–7; Lewy, p. 176. At the Auschwitz trial Lucas admitted only to having performed three sterilization operations; the others, he claimed, were faked.

p. 170. *Manfred's experiences must also have been wretched...*
Sophie and her husband, Josef, made statements about their experiences which are recorded in Ludwig Eiber's book *Ich wusste, es wird schlimm*, p. 100 and 106.

p. 170–1. *Nazi racial policy determined that people unworthy of procreation...should be subject to sterilization...*
Lifton devotes an entire chapter of *Nazi Doctors* to the doctors who performed experiments, especially sterilization. A detailed account of Dr Clauberg and Dr Schumann is given on pp. 269–84. A valuable summary account is given in Henry Friedlander's *The Origin of Nazi Genocide*, pp. 132–3.

p.171. *The women prisoners at Auschwitz were so terrified of Dr. Clauberg...*
This is described by Gilbert, p. 577

p. 171. *Clauberg fled to Ravensbrück in the beginning of 1945...*
Sterilization of Gypsy girls by Clauberg and Schumann is reported in Lifton, p. 277, *From Race Science to the Camps: the Gypsies during the Second World War*, pp. 93–4, and Yahill, p. 369.

p. 172. *Sterilization at Ravensbrück was most likely done by an injection into the uterus...*

*From Race Science to the Camps: the Gypsies during the Second World War*, gives a detailed description of the sterilization procedures, as well as the quote cited here, on pages 93–4. I also used Kenrick and Puxon's *Gypsies Under the Swastika*, p. 148, as a source.

p. 172. *Even girls as young as eight and ten years old were victims of these brutal procedures...*
The Czech prisoner-doctor is quoted in *From 'Race Science' to the Camps*, p. 94. Also, see Lewy, p. 176.

p. 172–3. *"For those women who were the victims of these operations, there was no liberation in 1945..."*
Fings writes this in *From Race Science to the Camps: the Gypsies during the Second World War*, p. 94.

In *Nazi Doctors*, Lifton writes that Dr. Clauberg was captured by the Russians in June of 1945 and imprisoned for three years in the Soviet Union before he was tried and convicted of war crimes. But his twenty-five year sentence was cut short in 1955 when he was repatriated with other Germans. He was unrepentant, boasting to the press that he had perfected "an absolutely new method of sterilization ... [which] would be of great use today in certain cases." Although pressure from survivor groups led to Clauberg's arrest in November 1955, the German Chamber of Medicine resisted divesting him of his title until a group of former prisoner physicians of Auschwitz decried his behavior there. When Clauberg died suddenly in his prison cell in August 1957 "the general belief was that he was in the process of naming names at the top of the medical hierarchy and that, consequently, medical colleagues helped bring about his death." (pp. 277–8).

### 18 – Their ways and our ways

p. 177–8. *Groups of Gypsies use different names to designate themselves...*
This explanation of the linguistic origin of the names is taken from Friedlander's *The Origins of Nazi Genocide*, pp. 248–9. Friedlander further explains that there were also linguistic subgroups, such as the Lalleri, who were generally considered Sinti. "Further, some Gypsies designated themselves by their profession, although they also belonged to one of the language groups. For example, the Roma Gypsies in Austria involved in itinerant horse trading, called themselves Lowara."

p. 178. *"Those Gypsies who arrived in Germany in the beginning of the fifteenth century call themselves Sinti..."*
Wolfgang Wippermann, "Nazi Racial Policy and the Roma and Sinti," *Roma and Sinti: Under-studied Victims of Nazism*. Center for

# End notes

Advanced Holocaust Studies, United States Holocaust Memorial Museum. 21 September 2000.

## 20 – Primitive people

p. 192. And this, I think, must be what Lawrence Langer calls "*humiliated memory*"... Lawrence Langer analyzes the different types of memory in *Holocaust Testimonies: The Ruins of Memory*

p. 193–6. *Sterilization of 'inferior' people was one of the first measures Nazis proposed to improve the 'race'*... I used several sources in telling the story about the Nazi's sterilization policies toward Gypsies:
Henry Friedlander's *The Origins of Nazi Genocide: From Euthanasia to the Final Solution* (29–31; 253–4; 292); Guenter Lewy's *The Nazi Persecution of the Gypsies* (146; 210–12, and 223); Robert J. Lifton's *The Nazi Doctors: Medical Killing and the Psychology of Genocide* (269–302) Benno Müller-Hill's *Murderous Science: Elimination by Scientific Selection of Jews, Gypsies, and Others, Germany 1933–1945* (13–14; 59–60); Jeremy Noakes' "Social Outcasts in Nazi Germany" (16–17) and Miriam Novitch's *Romani Genocide Under the Nazi Regime* (8)

p. 198. "*We do not know exactly how many Gypsies were sterilized*" Friedlander, p. 254.

p.201. *But perhaps Stramsee had heard that the federal government had determined that those who were sterilized were not entitled to compensation*...
Lewy writes about restitution policies for victims of sterilization, p. 204.

p.201–3. *And what happened to those racial scientists and researchers who had recommended sterilization or concentration camps...?*
Information on the racial scientists is from Lewy, pages 208–12 and Benno Müller-Hill's *Murderous Science*, pages 60–1. The Frankfurt magistrate decided that Justin hadn't known that Gypsies would be sent to concentration camps because of her research. She was "young and inexperienced," strongly influenced by Ritter. These findings ignored much evidence to the contrary, according to Lewy. Ritter died in either 1950 (Müller-Hill) or 1951 (Lewy). Müller-Hill attributes the death to a suicide and says Ritter was on trial at the time of his death.

Due to unfavorable press coverage of the decision to award Dr. Ehrhardt a grant, and a complaint by the Central Council of the Sinti and Roma Gypsies, she was required to deposit the material she had collected at the Federal Archives in Koblenz.

### *21 – A question of complicity*

pp.204–5. *Dachau was the first concentration camp established by the National Socialists in 1933…*

I found much of this information on Dachau in *Dachau Concentration Camp*, a booklet sold at the former Dachau concentration camp museum. It is written by Barbara Distel and published by Comité International de Dachau, Brussels. I also used Yahill's information on the establishment of Dachau, pp. 133–5.

pp. 205–6. *With this ready supply of human guinea pigs, the camp became a favored site…*

Information on Dachau's experiments is from the booklet mentioned above, as well as from Lewy, p.172, and from *The Doctors' Trial and the Nuremberg Code* (Annas and Grodin, editors), pp. 74–5

p. 206. *The brother of Julia Lentini, a Sinti survivor from Germany, was a victim of one of these experiments…*

I interviewed Julia Lentini by telephone, 11 September 2000.

p. 209. *Under the Night and Fog decree, people were taken from their homes at night and shot…*

From Persico's *Nuremberg*, p. 214 and 189

p. 209. *I read that a former pastry chef…worked at Dachau and killed 20,000 people…*

Persico, p.188

p. 211. *They "cast a pall of terror over the entire population…"*

Yahill, Leni, p. 135

### *26 – Friedhof/Judenfriedhof*

p. 244. *In October 1940, 2,000 of the remaining 3,000 Jews in Mannheim were arrested…*

The remaining 1000 Jews who had not been deported to Gurs in 1940 were deported directly to Auschwitz a year later.

### *Epilogue – A spool of thread*

p. 249. *Reading Reili's words years later makes me think of Gitta Sereny's words….*

From *Into that Darkness: From Mercy Killing to Mass Murder*, McGraw-Hill Book Company, 1974. p. 111.

p. 255. *"Conscience is formed by memory," wrote the authors of the Declaration of Repentence…*

The declaration was signed by Bishop Gaston Poulain of Perigueux, president of the French bishops' Committee for Relations With

Judaism; by Bishop Olivier de Berranger of St Denis, who read the declaration at the ceremony in October, 1997, and by some fifteen other bishops of dioceses that had internment camps, as well as by twelve bishops of the greater Paris region and the bishop to the armed forces. Another translation of this statement, by the Catholic News Service (Origins) reads: "As one of the major events of the twentieth century, the planned extermination of the Jewish people by the Nazis raises particularly challenging questions of conscience which no human being can ignore. The Catholic Church, far from wanting it to be forgotten, knows full well that conscience is formed in remembering, and that, just as no individual person can live in peace with himself, neither can society live in peace with a repressed or untruthful memory."

# Bibliography

Adelsberger, Lucie. *Auschwitz: A Doctor's Story*. Trans. Susan Ray. Boston: Northeastern University Press, 1995.

Alt, Betty and Silvia Folts. *Weeping Violins: The Gypsy Tragedy in Europe*. Kirksville, Missouri: Thomas Jefferson University Press, 1996.

Annas, George J. and Michael Grodin, editors. *The Doctors' Trial and the Nuremberg Code: Human Rights in Human Experimentation*. New York and Oxford: Oxford University Press, 1992.

Anne Frank Center. *Anne Frank in the World*. Amsterdam, Anne Frank Center, 1985.

Brearley, Margaret. "The Roma/Gypsies of Europe: A Persecuted People." Policy Paper. London: Institute for Jewish Policy Research: December 1996.

Burleigh, Michael and Wolfgang Wipperman. "The Persecution of Sinti and Roma, and Other Ethnic Minorities." In *The Racial State: Germany 1933-1945*, 113-35.Cambridge: Cambridge University Press, 1991.

Cargas, Harry James. "The Continuum of Gypsy Suffering" in *Reflections of a Post-Auschwitz Christian*, 75-90. Detroit: Wayne State University Press, 1989.

Delbo, Charlotte. *None of Us Will Return*. Trans. John Githens. New York: Grove Press, Inc., 1968.

Eiber, Ludwig. *Ich wusste es wird schlimm: die Verfolgung der Sinti und Roma in Munchen 1933-45*. Munchen: Buchendorfer Verlag. 1993. Personal Letter. Munich: December 12, 1994.

Ficowski, Jerzy. *The Gypsies in Poland: History and Customs*. Warsaw: Interpress Publishers, 1989.

Ficowski, Jerzy. "Gypsies on Polish Roads." Trans. Regina Gelb. Wydawnfictwo Literackie. Krakow-Wroclaw. 1985: 129-51.

# Bibliography

Frank, Anne. *The Diary of a Young Girl*. The Definitive Edition. New York: Anchor Books, 1991.

Friedlander, Henry. *The Origins of Nazi Genocide: From Euthanasia to the Final Solution*. Chapel Hill: The University of North Carolina Press, 1995.

Fings, Karola, Herbert Heuss and Frank Sparing. *From "Race Science" to the Camps: the Gypsies during the Second World War-1*. Interface Collection, Volume 12. Trans. Donald Kenrick. Hatfield: University of Hertfordshire Press, 1997.

Gilbert, Martin. *The Holocaust: A History of the Jews of Europe during the Second World War*. New York: Henry Holt and Company, 1985.

Goldhagen, Daniel Jonah. *Hitler's Willing Executioners: Ordinary Germans and the Holocaust*. New York: Vintage Books, 1997.

Hancock, Ian. *The Pariah Syndrome: An Account of Gypsy Slavery and Persecution*. Ann Arbor: Karoma Publishers, Inc., 1987.

Hancock, Ian. "The Roots of Anti-Gypsyism: To the Holocaust and After." Paper presented at "Confronting the Holocaust: A Mandate for the 21st Century." The University of St. Thomas. St. Paul and Minneapolis: 3–5 March, 1996.

Hancock, Ian. "Gypsy History in Germany and Neighboring Lands: A Chronology Leading to the Holocaust and Beyond," p. 11–13 in Crowe and Kolsti, *The Gypsies of Eastern Europe*. Armonk, New York and London: M.E. Sharpe, Inc., 1991.

Hilberg, Raul. *The Destruction of the European Jews, Student Edition*. New York: Holmes and Meier Publishers Inc., 1985.

Höss, Rudolf. *Commandant of Auschwitz: The Autobiography of Rudolf Hoess*. Cleveland and New York: The World Publishing Company, 1959.

Kenrick, Donald. *Gypsies Under the Swastika*. Interface Collection, Volume 8. Hatfield: University of Hertfordshire Press, 1995.

Kenrick, Donald and Grattan Puxon. *The Destiny of Europe's Gypsies*. New York: Basic Books, Inc., 1972.

Kenrick, Donald and Grattan Puxon. *In the Shadow of the Swastika: The Gypsies during the Second World War-2*. Interface Collection, Volume 13. Donald Kenrick, ed. Hatfield: University of Hertfordshire Press, 1999.

Langer, Lawrence L. *Holocaust Testimonies: The Ruins of Memory*. New Haven and London: Yale University Press, 1991.

Lewy, Guenter. *The Nazi Persecution of the Gypsies*. Oxford: Oxford

University Press, 2000.

Lifton, Robert Jay, *The Nazi Doctors: Medical Killing and the Psychology of Genocide*. New York: Basic Books, 1986.

Lindwer, Willy. *The Last Seven Months of Anne Frank*. New York: Pantheon Books, 1991.

Mehler, Barry. "In Genes We Trust: When Science Bows to Racism." *Reform Judaism*. Winter 1994: 10–14.

Milton, Sybil. "Holocaust: The Gypsies, Eyewitness Accounts." In *Genocide in the Twentieth Century: An Anthology of Critical Essays and Oral History*, edited by Samuel Totten, et al. pp. 209–64. New York: Garland Publishing, 1995.

Milton, Sybil. "Nazi Policies toward Roma and Sinti, 1933–1945" *Journal of the Gypsy Lore Society 5*, Vol. 2, No. 1 (1992): 1–18.

Milton, Sybil. "The Racial Context of the Holocaust." *Social Education*. February, 1991: 106–10.

Milton, Sybil. "Reassessing the Racial Context of the Holocaust." Paper presented to the American Historical Association. New York. December 30, 1990.

Müller-Hill, Benno. *Murderous Science: Elimination by Scientific Selection of Jews, Gypsies, and Others, Germany 1933-1945*. Trans. George R. Fraser. Oxford: Oxford University Press, 1988.

Noakes, Jeremy. "Social Outcasts in Nazi Germany." *History Today*. December, 1985: 15–19.

Nomberg-Przytyk, Sara. *Auschwitz: True Tales from a Grotesque Land*. Trans. Roslyn Hirsch. Chapel Hill and London: The University of North Carolina Press, 1985.

Novitch, Miriam. "Romani Genocide Under the Nazi Regime." Distributed by World Romani Union, Buda, Texas. 1968.

Persico, Joseph. *Nuremberg: Infamy on Trial*. New York: Viking, 1994.

Shirer, William L. *Berlin Diary: The Journal of a Foreign Correspondent 1934-1941*. New York: Alfred A. Knopf, 1941.

Stojka, Karl. *The Story of Karl Stojka: A Childhood in Birkenau*. Washington, D.C.: United States Holocaust Memorial Council, 1992. Thurner, Erika, editor. "A Plan for Persecuting Gypsies." In *The Apparatus of Death*, 40–7. Alexandria, Va.: Time-Life Books, 1991.

Tong, Diane. *Gypsy Folk Tales*. San Diego, New York, London: Harcourt Brace Jovanovich, 1989.

Tyrnauer, Gabrielle. *Gypsies and the Holocaust: A Bibliography and Introductory Essay*. Montreal: Montreal Institute for Genocide Studies, 1991.

Wippermann, Wolfgang. "Christine Lehmann and Mazurka Rose: Two 'Gypsies' in the Grip of German Bureaucracy, 1931–60." In *Confronting the Nazi Past: New Debates on Modern German History*, edited by Michael Burleigh, 112–24. New York: St. Martin's Press, 1996.

Yahill, Leni. *The Holocaust: The Fate of European Jewry*. Oxford: Oxford University Press, 1990.

Yoors, Jan. *Crossing*. New York: Simon and Schuster, 1971.

Zuccotti, Susan. *The Holocaust, the French and the Jews*. New York: BasicBooks, 1993.

# *Index*

# Index

# Index